The Economics of War

Paul Poast

 **McGraw-Hill Irwin**

McGraw-Hill
Irwin

THE ECONOMICS OF WAR

Published by McGraw-Hill/Irwin, a business unit of The McGraw-Hill Companies, Inc., 1221 Avenue of the Americas, New York, NY, 10020. Copyright © 2006 by The McGraw-Hill Companies, Inc. All rights reserved. No part of this publication may be reproduced or distributed in any form or by any means, or stored in a database or retrieval system, without the prior written consent of The McGraw-Hill Companies, Inc., including, but not limited to, in any network or other electronic storage or transmission, or broadcast for distance learning.

Some ancillaries, including electronic and print components, may not be available to customers outside the United States.

This book is printed on acid-free paper.

1 2 3 4 5 6 7 8 9 0 QPD/QPD 0 9 8 7 6 5

ISBN   0-07-313399-X

Publisher: *Gary Burke*
Executive sponsoring editor: *Lucille Sutton*
Editorial assistant: *Jackie Grabel*
Senior marketing manager: *Martin D. Quinn*
Lead producer, Media technology: *Kai Chiang*
Lead project manager: *Pat Frederickson*
Senior production supervisor: *Sesha Bolisetty*
Design coordinator: *Cara David*
Supplement producer: *Gina F. DiMartino*
Developer, Media technology: *Brian Nacik*
Designer: *Cara David*
Cover Image: *©Corbis Images*
Interior designer: *Rick Soldin*
Typeface: *10/12 Times New Roman*
Compositor: *Electronic Publishing Services, Inc., TN*
Printer: *Quebecor World Dubuque Inc.*

Library of Congress Cataloging-in-Publication Data

Poast, Paul.
     The economics of war / Paul Poast.
        p. cm.
     Includes bibliographical references and index.
     ISBN 0-07-313399-X (alk. paper)
     1. War--Economic aspects. 2. War--Economic aspects--United States. I. Title
HB195.P625 2006
330.9--dc22   2005041692

www.mhhe.com

This book is dedicated to the men and women who have, are, and will serve in the United States Armed Forces. Thank you.

About the Author

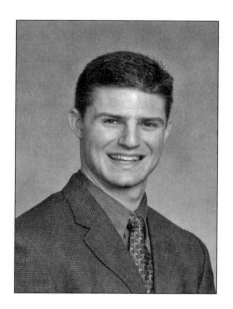

Paul Poast teaches economics and international studies at The Ohio State University. He began his research into the economic aspects of war in response to heightened student interest after the September 11, 2001, terrorist attacks on New York and Washington D.C. Paul holds degrees from Miami University (Oxford, Ohio) and the London School of Economics. He has published journal articles in both political science and economics journals. Paul and his wife Julie currently reside in Dublin, Ohio.

Contents

Contents

ACKNOWLEDGEMENTS

Many individuals offered help and encouragement during the writing of this text. First, I must thank my wife, Julie. It was through her ideas and encouragement that I came to write this book. Second, I would like to thank Lucille Sutton, Martin Quinn, Patricia Frederickson, and Gina DiMartino at McGraw Hill for their hard work and for giving me the opportunity to bring this book to life. Third, I must thank my personal editor, Jan Hall, my indexer, March Schaefer, and three former professors at Miami University for advice and cheerleading: James Brock; William R. Hart; and Thomas Hall. Next, there were several scholars who read and offered suggestions on portions of this text. They are:

Molly Cooper, *Ohio State University*
Geoffrey Forden, *Massachusetts Institute of Technology*
Leroy Gill, *Ohio State University*
David Hineline, *Miami University*
Anke Hoeffler, *Oxford University*
Vasilios Koesteas, *Cleveland State University*
Alexander Montgomery, *Harvard University*
John Mueller, *Ohio State University*
Gene Mumy, *Ohio State University*
Lt. Col. Daniel Olexio, *Defense Geospatial-Intelligence School*
Cindy Williams, *Massachusetts Institute of Technology*
Ronald Wintrobe, *University of Western Ontario*

PREFACE

War fascinates scholars, intrigues the general public, changes lives and shapes history. Yet, as important as it may be to study Lee's tactics at Fredericksburg, or Eisenhower's plans for the D-Day invasion, it can be forgotten that war is also an economic enterprise. "War is a matter not so much of arms as of expenditure, through which arms can be made of service," remarked the ancient Greek war historian Thucydides.[1] "Money," according to the first-century Roman historian Tacitus, "is the sinew of war." More directly, Louis XIV of France believed that "the last guinea will always win."[2] The crux of their statements is simple; throughout history, wars have been fought for money, and money has enabled wars to be fought.

This book offers an introduction to war economics. Though a single topic covered in one of this book's chapters could, by itself, fill an entire book or course, offering such detail is not the intention of this text. Instead, this text has two objectives. First, to enable all those interested in economics, political science, and related social sciences and humanities (both scholars and members of the general public) to understand how economics relates to warfare and national defense. Second, this text seeks to provide instructors of economics a tool by which they can offer exciting real-life applications of core economics concepts.

TEACHING POINTS

Geared to a wide audience of scholars and students, this book can serve as a stand-alone text or as an outstanding supplement to a variety of economics and political science courses, particularly principles and intermediate economics and international political economy. To bolster the text's pedagogic value, several educational features are provided. First, rather than simply summarizing the main points of a chapter, the final section of the chapter is called the "Key Points" section. This "Key Points" section specifies which major topics in the chapter are of a microeconomic focus, and which are of a macroeconomic focus. Next, the "Key Points" section offers a listing of the key terms found in the chapter. Finally, the section ends with a grouping of material-based and critical-thinking questions. The questions can serve as the basis for exam, homework, or bonus questions.

To assist instructors and students in matching key economic principles with the lessons of this book, please refer to Table I. It presents a listing of core macro and microeconomic concepts, the sections of the book in which those are addressed, and the defense issue used to instruct the concept.

Each chapter contains "Historical Perspective" boxes. Though the book is full of historical examples, these boxes use history to offer unique information that can be applied in or outside the context of the chapter's text. These perspectives are especially helpful for instructors of economic or military history.

---

[1] Thucydides, *The History of the Peloponnesian War,* Book 1, Ch. 83.
[2] Plender, John. "The Sinews of War." *Financial Times,* March 20, 2003.

Table I
Core Economic Concepts and Corresponding Defense Concepts

Core Macroeconomic Concept	Book Section	Defense Concept
Disposable Income	3.4	Economic Impact of Disarmament
Inflation (causes, impact, quantity theory of money, equation of exchange)	1.3	Impact of War on Economy
Production Function (National Security Function)	3.5	Economic impact of Arms Races
Crowding Out	2.3 and 3.4	Economic Impact of Disarmament
Phillips Curve	2.3	Financing of Vietnam War
Bond Market	2.2	Financing of World War II
Operation of the Federal Reserve	2.2, 2.3, and 7.6	Financing of World War II; Financing of Vietnam War; response to September 11, 2001 terrorist attacks
Unemployment	1.3	Impact of War on Economy
Gross Domestic Product	1.3	Impact of War on Economy
Macroeconomic Identity [C+I+G+(X-M)]	1.2 and 3.4	Impact of War on Economy, Crowding Out by Government Expenditures
Marginal Propensity to Consume	3.4	Economic Impact of Disarmament
Marginal Propensity to Save	3.4	Economic Impact of Disarmament

Core Microeconomic Concept	Book Section	Defense Concept
Comparative Advantage	4.3 and 8.5	Conscription vs. All-Volunteer Force; Supplying Countries with Nuclear Technology
Dead Weight Loss	5.3 and 5.4	Domestic Arms Market; Global Arms Market
Economies of Scale	5.4	Global Arms Market
Efficiency Wages	4.6	Private Military Contractors
Gains From Trade	8.5	Bartering to Supply Countries with Nuclear Technology
Game Theory	3.5, 7.4, and 8.6	Arms Races, Resorting to Terrorism; Failure of Treaties
Impact of Quotas and Transfer Payments (subsidy) on Supply and Demand	5.4	Global Arms Market
Indifference Curves	3.6 and 7.4	Economic impact of Arms Races; Suicide Bombing
Labor Demand and Labor Supply Curves	4.3	Conscription vs. All-Volunteer Force
Marginal Cost and Marginal Benefit Analysis	4.3 and 6.6	Military Labor Market; Peacekeeping
Marginal Productivity of Labor	4.3	Conscription vs. All-Volunteer Force
Monopoly and Monopsony	5.2 and 5.3	Domestic Arms Market
Opportunity Cost	3.3, 4.3, 6.3 and 8.5	Economic Impact of Disarmament, Conscription vs. All-Volunteer Force; Poverty and Civil War; Supplying Countries with Nuclear Technology
Principal-Agent Model	5.3	Domestic Arms Market
Production Possibilities Frontier	3.3 and 3.6	Economic Impact of Disarmament; Economic impact of Arms Races
Public Goods (free-riding, common resources)	4.6, 6.6, and 8.6	Private Military Contractors; Peacekeeping; Treaties
Supply and Demand Curves	5.3 and 8.5	Domestic Arms Market; Determinates of Nuclear Black Market Price

For ease of understanding, this text makes extensive use of graphs, figures, and tables. Graphical economic analysis is particularly important to students, because it is through graphs that many undergraduates become familiar with economics.

The book's bibliography contains a section dedicated to those sources that can be accessed, for free, via the web, along with web addresses.

TEXT ORGANIZATION

This book is divided into three units. Unit I explores the economics of war economies. Unit I seeks to lead students through a determination of whether or not war benefits the economy; and, if not, why not. Chapter 1 presents the economic theory underpinning the Iron Law of War—the idea that fighting wars can provide a boost to an economy (if the war is not fought on that country's soil). This theory will lead to the creation of a four-point scheme for evaluating the economic impact of war. Chapter 2 applies this scheme to a variety of major American wars from the 20th century and today. The evidence that these case studies present indicates that the Iron Law of War, though valid in the past, does not hold today. These case studies also bring out the two reasons why wars no longer induce the same strong, positive economic response of early 20th century wars: the existence of a permanent military industry and the nature of modern warfare.

Unit II explores the fact that because the United States is continually maintaining a military establishment, the onset of a war no longer induces massive mobilization and drastic increases in government expenditures. Prior to World War I, the U.S. government only incurred military expenditures at times of war. Today, military spending is the single largest discretionary (i.e., adjustable) expenditure of the U.S. government and many governments maintain high levels of military expenditures during times of war and peace. As such, modern war does not offer a large and sustained boost in government expenditures and mobilization of resources.

Chapter 3 details the level of military expenditures in the United States and around the world, the economic implications of military spending, and the reasons why countries will maintain such high levels of military expenditure. Chapters 4 and 5 look in-depth at what exactly is purchased with these expenditures, in both personnel and equipment. Chapter 4 surveys the economics of recruiting and training military personnel, while Chapter 5 looks into weapon systems procurement.

Unit III focuses on another reason why wars now lack the ability to boost an economy's performance—the unique and limited nature of modern warfare. At the close of the Cold War, political scientist John Mueller wrote, "From a rational perspective then, war among developed states seems to have become unthinkable—rejected because it's unwise [given the presence of nuclear weapons], a thoroughly bad and repulsive idea."[3] Though Mueller's thesis focuses primarily on the existence of nuclear weapons, he and others recognize that increasing economic interdependence through trade and financial flows have also contributed to war's irrationality: "Why would we [the U.S.] go to war with China? We would have to close all the Wal-Marts."[4] However, nuclear weapons and economic interdependence did not bring about the cessation of war.

As instances of international war have declined, many developing countries have more frequently succumbed to civil war. In turn, if these countries' central governments can no longer provide public goods and services, enforce the rule of law, and/or hold

---

[3] Mueller (1989), p. 219.

[4] Lawrence Korb, in an interview in Hallet, Joe and Tory, Jack. "Are World Wars Obsolete?" *Columbus Dispatch,* June 6, 2004, p. A1.

ultimate sovereignty, these countries can prove fertile grounds for housing terrorist organizations that have a global reach. The industrialized world has responded in two ways, by stabilizing failed states through peacekeeping operations, and by neutralizing terrorist organizations through cutting off their funding. Even still, a greater potential threat remains—the proliferation of weapons of mass destruction. Though the probability of a chemical, biological, and nuclear attack is smaller than a terrorist strike, the great destructive power of these methods makes imperative that developed countries seek to prevent such weapons from falling into the hands of terrorists, or states with a low threshold for deploying such weapons.

Chapter 6 considers the economic causes and consequences of civil conflict in the less developed world and the use of peacekeeping operations as a response to such conflicts. Chapter 7 uses economics to analyze terrorism's existence, impact, and prevention. Chapter 8 concludes the unit by outlining the economic costs and motivations faced by countries that wish to develop and proliferate weapons of mass destruction, particularly nuclear weapons.

The Economic Impact of War

Chapter 1:

The War Economy in Theory

1.1 INTRODUCTION

Shortly before the war in Iraq began in 2003, an unemployed man who was frustrated over his inability to secure a job told me, "What this economy needs is a good war!" Why would he say such a thing? Wouldn't war disrupt the peaceful process of wealth creation? Well, that depends; World War II, for example, is widely regarded as having helped pull the United States economy out of the Great Depression.

This brief chapter presents theoretical reasons for how war can help or hurt an economy. Section 1 explores the Iron Law of War—the idea that war produces economic booms. Section 2 presents a four-point scheme that can determine to what extent a war impacts an economy and, if so, whether that impact will be positive or negative. This scheme will create a framework for analyzing in Chapter 2 various major U.S. wars.

1.2 THE IRON LAW OF WAR

The man who spoke to me was reflecting on a common belief that I will call the **Iron Law of War**.[1] This law, conceived primarily from the experience of the United States during two world wars, asserts that war is good for the economy. The law's logic is simple: in order to fight a war, a government must raise an army and produce weapons. Both tasks put people to work, either directly in the armed forces or in a factory, producing armaments. Yet, is this piece of conventional wisdom true? Answering that question requires an exploration of the two ways that war influences the economy: first, that war scares people (**psychological effect**) and, second, that war is expensive (**real effect**). Both of these effects can be best captured by the standard macroeconomic relationship $Y = C + I + G + (X - M)$, where Y = national income, C = consumption, I = business investment in new equipment and factories, G = government spending, and $(X - M)$ is net exports (which, for the sake of simplification, is assumed to be relatively small).

1.2.1 War Scares People

The psychological effect of fear results in a decline in economic confidence (both of households and corporations). Consumer sentiment surveys since the 1970s have measured this effect. Unfortunately, such surveys are not available for earlier times. As an alternative, we can turn to stock market valuations. Because the valuation of company stock is based in large part on expectations about the future, the performance of the stock market can be a useful, though imperfect, indicator of economic expectations.[2] Table 1.1 shows the performance of the Dow Jones Industrial Average immediately following major U.S. national security crises. Because the onset of a crisis creates uncertainty about the future, the stock market typically declines. This fear reduces the willingness of people to spend, thereby lowering consumption, C, and business investment, I. If all other variables (G, X, and M)

Table 1.1
U.S. Stock Market Performance at the Onset of Major National Security Events
(Dow Jones Industrial Average)

Event	DATE	DAY	% Change for Day**	6 Months Later	1 Year Later
Invasion of Iraqi Freedom	3/19/03	Wednesday	0.26%	17.90%	25.60%
Invasion of Afghanistan	10/7/01	Sunday	−0.57%	12.63%	−18.61%
Terrorist Attack	9/11/01	Tuesday	−7.12%	10.47%	−10.66%
Oklahoma Bombing	4/19/95	Wednesday	0.68%	14.92%	32.46%
WTC Bombing	2/26/93	Friday	0.17%	8.41%	14.07%
Somali Crisis	12/4/92	Friday	0.57%	7.80%	12.63%
Operation Desert Storm	1/16/91	Wednesday	4.57%	18.73%	30.14%
Kuwait Invasion*	8/2/90	Thursday	−6.31%	−5.81%	3.69%
Panama & Noriega	12/15/89	Friday	−1.53%	7.17%	−5.32%
Hostage in Grenada	10/25/83	Tuesday	−0.69%	−7.1%	−3.31%
Reagan Shot	3/30/81	Monday	−0.26%	−14.56%	−17.12%
Iran Crisis	11/4/79	Sunday	−0.77%	−0.32%	14.44%
Tonkin Gulf Attack	8/4/64	Tuesday	−0.9%	7.58%	5.18%
Kennedy Assassination	11/22/63	Friday	−2.89%	12.04%	21.58%
Cuban Missile Crisis	10/22/62	Monday	−1.85%	25.05%	31.41%
Sputnik Launched	10/4/57	Friday	−2.01%	−4.59%	15.60%
Korean War	6/25/50	Sunday	−4.65%	2.36%	9.34%
Pearl Harbor	12/7/41	Sunday	−3.5%	−9.48%	−1.37%
Lusitania Sinks	5/7/15	Friday	−4.54%	36.01%	32.75%
U.S.S. Maine Explodes	02/15/1898	Tuesday	−2.14%	14.91%	24.90%

Source: Dow Jones Indexes at www.djindexes.com/jsp/events.jsp. Six-month and one-year values for Operation Iraqi Freedom calculated based on data from EconStats Stock Market data available at www.econstats.com/eqty/eq__d2.htm and Economagic Stock Prices data at www.economagic.com/sp.htm.

*The 6.31% drop is over three trading days: 1.2% on the day of the invasion, followed by a decline of 1.92% on Friday and 3.32% on Monday.
**If the event occurred after the U.S. market closed (or on a non-trading day), the percent change for day reflects the next trading day's activity.

are held constant, a crisis will force Y to decline. In short, crises initially scare people and this fear, in turn, forces the economy to slow down.

However, the initial dampening effect of fear on consumer spending soon dissipates. Table 1.1 shows that, with a few exceptions, the performance of the stock market typically improves over the six months and over the first year following the crisis. This dramatic result is either because the course of the conflict soon heads in a favorable direction or the public returns to a normal daily routine in spite of the ongoing conflict.

1.2.2 War is Expensive

The psychological effect of fear is typically overwhelmed by the real effect of wartime conversion. The real effect entails a large and sustained increase in government military expenditures, plus the mobilization of physical and labor resources. If such expenditures represent an increase in defense spending (and/or an increase in resource mobilization), then in the short term, the war-related boost in government spending, G, will increase national income, Y.[3] The exact process by which this real effect takes hold will be discussed next.

1.3 FOUR-POINT SCHEME FOR EVALUATING THE ECONOMIC EFFECTS OF WAR

A four-point scheme can help an economist determine the extent to which the above effects (psychological and real) impact an economy during any given conflict. Briefly, these points are the following:

1) State of a country's economy prior to the war
2) Location of the war
3) Extent of the mobilization of physical and labor resources
4) Duration of the war, the cost of the war, and the method of financing the war

1.3.1 Condition of the Economy Prior to the War

A country's **Gross Domestic Product** (GDP) is a good measure of an economy's performance. Specifically, GDP is the market value of the production of new, **final goods and services** (goods and services that are produced for their final purpose—like a car—not as a component of another good or service—like an engine) over the course of three months. More generally, it is the measure of the new national income generated in an economy in a given period of time. Because GDP is a measure of national income, then Y represents GDP.

Rise in GDP: GDP growth (or non-growth) is a measure of how quickly an economy's income is growing (or declining). When an economy's GDP is growing slowly, then that economy may not have enough jobs to employ new people entering the **labor force** (the number of people working or wishing to work in part-time or full-time jobs). This lack of job growth is called a **recessionary gap.** Additionally, GDP can also shrink! When the growth rate of GDP is negative, jobs are being eliminated. This is called a **recession.** When the economy is in a recession, economists want Y to grow. Y can grow when households consume more, firms invest more, the government spends more, or more exports are sold. Most economists would like to see the private sector increase its expenditures. However, sometimes firms see no need to invest in new capital because they are swamped with excess capacity. Alternatively, households may be reluctant to spend because of low confidence. Therefore, if Y is to increase, the government must step in and provide the spending. This is known as **Keynesian economics** (named after the founder of macroeconomics, John Maynard Keynes).

Typically, the government can increase its own spending by authorizing the funds for public works projects, like road construction. The government can also increase expenditures through the purchase of military equipment. This method is known as **Militaristic Keynesianism.**[4] Buying military weapons can be justified if the country is entering a war; and if the economy is below full employment when entering a war, then the additional government spending can pull the economy to full employment.

Rise in inflation:[5] But providing a boost to Y by any means, even Militaristic Keynesianism, is not always best economically. Consider a few scenarios. First, if Y is already growing, then a shortage of production capacity may exist. In such a scenario, if the government raises G and firms are unable to produce goods fast enough, the firms may raise prices as a means of slowing the public's consumption of goods.

Second, the government may ration goods produced at home, leaving more materials available for use in the war. This shortage of goods can result in a rise in prices as people bid up the price of existing goods (this rise can still occur even in the presence of price

Box 1.1
Historical Perspective
GDP per Capita and Victory During the World Wars

An important measure of a war's potential economic impact is the level of GDP per capita (per person) prior to a war. Consider the experiences of the major belligerents during the world wars of the 20th century.[1]

A high GDP per capita relative to other countries has several advantages. First, it implies a bigger surplus of resources over those needed for basic subsistence (level of production needed for survival). These excess resources can then be diverted from civilian to war use. Second, because the economy is well above the subsistence level, it can have industrial specialization in metallurgy (use of chemistry to devise different forms of metal) and engineering. Both specializations are essential in the manufacture of modern munitions. Third, societies with higher GDP per head commonly have more sophisticated technological, commercial, transportation, and administrative services infrastructure. Better infrastructure eases the ability of the economy to employ wartime regulation and mobilize resources toward the war effort. All three advantages mean that high GDP per capita countries can sustain mobilization. By contrast, large-scale mobilization can accelerate economic collapse in low-GDP per-capita countries.

Entering World War I, Russia, Germany, and Britain had GDPs of roughly equal size. Russia had more territory and population than either Britain or Germany, while Germany had more territory and population than Britain. However, Britain began the war with the highest GDP per head. Thus, it was able to supply its war effort with resources of superior quantity and quality, and maintain its civilian households with better personal health, living standards, and morale. Russia, with the lowest GDP per capita of the warring countries, was the first to economically collapse. The next two countries to experience economic collapse were Austria-Hungary and Germany, possessing the second-to-lowest and third-to-lowest GDP per capita, respectively.

Entering World War II, Britain, Germany, and the United States had the highest relative GDP per capita of the warring parties. As Table I illustrates, the average GDP per capita of the Allies surpassed that of the Axis powers, despite the Soviet Union (USSR) possessing the lowest GDP per capita overall.

Table I: Average GDP per Capita

Country	GDP per capita (1938), in 1990 U.S. $
Allies	
U.S.	6134
U.K.	5983
France	4424
USSR	2150
Average	*4673*
Axis	
Germany	5126
Italy	3244
Japan	2356
Average	*3575*

Source of data: Harrison, M. (ed.). *The Economics of World War II.* Cambridge, U.K.: Cambridge University Press. Cambridge. 1998.

In fact, economically speaking, the Soviet Union may have suffered the most from the war. Due to its low GDP per capita, machinery was relatively more expensive and agriculture was less productive than in Germany, Britain, or the United States. Consequently, even though Russia was on the winning side of both wars, its economy was severely weakened.

---

[1] Information from Harrison (1998), pp. 3, 7, 18–19, and 269–270.

controls as will be seen in Chapter 2). Third, even in a recession, once Y begins to grow and excess capacity is finally being put to use, the same factors can cause prices to rise.

In any of these scenarios, the end result is an increase in the price level, an event called **inflation.** This inflationary impact of war can also result from how the war is financed, which will be discussed more fully in section 1.3.3.

Impact of inflation: If unanticipated, inflation damages an economy by diminishing the **purchasing power** of money. Purchasing power is the quantity of goods that a given quantity of money can purchase. If the price of all goods rises, then the same quantity of money will no longer be able to purchase as many goods. If inflation is unanticipated, it leaves workers worse off because their wages will no longer purchase as many goods. It leaves creditors (people who are owed money) worse off because it reduces the purchasing power value of the **nominal interest rate.** This rate is the amount of additional money a creditor (someone who is owed money) must be given when lending money, as a percentage of the quantity of money lent.[6] Inflation makes it less attractive for creditors, such as banks, to lend.

However, if creditors and workers anticipate inflation, they can adjust to it. For example, if workers anticipate prices to rise by 5 percent in the next year, they can request that their next employment contract stipulates a 5 percent rise in their wages. If the inflation rate actually turns out to be 5 percent, then the workers are no worse off with regard to their purchasing power.

Additionally, banks can raise interest rates so as to prevent inflation from diminishing the purchasing power of the money paid back by the borrower. For example, assume there is no inflation. A bank lends $100 to a person for one year at 0 percent interest. When the bank receives its $100 back, the money will still have the same purchasing power. However, if there is 10 percent inflation, then when the bank receives its money back in a year's time, the $100 will have lost purchasing power. At that rate, an item that cost $50 a year ago will now cost $55. So how can the bank maintain the same purchasing power? It will ask the borrower to give it more money, by charging interest. The bank will charge 10 percent interest on the $100 loan so that, in a year's time, the borrower will pay the bank $110, not $100. So you can see that if the inflation is unanticipated, it can have a detrimental impact on the economy.

1.3.2 Location of the War

Where the war occurs is crucial to a war's economic impact. This fact is obviously true of the impact to the country where the war is located. A war fought in country A often physically decimates the economy of that country. For example, World War I and World War II devastated the economies of continental Europe.

Yet wars can economically harm countries far from the battle. Many countries are tied to each other through critically needed imports (or to sell exports). For example, wars fought in the Middle East and Persian Gulf, by disrupting oil distribution and adding to the international price of oil, have a deleterious effect on the U.S. economy. As Figure 1.1 shows, the real GDP growth rate of the U.S. economy has been closely tied to the world price for oil. As the price of oil rises, the real GDP growth rate tends to fall (and vice versa). In fact, a one-year increase of $10 in the price of oil can cause the U.S. real GDP growth rate to slow, on average, by approximately 0.5 percent.[7] "Real" GDP is an adjusted figure, so that the production levels in each period are measured using the same prices. This adjustment ensures that we are measuring just the changes in production, not changes in production AND changes in prices.

Figure 1.1
Impact of Oil Prices on the U.S. Economy

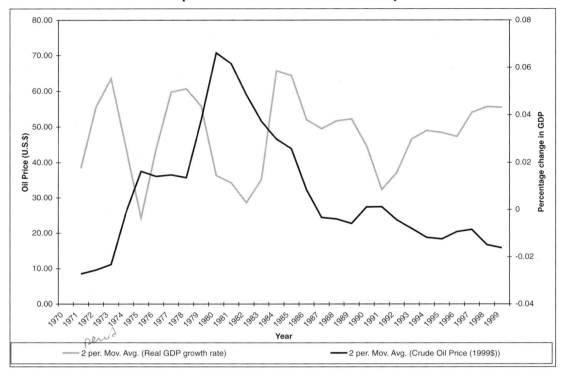

Source of data: Oil prices from Energy Information Administration (EIA), U.S. Department of Energy. Crude Oil Prices 1861–1999 from British Petroleum. Available at www.eia.doe.gov/emeu/international/petroleu.html#Prices. Real GDP from Federal Reserve Economic Data (FRED) database of the Federal Reserve Bank of St. Louis. Available at http://research.stlouis.fed.org/fred2/data/GDP.txt.

By the same token, a war in an export market could also prove economically beneficial. If the country at war requires additional raw materials and **intermediate goods** (goods that are part of a final good) in order to build weapons and feed its population, then the country will increase its purchases of such goods. This was the case of the United States during World War I and World War II, when U.S. exports of iron, steel, and coal to Europe rose dramatically (see the respective case studies in Chapter 2).

1.3.3 Duration, Budgetary Cost, and Financing of the War

War, an expensive enterprise, is seen economically by both its cost and duration. The war's cost is a direct function of the war's length; longer wars mean the cost continues to be incurred over more months. Table 1.2 summarizes the cost of several U.S. wars. As can be seen, the cost of war—both in dollars and as a percentage of GDP—has continually diminished with each war.

Financing a war: In addition to the war's cost, it is important to know how that cost is covered. Wars can be financed in a variety of ways. Governments can borrow money (war bonds), raise taxes, cut nonmilitary spending, create money (print currency or increase

Table 1.2
Cost of Major Wars to the United States

War	Duration	Total Direct Cost [in billions of current year dollars]	GDP in final war year [in billions of current year dollars]	Total GDP during war period [in billions of current year dollars]	Cost as a percentage of GDP in the final war year	Cost as an average of GDP per year [total cost/total GDP during war period]
World War I	2 years*	26	71.3	128	36%	20%
World War II	4 years**	288	218	923	132%	31%
Korea	3 years	54	380	1375	14%	4%
Vietnam	10 years	111	1383	9677	8%	1%
Persian Gulf	8 months	61	5917	5917	1%	1%
Iraq	1.5 years +	$4-5 billion/month	N/A	N/A	N/A	N/A
		$60 billion/year***				

Sources of data: The GDP from 1917–1991 is from Gordon (1998), Appendix A.
War cost data are from Nofi, Al. *Statistical Summary: America's Major Wars.* The United States Civil War Center. Available at www. cwc.lsu.edu/cwc/other/stats/warcost.htm.
$4 billion monthly cost of Iraq Operations from "Occupying Iraq." *The Economist.* August 7, 2003.
$5 billion monthly cost of Iraq Operations from Bennis, Phyllis "A Failed Transition: The Mounting Costs of the Iraq War." *Institute for Policy Studies* and *Foreign Policy in Focus.* September 30, 2004 available at http://www.ips-dc.org/iraq/failedtransition/. This estimate is also found in O'Hanlon, Michael. "Iraq–By the Numbers." *Los Angeles Times.* September 2, 2004 available through the Brookings Institute Website at www.brookings.edu/views/op-ed/ohanlon/20040903.htm.

* The United States did not officially enter the war until 1917.
** The United States did not officially enter the war until late 1941. However, they had already begun increasing military production earlier in 1941 in order to supply arms to the Allies (see Chapter 2's case study).
*** Estimates. Also see Section 2.3.3 in chapter 2 for further details on cost estimates.

bank reserves), receive reparations (receive payments from the defeated), and/or collect transfer payments from a third party. As the case studies of Chapter 2 will illustrate, though the U.S. government has used a combination of these methods, money creation is one of the most common.

Money creation leads to a rapid increase in the growth rate of the money supply. Figure 1.2 illustrates this trend during the 20th century. As can be seen, the growth rate of **M2** (the most widely used measure of the U.S. money supply, which includes currency, checking, and short-term time deposits) hit peaks during World War I, World War II, the Korean War, and later during the Vietnam War (though the growth rate of the money supply during this era was not completely related to financing the war).

The money supply and inflation: What has been the consequence of this rapid increase in the supply of money? A concept called the **quantity theory of money** provides an answer. This theory proposes that, in the long run, an increase in the quantity of money brings an equal percentage increase in the price level. This relationship is illustrated by the **equation of exchange.** According to this macroeconomic identity, the supply of money in the economy, *M,* multiplied by the number of times per year that the money is spent (called the "velocity of money," *V*), is equal to how many goods were produced in the economy in a given year, *Y,* times how much each of those goods cost, *P.* This creates the following equation: $M*V = P*Y.$

Figure 1.2

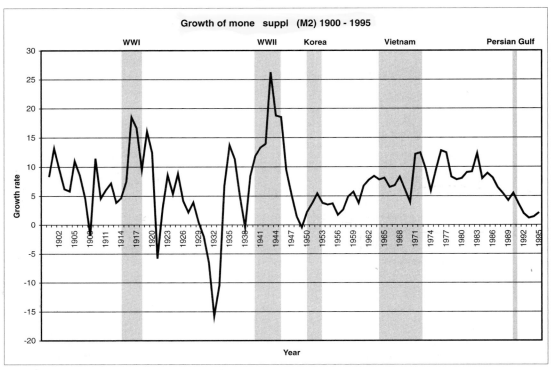

Source of data: Gordon, R. *Macroeconomics.* Seventh Edition. Addison-Wesley. New York. 1998, Appendix A.

The quantity theory of money takes the equation of exchange and makes two assumptions. First, the velocity of money is treated as a constant because it is primarily determined by patterns in payment methods (such as cash and checks) that gradually evolve over time.[8] Second, in the long run, barring a change in technology, the capital stock (machines or factories) or human capital (knowledge or labor), GDP, Y, is also considered constant. Therefore, as M rises, if the equation of exchange is to balance itself, then P must rise by an equal percentage. Consequently, increasing the rate of money creation leads to higher inflation.

The quantity theory of money and equation of exchange together illustrate another reason for the inflationary impact of war: money creation to finance a war. Money creation, combined with the other reasons mentioned in section 1.3.1, help explain why almost all wars in all countries have had an inflationary impact. Consider Figure 1.3. It shows the U.S. inflation rate during the 20th century. Notice that peaks coincide well with U.S. involvement in major wars in 1917–1918, 1941–1945, the late 1960s into the 1970s, and 1991. Though the post–World War II inflation may appear to be a notable exception to this trend, the inflation of that period was the direct result of lifting price controls after World War II. This lifting of controls allowed the money created to finance World War II to be spent by the private sector, thereby sparking inflation.[9]

Figure 1.3

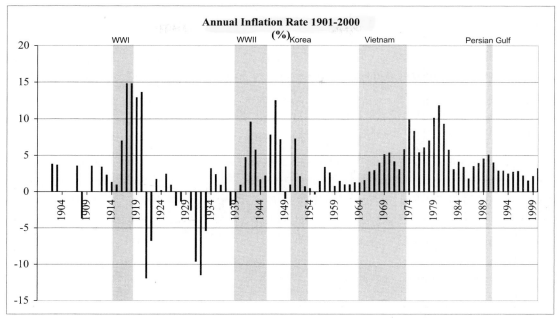

Source of data: Provided courtesy of Byron Chapman, Ohio State University. Data from 1900–1960 is from the U.S. Bureau of the Census, Historical Statistics of the United States. Data from 1960–2002 is from the Economic Report of the President, Table B-60 (2003). Data from 2003 is estimated by Byron Chapman, Ohio State University. All series adjusted to 2003=100.

1.3.4   Physical and Labor Resource Mobilization

When a war arises, the economy directs its **factors of production**—land, capital (machines and factories), and labor—toward the production of war supplies and weapons. The government may repossess land for factory construction or nationalize private industries so as to control production. Phrases like "war-capitalism" and "plowshares to swords" have been invoked to describe such government wartime economic control and mobilization.[10] For the purpose of evaluating this mobilization, the resources can be divided into two types: physical and labor.

Physical resource mobilization: Government-directed mobilization of physical resources can impact the economy both positively and negatively. It can have a substantial positive economic impact if the peacetime economy has extensive unused production capacity and/ or if wartime production far surpasses peacetime production.

However, even if there is very little unused production capacity, wartime physical resource mobilization might still prove highly inefficient to stimulate the economy. This is because producing civilian goods commonly adds value to the economy, but military goods may not. For example, when General Electric produces refrigerators, this generates revenue for the producing firm. But those sales also create value beyond the firm's revenue, because a refrigerator enables the buyer to store food. This, in turn, allows the buyer to purchase more food. In contrast, when General Electric produces bullets (as it did during World War II), this product generates revenue for the firm, but—unlike the

Table 1.3
Economic Stimulus from Defense Spending and Government Expenditure

War	Period Measured for Defense Expenditures	G as Percent of GDP Before	G as a Percent of GDP During	G as a Percent of GDP After	Percent Change of G From Before to During	Increase in Defense Spending as Percent of GDP	Real GDP Growth over Buildup Period (%)
World War I	1915-1919	10% (1910)	22% (1918)	6% (1920s)	120%	12.50%*	25%**
World War II	1939-1944	13% (1940)	45% (1945)	14.7% (1947)	246%	41.40%	69%
Korea	1950:3-1951:3	14% (1949)	20%(1953)	16.5% (lowest of 1950s)	42%	8.00%	11%
Vietnam	1965:3-1967:1	19% (1963)	21%(1968)	18.7% (lowest of 1970s)	10%	1.90%	10%
Persian Gulf	1990:3-1991:1	21% (1989)	22% (1991)	21.1% (by 1994); 18.6% (by 1999)	5%	0.30%	-1%
Iraq	2002:3-2003:2	19% (2001)	22% (2003)	N/A	14%	0.70%	2%

Source of data: Nordhaus, 2002, p. 74; St Louis Federal Reserve Bank FRED database.

Note: Quarters are designated by the number following the colon.
* Calculated by dividing real per-capita increase in defense and interest payments from 1915 to 1919; taken from Holcombe, Randall. "The Growth of the Federal Government in the 1920s." *The Cato Journal.* Vol. 16, No. 2 (available at www.cato.org/pubs/journal/cj16n2-2.html). Then, dividing this answer by the average real GDP per capita from 1915–1919 ($6,250).
** New value was 1918 real GDP, not 1919.

refrigerator—the bullets are not used again in an economically productive fashion. Instead, they are simply destroyed!

Not only does government expenditure, as a percentage of GDP, give an indication of a war's cost, but it can also estimate the magnitude of resource mobilization. This fact is because the greater the rise in government spending as a percentage of GDP during a war, the greater the government's involvement in the economy and the greater is its need to acquire resources to fight a war. One noticeable reason some wars gave the U.S. economy a substantial economic boost was the sharp and sudden rise in government expenditures as a percentage of GDP. Table 1.3, using real GDP growth as a measure of whether a war supported the Iron Law of War, shows that those wars with the highest increases in real GDP—and, hence, support the Iron Law—saw a tremendous rise in the size of government expenditure relative to the economy. Those wars not supporting the Iron Law, mostly later wars, did not.

Labor resource mobilization: Tables 1.4 and 1.5 tell a similar story with regard to labor resource mobilization. The percent of the population in the military (both active and reserve) and the drop in the **unemployment rate** during wartime are good measures of labor mobilization. The unemployment rate measures the number of people who are not working but who wish to work as a percentage of the labor force. Recall from section 1.3.1 that the labor force is the number of people with part- or full-time jobs, plus the number of people unemployed. Because a sustained rise in government expenditures during wartime

Table 1.4
Labor Resource Mobilization in the U.S. (% of population in armed forces)

War	Population (millions)	Military Personnel Thousands	% of pop.	Fatalities Numbers	% of pop.
World War II	134	16,354	12.20%	292,131	0.219%
Korea	152	5,764	3.80%	33,651	0.022%
Vietnam	205	8,744	4.30%	47,369	0.023%
Persian Gulf	260	2,750	1.10%	148	0.00%
Iraq	282	2,614	0.90%	N/A	N/A

Source of data: Nordhaus. W. "The Economic Consequences of a War with Iraq," (2002), Table 1, p. 6. Available at www.econ.yale.edu/~nordhaus/homepage/AAAS_War_Iraq_2.pdf.

Table 1.5
Labor Resource Mobilization in the U.S. (Changes in Unemployment Rates)

War	Avg. Unemployment Rate (during two years prior)	Lowest Unemployment Rate (during war period)	Change (points)
World War II	15.9	1.2	-14.7
Korea	4.9	2.9	-2
Vietnam	6.1	3.5	-2.6
Persian Gulf	5.3	5.6	+0.3
Iraq	6.0	5.6 (as of April '04)	-0.4

Source of data: Federal Reserve Economic Data (FRED) database of the Federal Reserve Bank of St. Louis. Available at http://research.stlouis.fed.org/fred2/data/GDP.txt .

can cause factories to produce more, the factories will eventually have to offer overtime to existing workers and, most importantly, hire additional workers. Thus, Militaristic Keynesianism can serve to lower the unemployment rate. Table 1.4 shows that the unemployment rate has declined substantially during earlier 20th century U.S. wars, but this decline has diminished with later wars.

Additionally, if more soldiers enter the military, then there are fewer people available to work (military personnel are not counted in the labor force). More soldiers going to war has two effects on the unemployment rate, one statistical and one practical. Statistically, by decreasing the size of the labor force, soldiers leaving will place a downward bias on the unemployment rate. Practically, if the soldier is no longer available to work, then (particularly if the person will be gone for a substantial amount of time) someone else must do his or her job. Additionally, if new jobs are created, then more soldiers in the military means less people in the civilian sector to compete for the job. However, mobilization can harm the economy if the soldiers called to fight were active workers in the economy. Economically speaking, this removes human capital from the economy that, in the short-run, is difficult to replace. This is known as **allocational inefficiency.**

One can see in Table 1.5 that the percentage of the population in the military has declined steadily with each war. The reasons for this decline will be discussed in Chapter 2. At this point, note how the numbers in Tables 1.4 and 1.5 illustrate that later wars have (much like the case of physical resource mobilization) induced less labor mobilization.

Box 1.2
Historical Perspective
Value of Human Lives Lost in War

Although this text focuses on the economy of war, it is wise to stress war's human tragedy. People die. Though the deaths of soldiers and civilians caught in the fighting can be considered from many angles, economists approach this issue from the standpoint of economic cost—what economic value is lost due to the individual's death. The table below tabulates the number of soldiers killed in several major American wars.

Table I: American Casualties from Major American Wars

War	Fatalities	Percent of Population (%)
Revolutionary War	4,435	0.127
War of 1812	2,260	0.030
Mexican War	1,733	0.008
Civil War (combined)	184,594	0.538
Spanish American War	385	0.001
World War I	53,513	0.052
World War II	292,131	0.219
Korean War	33,651	0.022
Vietnam War	47,369	0.023
1991 Persian Gulf War	148	0.000

Source of data: Nordhaus. W. "The Economic Consequences of a War with Iraq." (2002), Table 1, p. 6. Available at www.econ.yale.edu/~nordhaus/homepage/AAAS_War_Iraq_2.pdf.

What was the economic cost of losing the lives of these soldiers? Many studies have sought to place a dollar figure on the value of human life. Though such studies base their dollar estimates on a number of factors, two factors are fairly common throughout the studies. One factor is the value employers and employees place on reducing the risk of workplace injury and fatality. This is done by using evidence from activities that involve an implicit tradeoff between risk and money, such as joining a union, purchasing cigarettes, or accepting riskier lines of work in order to receive higher pay. The second factor is the value of wages and benefits earned over the work life of a prime-aged worker.[1]

W. Kip Viscusi of Harvard Law School, an expert on estimating the value of lives for insurance compensation, estimates that the average economic value of an American blue-collar male worker in the year 2000 was $7.5 million.[2] Table II uses the Viscusi estimate to calculate the total loss of life economic cost during the wars listed in Table I.

These values are useful to consider, but $7.5 million in the year 2000 is much different than $7.5 million in, for example, 1862. Therefore, we can adjust this figure for inflation in order to see the estimated total war cost due to the loss of life in terms of the prices at the time of the war. Adjusting the value of money for inflation requires taking the Consumer Price Index (a measure of the average cost of consumer goods—see Chapter 2 for more on the CPI) for 2000 (the year of Viscusi's estimate) and using it in the following equation:

$$\text{Value of one life in war year} = \text{Value of one life in 2000} \times (CPI_{war\ year} / CPI_{2000})$$

For example, the CPI in 2000 was 515.8 and the CPI in 1968 (during the Vietnam War) was 104.2. Therefore, the value of one life during the Vietnam War requires taking $7.5 million and multiplying it by 0.20201 (104.2 / 515.8). This computation generates a value of $1,515,122. This means $7.5 million in 2000 was the equivalent of about $1.5 million in 1968. If this figure is multiplied by the 47,369 military fatalities during the Vietnam War, then the Vietnam War generated a total loss of life economic cost of $71 billion at 1968 prices (see Table III). This is in contrast to more than $355 billion if measured in year 2000 prices.

(continued)

Box 1.2 *(concluded)*

Table II: Value of Lives Lost in Major American Wars (in year 2000 prices)

War	Number of Fatalities	Total Estimated Cost from Loss of Life
Revolutionary War	4,435	$33,262,500,000
War of 1812	2,260	$16,950,000,000
Mexican War	1,733	$12,997,500,000
Civil War (combined)	184,594	$1,384,455,000,000
Spanish American War	385	$2,887,500,000
World War I	53,513	$401,347,500,000
World War II	292,131	$2,190,982,500,000
Korean War	33,651	$252,382,500,000
Vietnam War	47,369	$355,267,500,000
1991 Persian Gulf War	148	$1,110,000,000

Non adjusted

4.435 × 7500000

(2800 × 7,500,000)
21,000,000,000
20,000 2

Source of data: Fatalities from Table I. The $7.5 million average lifetime value of blue-collar worker taken from Viscusi, W. Kip. "The Value of Life: Estimates with Risks by Occupation and Industry." *Economic Inquiry.* January 2004, pp. 29–48. Available at papers.ssrn.com/sol3/papers. cfm?abstract_id=416600. Available at papers.ssrn.com/sol3/papers.cfm?abstract_id=416600.

Table III: Value of Lives Lost in Major American Wars (at prices in war year)

War	CPI Year	CPI	CPI Year/ CPI 2003	Value of Single Life (in CPI year)	Number of Fatalities	Total Estimated Cost from Loss of Life
Revolutionary War	1800 *	51	0.0989	$741,566	4,435	$3,288,847,421
War of 1812	1813	58	0.1124	$843,350	2,260	$1,905,971,307
Mexican War	1848	26	0.0504	$378,054	1,733	$655,166,731
Civil War (combined)	1863	37	0.0717	$537,999	184,594	$99,311,428,848
Spanish American War	1900	25	0.0485	$363,513	385	$139,952,501
World War I	1917	38	0.0744	$558,356	53,513	$29,879,302,055
World War II	1943	52	0.1004	$753,199	292,131	$220,032,752,036
Korean War	1952	80	0.1541	$1,155,971	33,651	$38,899,590,442
Vietnam War	1968	104	0.2020	$1,515,122	47,369	$71,769,820,667
1991 Persian Gulf War	1991	408	0.7910	$5,932,532	148	$878,014,734

adjusted for inflation

Source of data: The CPI data is from the Federal Reserve Bank of Minneapolis—Consumer Price Index (Estimate) 1800–2000. Available at minneapolisfed.org/Research/data/us/calc/hist1800.cfm. Fatalities from Table I. The $7.5 million average lifetime value of blue-collar worker taken from Viscusi, W. Kip. "The Value of Life: Estimates with Risks by Occupation and Industry." *Economic Inquiry.* January 2004, pp. 29–48. Available at papers.ssrn.com/sol3/papers.cfm?abstract_id=416600. Available at papers.ssrn.com/ sol3/papers.cfm?abstract_id=416600.

* Earliest estimate available.

---

[1] See Viscusi and Aldy (2003) for a thorough review of the literature and methods used in life-value estimation.

[2] Viscusi (2004).

CPI₂₀₀₀ = 515.8

1.4 KEY POINTS

Key Macroeconomic Points:
- War has two economic effects: psychological and real.
- Using military expenditures to boost aggregate demand can bring the economy out of a recessionary gap, but such expenditures can also cause inflation.
- Governments have a variety of ways to finance wars: raising taxes, cutting non-military spending, printing currency, issuing debt, collecting reparations, and receiving third-party transfer payments.

Key Microeconomic Points:
- The degree to which the factors of production are mobilized (particularly capital and labor) will ultimately play a major role in determining the economic impact of the war.
- If the war's location disrupts the flow of goods and services from trading partners, this disruption will cause the war to negatively impact economies outside the war zone.

Key Terms

Iron Law of War	Inflation
Psychological effect	Purchasing power
Real effect	Nominal interest rate
Gross Domestic Product	Intermediate goods
Final goods and services	M2
Labor force	Quantity theory of money
Recessionary gap	Equation of exchange
Recession	Factors of production
Keynesian economics	Unemployment rate
Militaristic Keynesianism	Allocational inefficiency

Key Review Questions:
1. If the psychological effect has always dampened economic growth, then why do you suspect the U.S. economy still performed well during early 20th century wars?
2. When is Militaristic Keynesianism not beneficial? Explain.
3. What are the various methods of financing a war?
4. Consider the four-point scheme for evaluating the economic impact of war. What two points can government expenditure (as a percentage of GDP) measure? Explain.
5. On the basis of location, was the Iraq war started in 2003 good for either the Iraqi or U.S. economy? Explain.

Endnotes
1. Nordhaus (2002), p. 74, refers to this as the "iron law of wartime booms."
2. For an instructive discussion of how stock prices are based on expectations, see Mishkin (2004), Chapter 7, particularly p. 147. For analytical work on the relationship between stock market value and consumer sentiment, see Jansen and Nahuis (2003) and Fisher and Statman (2003).
3. Kapstein (1992), pp. 43, 49.
4. Term from Mosley (1985), Chapter 1.
5. See Rudiger Dornbusch "War and Inflation" handout. Available at web.mit.edu/rudi/www/media/PDFs/WARANDINFLATION.pdf.

6. Mishkin (2004), Chapter 4, provides a more extensive definition of the interest rate.
7. Estimates by the International Monetary Fund, Organization for Economic Cooperation and Development, and the International Atomic Energy Agency. Cited in Crooks and Morrison. "This is not the next great oil shock—at least, not yet," *Financial Times,* May 16, 2004. For a more scholastic analysis see, Hamilton and Herrera (2004).
8. Gordon, Robert. *Macroeconomics.* (1998), p. 211.
9. More on this process will be discussed in Chapter 2.
10. See, for example, Eisenhower's farewell address to the nation, 1/17/1961, from the Dwight D. Eisenhower Presidential Library. Available at http://www.eisenhower.utexas.edu/farewell.htm.

Chapter 2

The War Economy in Reality:
Case Studies of Major U.S. Wars

2.1 INTRODUCTION

This chapter will examine the Iron Law of War applied to numerous U.S. wars. The discussion will use the four-point scheme outlined in Chapter 1. The United States provides interesting cases for evaluating the economic impact of war on industrialized economies.[1] This is for two reasons. First, in addition to having considerable military prowess, both today and during most of the 20th century's major wars, the United States has a fully developed economy. Second, although the United States fought numerous wars during the last century, almost none were on its own territory.

In Section 2, the Iron Law of War is examined with regard to World War I, World War II, and the Korean War. These three wars appear to support the Iron Law of War. Section 3 looks at the Vietnam War, the 1991 Persian Gulf War, and the 2003 Iraq War, three wars that do not support the Iron Law. Finally, the Key Points in Section 4 will summarize the major findings of these case studies, particularly, what conditions are necessary for a war to support the Iron Law. To briefly review, war is economically beneficial to a country under the following circumstances: when that country has slow economic growth and low use of resources prior to the war; when there are large and sustained government expenditures during the war; when the war is not local, is of moderate duration, and is financed responsibly.

2.2 CASES THAT SUPPORT THE IRON LAW OF WAR

Figures 2.1 and 2.2 show the real GDP growth and unemployment during three wars considered by most economists to validate the Iron Law of War: World War I, World War II, and the Korean War. These wars also illustrate the Iron Law's down side: a post-war recession. The U.S. economy experienced recessions after World War I, World War II, and Korea as military expenditures returned to pre-war levels and as the economy converted back to peace-time production. This section will evaluate the economic impact of each of these three wars. When reading this section, please notice that the heading for each war includes the dates of U.S. involvement.

2.2.1 WORLD WAR I (1917–1918)

Condition of the economy prior to the war: In 1913, U.S. citizens were in the midst of the fourth recession in nearly 10 years (1902–1904, 1907–1908, 1910–1912, and 1913–1914).[2] This recession, coupled with the threat of war in Europe, created public uncertainty as U.S. real GDP shrank 7.6 percent in 1914.

Then in 1916, President Woodrow Wilson won reelection on the promise that he would continue to keep out of the European war. Consequently, there was virtually no military

Figure 2.1

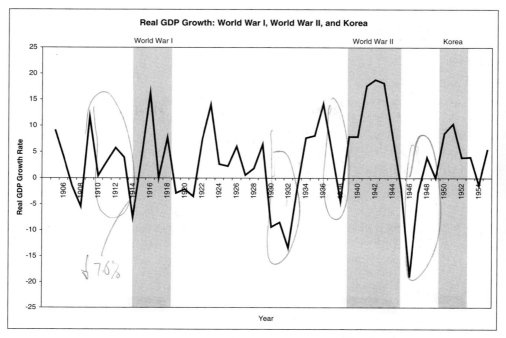

Source of data: Gordon, R. *Macroeconomics.* 7th Edition. New York: Addison-Wesley. 1998, Appendix A.

Figure 2.2

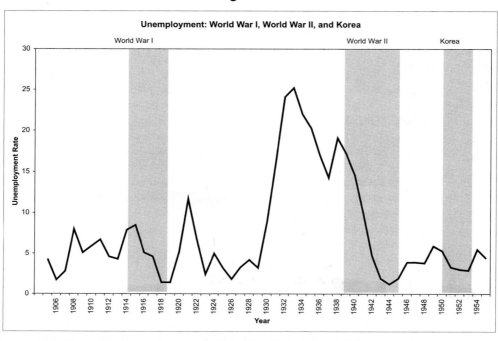

Source of data: Gordon, R. *Macroeconomics.* 7th Edition. New York: Addison-Wesley. 1998, Appendix A.

Figure 2.3

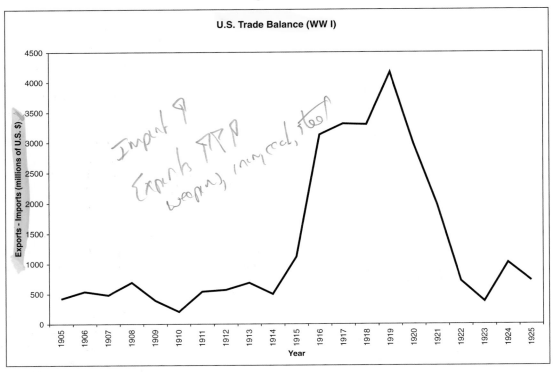

Source of data: Mitchell, Brian R. *International Historical Statistics: 1750–2000*. New York: Palgrave Macmillan. 2003, p. 427.

production prior to the war as government spending was only 3 percent of GDP in 1900 and 6 percent in 1910. The end result was that the predominately agrarian economy of the United States still exemplified that of a less-developed economy (particularly in the South). Despite all of these factors, the country gradually emerged as a world power in international politics, thanks to healthy growth in trade to Europe.

Location of the war: Even though the war was fought in a major U.S. export market, the war benefited the U.S. **trade balance** (the trade balance is the difference between **exports,** goods sold to other countries, and **imports,** goods purchased from other countries). As Figure 2.3 illustrates, the U.S. trade balance rose dramatically during the war years. Both U.S. imports (in the form of purchases of foreign military goods and raw materials, primarily from Mexico) and exports (in the form of U.S.-built weapons, iron, steel, and coal) rose at this time. But strong European demand for iron, steel, and coal prompted exports to rise by a greater amount than imports.[3]

Although the U.S. economy was unscathed by the war, the war in Europe severely devastated the European economy. As shown in the first column of Table 2.1, between 1913 and 1929 the war's primary belligerents sustained growth rates far below that of the United States. Also, in all of those countries, demand increased while supply remained limited. This result of the war is evident by observing the change in these countries' **Consumer Price Index** (CPI). The CPI tracks changes in the cost of a basket of commonly consumed household goods. When prices rise, the CPI value is high. If the CPI for all countries

Table 2.1
Economic Impact of World War I on Europe

Country	1913-1929 Average GDP Growth Rates	CPI in 1918 (1914 = 100)
Austria	0.3	1,163
Germany	1.2	304
Belgium	1.4	1,434
France	1.9	213
U.K.	0.7	200

Source of data: Feinstein, C. H.; Temin, P.; and Toniolo, G. *The European Economy Between the Wars*. Oxford, U.K.: Oxford University Press, 1997, pp. 13, 39.

in 1914 was 100, then in 1918 the CPI had increased dramatically in every country (as depicted in the second column of Table 2.1). Thus, the citizens of those countries were faced with much higher prices after the war.

Cost and financing: The total cost of the war approached 36 percent of U.S. GDP in 1918 (or 20 percent of GDP per year).[4] Though the war itself had been an unanticipated economic shock, two measures in particular had already been put in place to ensure that the government could afford to finance any prospective foreign entanglement.

First, nearly 33 percent of the war's cost was financed through the income tax created by the passage of the 16th amendment in 1909 (ratified in 1913). Though many domestic political factors explain the eventual adoption of the income tax, Congress was also aware that a European war could disrupt international trade, thereby reducing government revenue gained through **import duties** (a government tax placed on imports). The need for self-sufficient government finance in case of war was stated clearly in 1910 by then-Congressman Cordell Hull of Tennessee (later Secretary of State):

"During the great strain of national emergencies, an income tax is absolutely without rival as a relief measure. Many governments in time of war have invoked its prompt and certain aid....We cannot expect always to be at peace. If this nation were tomorrow plunged into a war with a great commercial country from which we now receive a large portion of our imports, our customs revenues would inevitably decline and we would be helpless to prosecute that war or any other war of great magnitude without taxing the wealth of this country in the form of incomes."[5]

Second, the war's cost was financed through the issue of Liberty Bonds facilitated by the banking sector. Banks purchased approximately 20 percent of these bonds, while the non-banking public purchased the rest (the patriotic public ate up the bonds).[6] The banking sector was capable of this feat thanks to the passage of the Owen-Glass Act of 1913 that created the **Federal Reserve System** (the Fed). The Fed was created in response to the banking crisis that befell the United States in 1907 (which required the wealthy J.P. Morgan to bail out the U.S. government). The creation of the Fed began the movement toward rationalizing banking and currency (i.e., making these factors more organized and bringing them under more centralized control), which enabled the national banking system to pool together finances and reserves to purchase the Liberty Bonds.

Resource mobilization: The war fundamentally changed the U.S. economy. As government expenditures rose to account for over 20 percent of production by 1918, the economy became characterized as "war socialism" or "state capitalism."[7] President Wilson created the War Industries Board to organize production, industry by industry. Railroads were seized and brought under one gauge so as to eliminate bottlenecks that threatened to prevent men and materials from reaching Europe. Millions of federal money went into shipbuilding. So many ships were produced that those vessels not ready for service by the war's end were sold at bargain prices. A large dam was built on the Tennessee River to supply the necessary power for nitrate extraction (nitrates and nitrogen are needed for fertilizer and explosives). As much as 30 percent of car production was switched to tank production. Farmers bought more machinery and farmed more land during the war. From the labor perspective, though only 5 percent of the population fought in the war, the increased farming and government-financed industrial production drove the unemployment rate down to 1.4 percent (see Figure 2.2).

Result: Because many countries purchased weapons and munitions from the United States, by the war's end the United States had become the world's largest creditor country. Interestingly enough, the economic impact of World War I on the United States is highly analogous to the experience of the United Kingdom during the Napoleonic wars at the beginning of the 19th century (see Box 2.1).

However, even though the war led to massive growth in the U.S. economy, this war "growth" came at a price. The U.S. and the world economy experienced a severe recession immediately after the war. How did this recession happen? The perception that "The Great War" was the "the war to end all wars" meant much of the military apparatus was dismantled after the war. As a consequence, the industrial and farming capacity created during the war became unnecessary afterwards as the economy began the slow and painful process of conversion back to a peacetime economy.

2.2.2 WORLD WAR II (1941–1945)

Condition of the economy prior to the war: The average real GDP growth rate of the U.S. economy in 1940 and 1939 was 7.9 percent. However, remnants of the Great Depression still remained, as the economy had shrunk 4.5 percent as late as 1938; and average unemployment, though lower than its peak of 25 percent during the 1930s, still stood at 15.9 percent.

Location of the war: Although Hawaii and Alaska were impacted by the war, for the most part the war was fought in Asia, Europe, and Northern Africa. Thus, this war was mainly somewhere else other than the United States. However, much like with World War I, this did not reduce U.S. exports. As Figure 2.4 illustrates, the U.S. trade balance improved dramatically during the war years, as the U.S. sold weapons to its allies, particularly to the United Kingdom and Russia (see the **Resource Mobilization** section).

Cost and financing:[8] The total cost for the United States, in terms of military expenditures, of this war was over 130 percent of U.S. GDP in 1945 (or 31 percent of GDP per year).[9] At peak level, military expenditures accounted for more than one-third of GDP (37.9 percent

Box 2.1
Historical Perspective
Britain during the Napoleonic Wars

The British and French fought seven major wars between 1689 and 1815.[1] Of special economic interest are the French Wars (1793–1815), which include the French Revolutionary Wars (1793–1802) and the Napoleonic Wars (1803–1815). As Paul Kennedy writes, these wars "more than ever before [had]…economic factors intermeshed with strategy."[2]

Condition of economy prior to war: Industrial revolution had already taken hold in Britain around the middle of the 1700s, but the British economy was still primarily agricultural, as can be seen by the mean growth rate of the cotton industry compared to the iron and coal industries from 1780–1790 (see Table I):

Table I: Mean Output Growth by Industry (1780–1790)

Industry	Growth per year
Cotton	12.8
Iron	3.8
Coal	2.4
13 Industry average	3.7

Source of data: Dickenson, H.T. *Britain and the French Revolution, 1789–1815*. New York: St. Martin's Press. 1989, p 200.

Location: The war's location was on the continent of Europe, not England. In a sense, this fact not only allowed England to serve as the "nation of shopkeepers" during the war, but it also contributed to the wars' length. England had a dominant Navy; France, a dominant Army. Therefore, the English were never able to bring their full military power to bear on the French. When they did, as in the famous 1805 Battle of Trafalgar, the British won. Instead, the British relied heavily on funding the troops of the other continental powers. This last point would prove expensive for England.

Cost and financing: The total cost (in 1989 prices) was approximately £1.657 billion. This sum includes subsidies to its allies, particularly Prussia, from 1793–1801 to assist the ground war. On a per-year basis, the state's expenditures during the peak years of the war, 1808–1815, amounted to nearly 25 percent of the national income compared to a government share of 6 percent in the late 1780s and early 1790s.[3]

Initially, these costs were financed through borrowing. Taxes (primarily through customs, land taxes, and excise taxes on certain goods) were increased only enough to pay the interest on the added debt. This increase was in place so as to prevent an escalation of debt (as was incurred during the American Revolutionary war) and to continue to pay down existing debt. The British government (particularly Prime Minister William Pitt) thought it a sustainable policy because he assumed the war would not last long.

This assumption was mistaken, as the war would last for over 20 years! As the war advanced, taxation increased every year. In 1793, the taxes necessary to pay the interest amounted to £250,000. For the second year, £650,000 was needed and for the third year, £1.1 million was required to pay the interest. As the debt continued to accumulate, Pitt finally resorted to higher taxation. In particular, he implemented taxes on income, first through an assessment tax (flat tax on declared income) and then through a 10 percent income tax.[4]

As a result, taxes as a percentage of commodity output soon rose. Taxes stood at approximately 20 percent in 1795, but reached nearly 50 percent by 1815. Still, even these increases in tax revenue could not prevent the British government from generating its largest deficits during this period. The deficit's largest value, of just around £35 million, occurred near 1800 and 1815, but deficits never dropped below £10 million for the entire war. This compares unfavorably to a surplus in the early 1790s and to a maximum pre-war deficit peak of just under £30 million (during the American Revolutionary War).[5]

Resource mobilization: According to Crouzet (1989), the war effort in Britain mobilized by the British government was considerably large at the time for a traditional economy of low per-capita income. Some statistics do highlight the shift in the economy's composition due to the war. Iron and coal production rose sharply, whereas cotton's growth slowed considerably (Table II).

The labor mobilization was quite significant, approaching U.S. World War I levels. In 1792, England had only 100,000 men in its Navy and Army; but this number would rise to 500,000 by 1815. These forces absorbed over 10 percent of the men in the 18–45 year age group.

Because men were typically fed better in the Army and Navy than in civilian life, this requirement placed additional demand on foodstuffs and, consequently, agricultural output increased faster during the wars than during the two or three preceding decades. Specifically, the increase in output was placed near 25 percent. Despite the presence of the

(continued)

Box 2.1 *(concluded)*

Table II: Mean Output Growth by Industry (1790–1811)

Industry	Growth per Year
Cotton	5.6
Iron	7.0
Coal	2.9
13 Industry average	2.6

Source of data: Dickenson, H.T. *Britain and the French Revolution, 1789–1815.* New York: St. Martin's Press. 1989, p 200.

Industrial Revolution, agriculture's contribution to national income rose from 26 percent in 1801 to 33 percent in 1811. However, high grain prices had begun to fall in 1813 and agriculture's share of national income fell back to 26 percent by 1821.

Results: There is mixed evidence as to whether the wars had a positive or negative impact on the British economy. There was sharp, though not runaway, inflation. The Gayer index of wholesale prices of domestic and imported commodities rose from 89 in 1790 to a peak of 169 in 1813 (a

90 percent increase). Many economists argue that private investment and private consumption were crowded out by the large increases in government borrowing. On a per capita basis, private consumption fell 10 percent. On the other hand, by disrupting established patterns of continental finance to Amsterdam and Frankfurt, the war helped cement London's position as the world financial center, as evidenced by the surge in British exports during the war (Figure I). Finally, the fact remains that British productivity and wealth rose during the war and the economy could bear the burdens of financing the war for itself and its allies.

Figure I

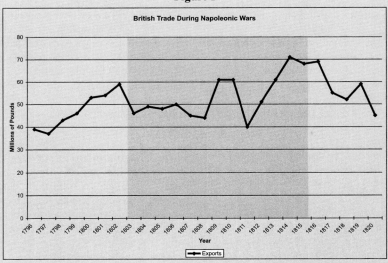

Source of data: Mitchell, Brian R. *International Historical Statistics: The Americas 1750–2000.* New York: Palgrave Macmillan. 2003.

---

[1] Primary sources are these three:
Kennedy (1988), pp. 115–129.
[2] "War Against Napoleon." Channel 4 United Kingdom. History site. At www.channel4.com/history/microsites/H/history/napoleon/against1.html .
"French Revolutionary Wars." The Columbia Encyclopedia on-line (2001).
[3] O'Brien, P.K. "Public Finance in the War with France: 1793–1815" in Dickenson, H.T. (ed.) *Britain and the French*

Revolution, 1789–1815. New York: St. Martin's Press.1989.
[4] Cooper, Richard. "William Pitt, Taxation, and the Needs of War." *Journal of British Studies.* Vol. 22. Autumn 1982, pp. 94–103.
[5] Bordo, M.D., and White, E.N. "A Tale of Two Currencies: British and French Finance during the Napoleonic Wars." *Journal of Economic History.* Vol. 51. June 1991, pp. 303–316.

Figure 2.4

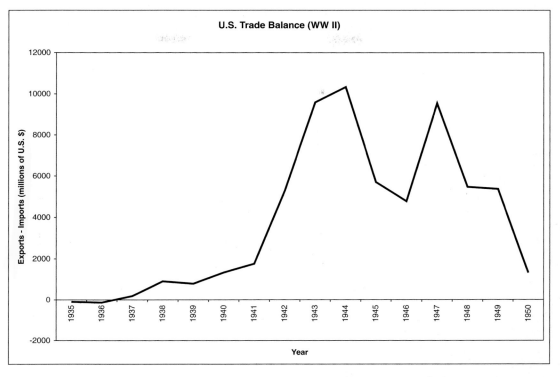

Source of data: Mitchell, Brian R. *International Historical Statistics: 1750–2000.* New York: Palgrave Macmillan. 2003, p. 427.

in 1944); non-military government expenditures fell to less than half of their pre-war level (3.0 percent of GDP in 1945, compared to 7.2 percent in 1940). The budget deficit rose from a 3.0 percent deficit in 1940 to a 30.3 percent deficit by 1943.

Some tax increases were implemented (The Revenue Act of 1942, The Current Tax Payment Act of 1943, the Revenue Act of 1943, and the Individual Income Tax Act of 1944). However, because financing such massive increases in government spending through taxation would have required impossibly large tax increases, the government relied primarily on inducing the private sector to save, while simultaneously creating money to pay for debt. First, the prices of consumer goods were fixed and controlled from 1942 through 1945. This control kept the increase in prices below the increase in salaries. At the same time, consumer goods were rationed through the use of purchase coupons. These dual policies artificially created a higher private savings rate, which generated excess funds for households to purchase war bonds.

Next, in 1942 the Fed (through the request of the Treasury) formally committed to maintaining a low interest rate on the government bonds. This commitment served to keep interest rates low, which enabled the federal government to engage in cheaper debt financing.[10]

When the government issues a bond to borrow money, it must pay the holder of that bond interest, as a reward for the loan. For example, a 10 percent interest rate means that if the government borrows $1,000 from a household, then it must eventually pay back to the household its initial $1,000 plus $100 in interest. If the rate were 5 percent instead of 10 percent, then the government would only have to pay back an additional $50.

Figure 2.5

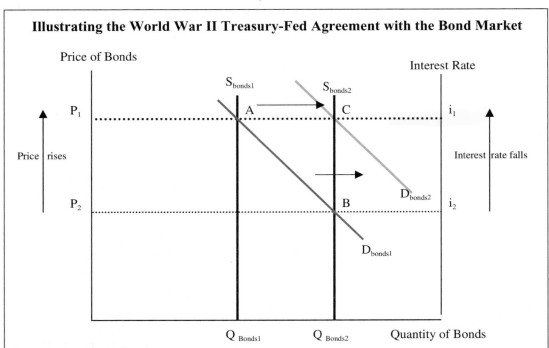

Illustrating the World War II Treasury-Fed Agreement with the Bond Market

For a simple depiction of how the Treasury-Fed agreement worked, consider the market for government bonds illustrated in Figure 2.5. Keep in mind that the price for bonds and the interest paid on bonds have an inverse relationship: when the price of bonds increases, the interest rate on bonds decreases; when the price of bonds decreases, the interest rate on bonds increases. The left-hand vertical axis shows the prices on bonds, while the right-hand vertical axis shows the interest rates of bonds. The higher you go on the left-hand vertical axis, the higher the price of the bond. The higher you go on the right-hand vertical axis, the lower the interest rate of the bond.

Next, notice that the demand curve for bonds (D_{bonds}), like the demand curve for any other good, is downward sloping. For a given level of income, as the price of bonds rise, households will purchase a lower quantity. The supply of bonds (S_{bonds}) is vertical to indicate that the amount of bonds issued by the government is a function of the government's need to borrow money. The amount of government bonds issued is not dependent on the price of the bonds themselves. For instance, if the government needs to acquire the funds to fight a major war, it will issue more bonds, regardless of the price offered for those bonds.

Starting at point *A* on Figure 2.5, the government is shown to increase the supply of bonds, as it did to finance World War II. S_{bonds} shifts right from S_{bonds1} to S_{bonds2}. Because bonds are now more numerous, this increase places downward pressure on the price of bonds and, consequently, upward pressure on the interest rates of bonds. The market is now at point *B*. The higher interest rate could make it more expensive for the government to pay for the debt it is issuing. However, the Federal Reserve can reduce the interest rate by printing money and purchasing these bonds. This strategy increases the demand for bonds, thereby shifting D_{bonds} from D_{bonds1} to D_{bonds2}. This shift raises the price of bonds and returns the interest rate to its lower level (point *C*).

Table 2.2
United States Trade Balance, 1938–1948 ($ millions)

Year	Export	Imports	Balance of Goods and Services
1938	4336	3045	1291
1939	4432	336	4096
1940	5355	3636	1719
1941	6896	4486	2410
1942	11769	5356	6413
1943	19134	8096	11038
1944	21438	8986	12452
1945	16273	10232	6041
1946	14792	6985	7807
1947	19819	8202	11617
1948	16861	10343	6518

Source of data: Harrison, M. (ed.). *The Economics of World War II.* Cambridge, U.K.: Cambridge University Press, 1998, p. 96.

Resource mobilization: The war's physical resource mobilization was so massive that the structure of the U.S. economy fundamentally changed. Americans began the war with a market economy; they ended up with a centrally planned economy with price controls, rationing, and the government using nearly half of all the economy's output. Though the attack that finally pulled the United States into the war was Pearl Harbor in 1941, the Roosevelt administration had actually begun the military build-up in 1940. Specifically, the United States was supplying weapons and munitions to the allies through a variety of programs.

For example, in the spring of 1940, the British began placing large-scale orders with American factories for weapons.[11] Britain initially paid for the bulk of these orders with the transfer of over $2 billion in gold (known as the **'Cash and Carry' policy**). Technically, up until 1941, Germany could also have purchased weapons. However, because U.S. neutrality laws required countries to pay in *cash*, and *carry* the weapons away in non-U.S. shipping boats, Germany's government could not buy due to a lack of dollar reserves and little freedom of surface shipping movement on the Atlantic. Next, the **Lend-Lease Act** (enacted in March of 1941 and lasting until June 1945) allowed a loan of $50 billion worth of weapons to the British, with the expectation that these weapons would be returned after the war. This loan contributed to a near doubling of U.S. exports from 1941 to 1942 (see Table 2.2).

The attack on Pearl Harbor provoked the Americans to expedite and increase weapons production. Table 2.3 uses aircraft production numbers to illustrate the rapid rise after Pearl Harbor of U.S. production relative to other belligerent countries. From 1942 through 1944, there is noticeable growth in aircraft production.

Similar trends can be seen with U.S. tank production. Between 1918 and 1933, the United States produced only 35 tanks. In 1940, the United States produced 309 tanks; and 29,500 in 1943. Altogether, the United States produced 88,430 tanks during World War II. This number of U.S. tanks compares to only 24,800 for the U.K., and 24,050 for Germany.[12]

Table 2.3
Annual Aircraft Production During World War II

Country	1939	1940	1941	1942	1943	1944	1945
U.K.	7,940	15,049	20,094	23,672	26,263	26,461	12,070
U.S.	2,141	6,086	19,433	47,836	85,898	96,318	46,001
U.S.S.R.	10,382	10,565	15,735	25,436	34,900	40,300	20,900
Germany	8,295	10,826	12,401	15,409	24,807	40,593	7,540
Japan	4,467	4,768	5,088	8,861	16,693	28,180	8,263

Source of data: Gropman, Alan. *Mobilizing U.S. Industry in World War II.* McNair Paper Number 50. National Defense University. 1996, Chapter 9.

Table 2.4
The Working Population of the United States, 1938–1946
(thousands, annual average of monthly series)

	1938	1939	1940	1941	1942	1943	1944	1945	1946
Employed population total (civilian)	44,142	45,738	47,520	50,350	53,753	54,470	53,960	52,820	55,250
Unemployed population total	10,390	9,480	8,120	5,560	2,660	1,070	670	1,040	2,270

Source of data: Harrison, M. (ed.). *The Economics of World War II.* Cambridge, U.K.: Cambridge University Press. 1998, p. 101.

The magnitude of labor mobilization meant females and minorities became more involved in the U.S. economy and in the military. In this sense, World War II may have created the conditions for the women's movement and the civil rights era. To place into context the size of the labor resource mobilization, consider that prior to 1939 the U.S. Army had less than half of the 280,000 troops authorized by the 1920 National Defense Act; but by 1942, the army had well over nine million troops.

Similar evidence of massive labor mobilization can also be seen on the civilian side, with a large increase in the employed population (and decline in the unemployed population) during the war (Table 2.4).

Result: The large percentage of the population fighting and working during the war drove the unemployment rate down to an average of 3.92 percent from 1941–1945. Average annual real GDP growth stood at nearly 11 percent per year from 1941–1945 and inflation rose from −1.4 percent in 1939 to 7.9 percent by 1946. In short, World War II epitomizes both the Iron Law of War and the inflationary impact of war.

2.2.3 KOREA (1950–1953)

Condition of the economy prior to the war: During the two years prior to the Korean War, the U.S. economy was still coming out of a post-World War II slump. Average GDP growth was a mere 1.88 percent over the two years prior to the war. Unemployment had averaged an economically sound 5 percent per year for the two years prior to the war, and in 1949 inflation had actually been negative (−1.2 percent).

Location: From the United States' perspective, the Korean Peninsula was not an economically sensitive region. The war began in June 1950 when Kim Il-Sung, leader of the Democratic People's Republic of Korea (North Korea) secured the backing of the Soviet Union and invaded the South in an effort to unify the Peninsula (which was split after World War II). The Truman administration had originally not considered Korea an American defense priority in the Pacific. However, the United States quickly dispatched troops from Japan to the Southern Republic of Korea after the North's invasion. Truman, after coming under criticism for not stopping China from becoming communist, took his country to war primarily to follow through on his pledge to fight communism anywhere in the world (the **Truman Doctrine**).

Cost and financing:[13] The total cost, in terms of military expenditures, of this three-year war (1950–1953) reached 14 percent of U.S. GDP in 1953 (or 4 percent of GDP per year), a significant figure, given the brief duration of the war.[14] The administration of U.S. President Harry Truman did not wish to rely on the practices of extensive borrowing and money creation used during World War II. Throughout the late 1940s, the Treasury and Fed had maintained the practice of directing monetary policy toward the maintenance of low Treasury bond interest rates. The switch to wartime financing in 1950–1951 made evident that continuing such a policy would prove highly inflationary. Therefore, the **Fed-Treasury Accord of 1951** allowed the Federal Reserve to focus on maintaining price stability, rather than interest-rate stability.

As a result, President Truman financed the war largely through taxation and reductions of non-military government expenditures. Non-military government expenditures fell from 8.8 percent of GDP in 1950, to 5.4 percent in 1951, to 4.9 percent in 1952. The Revenue Act of 1950 increased income-tax revenue by 1.3 percent of GDP; while the Revenue Act of 1951, by further increasing income and corporate taxes, raised an additional 1.9 percent of GDP in tax revenue. Such fiscal prudence is evident by low budget deficits (–1.1 percent of GDP in 1950; +1.9 percent in 1951; –0.4 percent in 1952), the lowest of any of the wars evaluated in this chapter.

Resource mobilization: Resource mobilization for the Korean War will be discussed further in Box 3.1 in Chapter 3. For now, it is important to know that resource mobilization for fighting this war was a crucial component of U.S. Cold War strategy and played an instrumental role in creating a permanent military industry in the United States. The physical resource mobilization was quite significant. For instance, by using growth of defense expenditures to reflect physical resource mobilization, in the third quarter of 1951 there was a 110 percent rate of annual defense spending growth. That rise in growth has never again been matched.

Result: The Truman administration could afford to raise taxes dramatically during the war in part because the Korean War was short and less costly than World War II. Truman also had the benefit of an economy that was experiencing strong growth. Real GDP growth averaged approximately 6.2 percent a year during the three years of the conflict and unemployment stood at 3.61 percent. Unfortunately, tax increases and even price controls could not prevent inflation from rising in 1951 to 7.3 percent. Therefore, the Korean War not only supports the Iron Law of War, but also the inflationary impact of war.

2.3 CASES THAT DO NOT SUPPORT THE IRON LAW OF WAR

Figures 2.6 and 2.7 show the performance of real GDP growth and unemployment during the 1991 Persian Gulf War and the initial stages of the 2003 Iraq War. Along with the Vietnam War, these wars offer little support for the Iron Law of War. In fact, throughout history, even as far back as ancient history, war has proven economically devastating for many societies (see Box 2.2).

2.3.1 VIETNAM (1964–1973)[15]

State of economy prior to war: As a result of the plastics revolution, highway construction, and government spending for the space program, the economy was growing strongly in the early 1960s. Specifically, in 1962 and 1963 the U.S. real GDP grew at an average rate of 4.18 percent and the unemployment rate averaged 6.10 percent. In 1962 inflation stood at only 1 percent.

Location: The Vietnam War was fought in Southeast Asia in order to prevent a "domino" conversion of former French colonies to communism. This region was not economically sensitive to the Americans, but the administration of U.S. President Lyndon Johnson feared that losing South Vietnam would diminish U.S. credibility and threaten the stability of American alliances, particularly its commitment to the Southeast Asian Treaty Organization (SEATO).

Cost and financing: The total cost of the war, in terms of military expenditures, reached 8 percent of U.S. GDP in 1973. However, this cost was incurred over a decade (1964–1973), thereby equating to an average per year cost of approximately 1 percent of GDP.[16] In fact, unlike in World War II and the Korean War, nonmilitary government expenditures rose during the Vietnam War as President Johnson sought to expand the U.S. welfare system through his Great Society program (begun in 1964). Consequently, average yearly growth of non-military government spending was 14 percent from 1965–1971. This spending growth is in contrast to a negative 11 percent for World War II and a negative growth of 6 percent for the Korean War.[17]

To compensate for the rise in nonmilitary expenditures, the White House escalated U.S. involvement in Vietnam gradually and did not fully divulge the expected cost of the war. For instance, during the early years of American engagement, the Department of Defense refused to supply separate figures for the costs associated with the war. As reported by *Fortune* magazine, "The official position of the Defense Department is that it does not know what the costs of the war are, and that it does not even try to compute them. We have no intention of cost-accounting the war in Vietnam. As one Pentagon official said, 'Our business is to support the conflict there....We have no estimate of costs.'"[18] In 1966, Congress became intolerant of this approach and so by 1967, the Pentagon began to provide the 'incremental cost' of the war—i.e., the costs over and above the normal cost of the defense establishment—which peaked in 1968 at $23 billion (the same year troop deployment peaked at 534,700).[19]

Initially, the Johnson administration was unwilling to push for tax increases to finance the war and other programs. Instead, the U.S. government began borrowing. The budget deficit rose from 0.8 percent of GDP in 1963 to 2.9 percent in 1968. In 1968, Johnson finally acquiesced to raising taxes. First, he installed a temporary 10 percent surcharge on income taxes. Second, the Tax Reform Act of 1969 repealed the investment tax credit, restricted the tax-exempt status of foundations, and broadened the individual tax base.

Figure 2.6

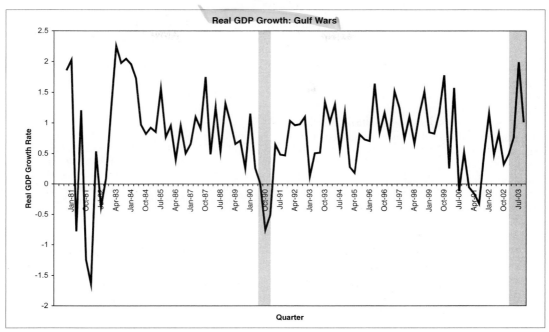

Source of data: Federal Reserve Economic Data (FRED) database of the Federal Reserve Bank of St. Louis. Available at http://research.stlouis.fed.org/fred2/data/GDP.txt.

Figure 2.7

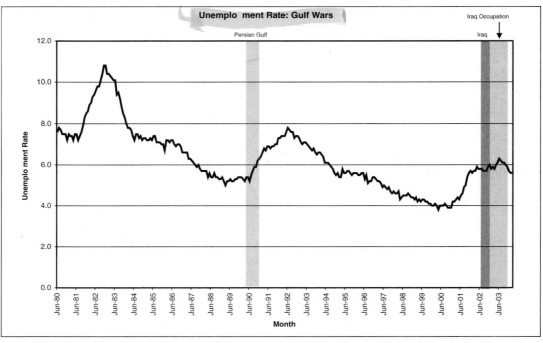

Source of data: Federal Reserve Economic Data (FRED) database of the Federal Reserve Bank of St. Louis. Available at http://research.stlouis.fed.org/fred2/data/GDP.txt.

Box 2.2
Historical Perspective
Athens during the Peloponnesian Wars

Background and state of the economy prior to war: The outbreak of what was actually the second, but longer and more devastating Peloponnesian War (431 B.C.E. to 404 B.C.E.) has drawn frequent comparisons to that of World War I. Both Athens and Sparta were dominant Greek city-states that had forged and led alliances comprised of other city-states.

Athens the city, located in the relatively mountainous and poor region of Attica, was actually quite wealthy. Early wars had built up its coffers (at one point holding over 6,000 talents–a form of currency—in the 430s), which it used to beautify the city (such as constructing the Parthenon) and import food from Ukraine and the Black Sea (which was actually more than the food grown in Attica itself). Athens also built a large wall around its city and its port.

Athens's central location in the Aegean Sea enabled it to become a large maritime empire. Athens's Navy and merchants accrued large sums of revenue from trade and, more so, from levies paid by members of the Delian League. This League comprised what is often referred to as the Athenian Empire. Its primary constituents included the islands of Chios, Lesbos, and Samos. These city-states would pay tributes to Athens. The tribute revenue enabled Athens to have over 342 triereis (ships), pay rowers to stay at their oars eight months out of the year, and as a result, "the Athenian Navy became by far the biggest and best fleet ever known."[1] In return, the Athenian Navy maintained security along the Aegean Sea's trade routes.[2] Though the provision of security on the Aegean Sea was a public good susceptible to free-riding (see section 6.6 for a thorough discussion of free-riding and public goods), this situation was tolerable to the larger member city-states as long as the tribute burden imposed by Athens was light (which was not always the case) and the protection secure (which, again, was not always the case).

Much like World War I, a confluence of factors contributed to the regional powers entering war. However, a widely accepted explanation (and one that allows us to move on with our economic analysis) is that the bipolar system created by the Athenians and Spartans became unstable when the Spartans feared the growing economic and diplomatic might of Athens.

Location: The war was fought throughout the Greek world, but Attica's countryside in particular incurred substantial damage. This toll on Attica was due largely to the strategy proposed by Pericles, a general who was a member of the Athenian assembly. Through his charisma and reputation for successful policymaking, he became the de facto leader of the Athenians.[3] His strategy was agreed to by the Greek citizens and is described here by Kagan (1995):

> "He [Pericles] understood the likely outcome of a traditional war in the same way as did the Spartans, so he devised a novel strategy made possible by the unique character and extent of Athens's power. It was naval power that permitted the Athenians to rule over an empire that provided them money with which they could sustain their naval supremacy and to obtain what they needed by trade or purchase. Its lands and crops were open to attack, but Pericles had all but turned Athens into an island by constructing long walls that connected the city with its ports and naval base at Piraeus. In the current state of Greek siege warfare these walls were invulnerable when defended, so that the Athenians could safely move within them and allow their fields to be ravaged, using the income from the empire to provide them with necessities and to maintain the fleet. If the Athenians were willing to withdraw within the walls the Spartans could neither get at them nor defeat them."[4]

Ironically, this strategy actually contributed to Athens's eventual defeat.

Duration, cost, and financing:[5] The second war lasted 27 years (431 B.C.E–404 B.C.E.) at a total cost for Athens between 35,000 and 47,500 talents.[6] Taking the middle number (41,250 talents) and dividing it by 27 (number of years) gives an annual cost of 1527 talents: a cost that, according to Thucydides, shocked most Athenians.

Athens relied primarily on the tributes collected from its Athenian League allies to finance its Army and Navy. In 477 B.C.E., Athens collected 460 talents and from 470–454 B.C.E. Athens collected 400–560 talents annually. Unfortunately for Athens (but fortunately for visitors of Greece today), these tributes neither served to build an adequate treasury coffer—because much was spent on beautification projects and the wall[7]—nor covered the fleet's expenses even in the few years without major wars. In fact, most of the money for the beautification projects came from the spoils of smaller wars against Persia dating back to 490 B.C.E.

(continued)

Box 2.2 *(concluded)*

In 431 B.C.E. (the year war with Sparta began), tributary collection rose to 600 talents. Between 429 and 420 B.C.E. Athens collected 1,300 talents annually. This gradual increasing of the tribute had two negative consequences. First, it increased the transaction costs of collecting tributes. Athens now had to commit troops to special collection ships. Second, and most importantly, it left a gap of 227 talents between war costs and revenue. So from 433 through 423 B.C.E., Athens borrowed an average of 600 talents per year from Polinas and Nike.

Because Athens had to borrow such funds, the citizens of Athens voted in 428 B.C.E. to impose a tax on itself (though who exactly paid the tax is unknown) as a means to generate revenue that could eventually pay back the loans. In 413 B.C.E., Athens replaced the tribute system with a 5 percent tax on all goods passing through ports. When this tax still proved inadequate to meet the war's cost, in what now appears to be an act of desperation, in 410 the tribute system was reestablished *and* the tax on all goods passing through ports was raised to 10 percent.

Resource mobilization and result: The exorbitant cost of the war and the strategic approach adopted by Athens created three conditions that led to Athens's defeat. First, the budgetary problems of Athens and the subsequent 'squeezing' of its allies for revenues weakened Athens economically and diplomatically. Second, the siege strategy adopted by Athens led to the devastation of its crops on the countryside, the onset of plague in the city, and an inability of Athens to take the war to Sparta. Thus, by 413 B.C.E., nearly half of the Athenian population was either enslaved by the Spartans, or dead. Third, if the ships were not fighting, they were collecting money. This activity not only lessened the ability of Athens to provide security, but

it also required a large number of troops. For example, the campaign in Sicily initially required 134 ships and nearly 40,000 persons. Unfortunately, the budgetary problems created difficulties in continually financing such large naval campaigns, particularly against such a militarily adept foe as Sparta. Soon, this naval over-stretch, coupled with the lack of financing, led to the Athenian Navy's final defeat in 405.

In short, the experience of Athens during the Peloponnesian War illustrates that, as Neal points out, "a society's ability to finance for long periods of time a substantial diversion of resources from useful economic activity is obviously a major determinant of its probable success at war, as much as its martial spirit and its command of weaponry, logistics, and personnel."[8] In addition, the overall impact of the war, according to Yale historian Donald Kagan, was bad for all of Greek society:

"The war was a terrible watershed in Greek history, causing enormous destruction of life and property, intensifying factional and class hostility, dividing the Greek states internally and destabilizing their relationship to one another, ultimately weakening the Greek capacity to resist conquest from outside."[9]

---

[1] Kagan (1995), p. 23.
[2] Neal (1994), Introduction.
[3] Kagan (1995), pp. 26-27.
[4] Kagan (1995), p. 63.
[5] Primary source: Morris (2003), available at www.stanford.edu/group/sshi/empires/morris.pdf.
[6] Know that 1 talent would be the approximate equivalent of $15,000 in 1996 U.S .dollars.
[7] Garraty and Gay (1972), p. 171
[8] Neal (1994), Introduction.
[9] Kagan (1995), p. 16.

Though these measures raised government revenue by 0.2 percent of GDP by 1970, the budget remained at a deficit of 2.0 percent of GDP. Furthermore, the taxes served to make the war more unpopular.

Inflationary pressures began to percolate in the economy. Inflation had risen to 4.5 percent in 1969, 5.5 percent in 1970, and 5.0 percent in 1971. Though the Federal Reserve had not been obligated since 1951 to use money creation to finance U.S. government debt (**monetizing the debt**), the inflation was due in large measure to debt monetization. For instance, consider Figure 2.8. This figure shows the growth rate of M1, a measure of the currency in circulation. Notice that the growth rate of the money supply increased dramatically starting in the mid-1960s.

Why was the Fed monetizing the U.S. budget deficits? To answer this, refer back to Figure 2.5. One can see that when the U.S. government issues more bonds in order to borrow money, this increase in the supply of bonds places upward pressure on interest

Figure 2.8

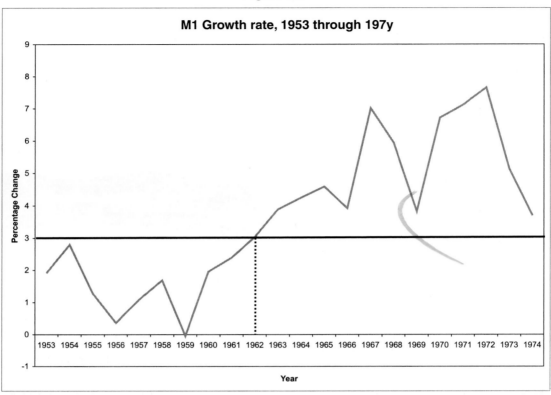

Source of data: Federal Reserve Economic Data (FRED) database of the Federal Reserve Bank of St. Louis. Available at http://research.stlouis.fed.org/fred2/data/GDP.txt.

rates in the bond market. Higher interest rates in the bond market will, in turn, lead to higher interest rates in the **loanable funds market** (the market in which the private sector borrows money for such things as homes, education, and business expansion). This result occurs because as the government issues bonds, the bonds are purchased with money that could have been lent to other people. Consequently, funds available for the private sector have diminished. This lack of funds is called the **Crowding Out Effect.** Because there are now fewer funds available in the loanable funds market, people in the private sector will start competing more vigorously for the remaining funds. This competition for loans will drive up the 'price' of the remaining funds (the price is the interest rate). The private sector may begin to reduce expenditures, due to fewer funds and higher interest rates in the loanable funds market. This reduction could slow down the economy and lead to higher unemployment. Therefore, during the late 1960s, the Federal Reserve wished to counter the Crowding Out Effect by keeping funds available and interest rates low.

Unfortunately, the Fed's approach for pursuing this objective was conceptually flawed. At that time, conventional economic wisdom held that there exist a permanent tradeoff between unemployment and inflation.[20] Figure 2.9 illustrates the tradeoff between inflation and unemployment, what is called the **Phillips Curve.** Moving from point *A* to point *B* shows that, in this theory, as inflation rises, unemployment falls.

Figure 2.9

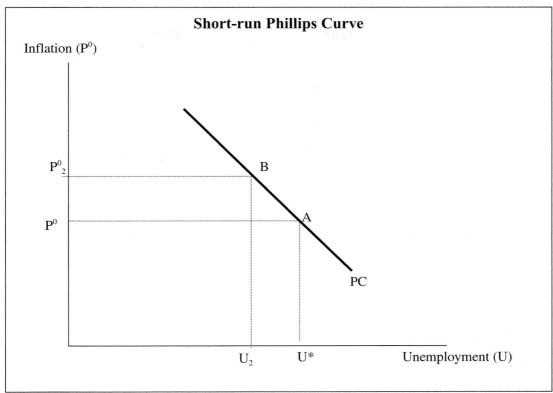

Short-run Phillips Curve

Therefore, even though the Fed knew that keeping unemployment low (through the creation of money) would also cause inflation, the Fed was willing to tolerate the higher inflation because it believed unemployment would stay low. However, it was only in the 1970s that economists came to fully accept the findings of Milton Friedman and Edmund Phelps. Each scholar had argued that the Phillips Curve depicted in Figure 2.9 only illustrates a short-term phenomenon. According to the **Friedman-Phelps Phillips Curve** model, the tradeoff between inflation and unemployment disappears in the long run. In the long run, workers and firms will adjust prices and wages to account for the higher inflation rate.

Two things occur as a result. First, workers become more expensive, which means firms will not be as willing to hire. Second, products become more expensive, which means households will be less willing to purchase these items. As fewer items are purchased, fewer items are produced. Unemployment increases. Unemployment returns to the level at point A, but now at a higher rate of inflation. This result is shown in Figure 2.10 by the movement to point C. Connecting points A and C of Figure 2.10 creates a vertical line. This line is the **long-run Phillips Curve** (*LPC*). The downward sloping line connecting points A and B (the original Phillips Curve) is the **short-run Phillips Curve** (*SPC*).

In summary, because the Fed miscalculated how the factors of money creation, unemployment, and inflation interact, the Fed believed that it could keep interest rates low for a much longer time than was truly practical.

Figure 2.10

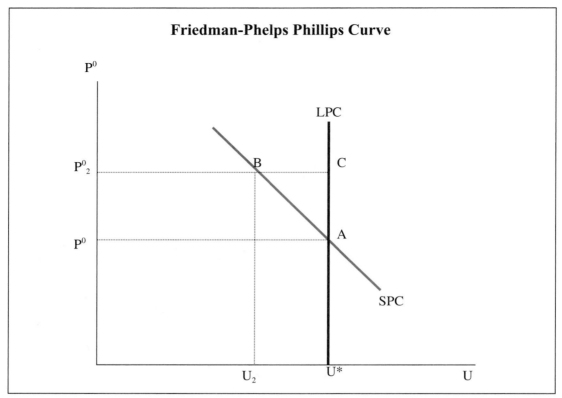

Friedman-Phelps Phillips Curve

Resource mobilization: The mobilization of resources was very gradual. With regard to labor resources, it took almost a year and a half for the United States to amass 185,000 troops in Vietnam. This troop number can be compared to the 250,000 troops more quickly amassed in the Persian Gulf region in the months just prior to the 2003 war with Iraq (which, it should be noted, was considered to be a "small" army). Yet, by the end of 1966, there were 385,000 troops in Vietnam and 535,000 by the end of 1967. Total military personnel were 4.3 percent of the population. This number was significantly less than the 12.3 percent of World War II, but only 0.3 percent lower than that of World War I. The physical resource mobilization, as indicated by the cost figures discussed above, was rather modest considering it was spread out over a decade. However, eventually the United States would drop more bombs from 1965 to 1973 than were dropped in World War I, World War II, and the Korean War combined (and all in an area slightly larger than New Mexico).

Result: Figures 2.11 and 2.12 illustrate the performance of real GDP growth and unemployment during the Vietnam era.

Unemployment did drop significantly during this period, reaching a low of 3.5 percent and an average of 4.55 percent over the duration of the war. Yet, the prolonged nature of the war soon became a drag on a vibrant economy. By overheating the economy, the Vietnam War, coinciding with a time of full employment in the U.S. economy and an expansion of social programs, arguably laid the basis for the "Great Inflation" of the 1970s.[21] Admittedly,

Figure 2.11

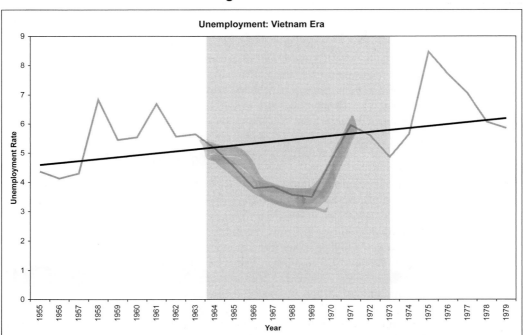

Source of data: Federal Reserve Economic Data (FRED) database of the Federal Reserve Bank of St. Louis. Available at http://research.stlouis.fed.org/fred2/data/GDP.txt.

Figure 2.12

Source of data: Federal Reserve Economic Data (FRED) database of the Federal Reserve Bank of St. Louis. Available at http://research.stlouis.fed.org/fred2/data/GDP.txt.

Figure 2.13
University of Michigan Consumer Sentiment Index, by Month (1987–2003)

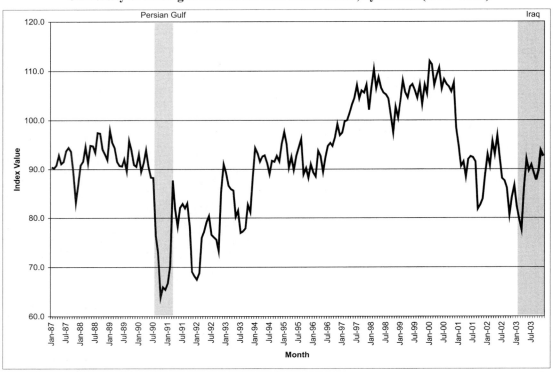

Source of data: Federal Reserve Economic Data (FRED) database of the Federal Reserve Bank of St. Louis. Available at http://research.stlouis.fed.org/fred2/data/GDP.txt.

because the war did not dominate the economic policies of the day, it is difficult to separate the economic impact of the Vietnam War from other factors. However, it does seem reasonable to suggest that while the Vietnam War initially supported the Iron Law of War, its protracted nature, coupled with overall government profligacy and overly loose monetary policy, eventually harmed the economy.

2.3.2 1991 PERSIAN GULF (1990–1991)

State of economy prior to war: The savings and loan scandals of 1988 and the overhang of large government deficits during the 1980s contributed to unsteady consumer confidence in the U.S. economy prior to Iraq's invasion of Kuwait. The University of Michigan's **Consumer Sentiment Index** (an index that measures how consumers view the health of the economy; higher scores indicate more consumer confidence) had fallen from a rating of 97.9 in January 1989 to 93.0 in January 1990, and then further to 88.2 in July 1990 (Figure 2.13). When Iraq invaded Kuwait in August, consumer sentiment fell to 76.4. Real GDP growth, though still positive, was lower than during the mid-to-late 1980s.

Location: This war was fought in the Persian Gulf, a region critical for determining the world price of oil because it is where a large portion of the world's oil supply is extracted. Therefore, the war was fought in an economically sensitive region for the global economy

Figure 2.14
World Crude Oil Futures Prices during the 1991 Persian Gulf War

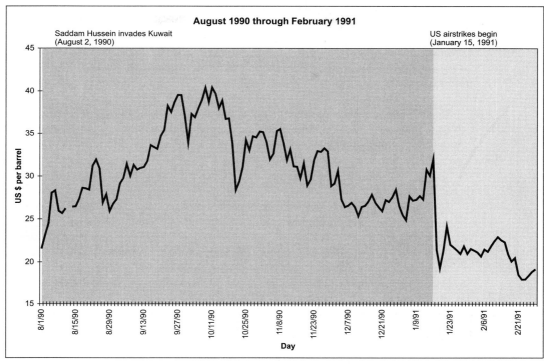

Source of data: Oil prices from "Daily NYMEX Light Sweet Crude Oil Futures Prices," the Energy Information Administration (EIA), U.S. Department of Energy. Available at www.eia.doe.gov/emeu/international/petroleu.html#Prices.

and particularly for the United States. Even though the United States only receives approximately 24 percent of its imported oil from the Gulf States (2.2 million barrels per day, out of 9.1 million barrels per day), the oil emanating from this region drastically impacts the world price of oil.[22] Therefore, any turmoil in this region will disrupt oil production and, in turn, raise the price of crude oil world-wide. When Iraqi President Saddam Hussein authorized his forces to invade Kuwait, the United States and United Nations (U.N.) responded with a military buildup in the region that forced the price of crude oil to rise dramatically. Yet once the war began, prices quickly returned to their initial levels (Figure 2.14).

Cost and financing:[23] The cost of the war, in terms of military expenditures, was approximately 1 percent of U.S. GDP in 1991 or $60 billion ($31.5 billion for the major combat phase, $30 billion spent in the wrap-up phase—i.e., shipping troops and equipment home or back to Europe).[24] However, this cost does not include maintaining no-fly zones in northern and southern Iraq after the war (see the Iraq 2003 case study).

The financing of this war is the most unique and perhaps most interesting of the 20th-century U.S. wars. Whereas other wars required borrowing, tax increases, or reductions in nonmilitary expenditures, this war was paid primarily by other countries. In effect, the United States did the fighting while other countries paid the bill. Because the administration of U.S. President George H.W. Bush had secured a U.N. mandate for operations in the Gulf region, it successfully concluded a series of bilateral agreements that encouraged U.S.

allies—particularly Germany and Japan, who for constitutional reasons could not send troops—to pledge funds amounting to $44 billion. Kuwait and Saudi Arabia contributed another $9.5 billion upon the completion of major combat operations.

Resource mobilization: Resource mobilization was minimal. There were low levels of government military expenditures and only a small increase in federal spending. Only about 1 percent of the U.S. population was in the military. Most telling, the unemployment rate rose.

Result: Because the resource mobilization was low, the primary impact on the American economy was a rise in oil prices and psychological dampening. These factors served to tip the economy from a slow-growth phase to a recession.

2.3.3   IRAQ (2003–present)

State of economy prior to war: Prior to the war, the U.S. real GDP growth rate was positive, but slow (real GDP growth was 1.8 percent in second quarter of 2002, 3.3 percent in third quarter of 2002 and 1.5 percent in fourth quarter of 2002).[25] This slow growth, combined with close to 30 percent of production capacity going unused (normal level is approximately 15 percent), meant that the economy was not growing fast enough to reduce unemployment. In fact, the unemployment rate had been increasing over the preceding year (4 percent to nearly 6 percent).

As the unemployment rate increased, the prospect of war became ever more evident. The combination of these forces contributed to a dip in consumer confidence. In March of 2003, the University of Michigan's Consumer Sentiment index fell from 86.7 in December of 2002 (the recent peak had been 96.9 in May 2002) to a rating of 77.6, its lowest level since 77.3 in August of 1993 (see Figure 2.13). For perspective, the index was constantly above 100 from 1997 until late 2000. In short, the impending conflict caused a negative psychological impact.

Location: Unlike the oil price increase incurred during the Persian Gulf War of 1991 (see section 2.3.2 above) the rise in oil prices during this war was not due exclusively to the U.S. military buildup near Iraq. When oil market futures prices closed above $30 per barrel on August 20 of 2002 (a record high at the time), this high was due as much to turmoil in Venezuela and Nigeria (major non-Gulf oil-producing states) as to a concern over a U.S. invasion of Iraq.[26] What concerned traders in the oil markets most was the possibility that Saddam Hussein would damage his oil fields (as happened after the 1991 Persian Gulf War), which would have caused an extended rise in the price of oil. The combination of all these factors eventually drove the price of crude oil above $40 per barrel.

Cost and financing:[27] Prior to the war, the U.S. defense-related expenditures had already been experiencing a steady rise due to stabilization and reconstruction operations in Afghanistan and new homeland security programs. For example, defense spending in general was already 66 percent above what it was in 1997 (an increase of $120 billion), with only a portion of this spending increase going directly toward facilitating the war in Iraq. This steady increase, combined with the unknown duration or nature of the conflict, meant pre-war cost projections varied widely (see below).

The invasion phase of the war lasted from March 20, 2003 until May 1, 2003, although no official cease-fire agreement was signed. Instead, this timing coincides with U.S. President George W. Bush's declaration that "major combat operations" were over. Given this time period, the cost of the invasion was approximately $28-$30 billion. This cost includes $11 billion for moving and setting up troops and equipment (the airlift and sealift of troops and equipment, troop support, housing and feeding, and maintenance of equipment); $9 billion for the first three and a half weeks of conflict; another $5–$7 billion for returning troops and equipment home; and an estimated $2 billion in combat and support costs during the final two weeks of April.

The subsequent occupation added a further $4–$5 billion a month or an additional $52–$65 billion total by the end of June 2004 (when Iraq regained its sovereignty). This figure places the total cost at approximately $80–$95 billion by July 1 of 2004 and $100–$120 billion by December 1, 2004. Both figures represent less than 1 percent of U.S. GDP in 2003 (not including interest payments).[28] Though both costs are very small relative to the cumulative costs of previous American wars, it is interesting to consider these costs in context:

Cost relative to pre-war estimates: [29] Prior to the war, the estimated cost of the war and occupation ranged from $27 billion (Congressional Budget Office estimate) to $688 billion (Center for Strategic and Budgetary Assessments estimate). William Nordhaus of Yale University attempted estimates that went beyond the budgetary financing of the war. His estimates factored in the reaction of oil markets and potential losses to the U.S. economy. Nordhaus's estimates ranged from a favorable-scenario cost of $99 billion to a worst-case scenario cost of nearly $2 trillion.

Cost relative to continuing containment policy: [30] After the 1991 Persian Gulf War, in an effort to prevent Saddam Hussein from acquiring the revenue to construct and operate a weapons-of-mass-destruction program, the United States and U.N. imposed **economic sanctions** on Iraq (economic sanctions are the denial of exports to, imports from, or financial relations with a target country in an effort to change the country's laws or policies).[31]

Additionally, in order to protect Iraq's neighbors and the minority ethnic groups within the country (particularly the Kurds living in the northern portions of the country), the United States and United Kingdom established and monitored regions in the northern and southern portions of the country (called "no-fly" zones). Iraqi planes were not permitted to fly within these zones.

The combination of sanctions and no-fly-zone monitoring formed a policy called **containment.** Accounting for per-person per-year deployment, operating costs, and depreciation of equipment (30,000 troops, 30 ships, and 200 aircraft), the U.S. spent approximately $13 billion per year on containment. This cost is significantly less than that of the invasion phase of the Iraq War, but this cost would have been incurred annually for as long as the Hussein regime remained in power. Given the failure of sanctions to induce regime change in countries such as Cuba and North Korea, conservative estimates project that the policy of containment would have continued for nearly 33 years. With these figures (and without discounting the expected present value of future expenditures), the cost of containment approaches an estimated total cost of $300-$400 billion. Also notable, these costs do not account for the devastation wrought upon the Iraqi people and economy by the sanctions.

Financing: The Bush administration and the Congress agreed to several rounds of tax reductions in 2001/2002. Therefore, though the Iraq War bears little resemblance to the Vietnam War in terms of political and military reality, parallels can be drawn between the financial consequences of the two wars (see section 2.3.1). Specifically, history suggests that the cost of the war, the continued U.S. military involvement in other regions, and the expansion of domestic social programs make sustaining such tax reductions problematic.

Furthermore, because the U.S. invaded Iraq without U.N. authorization, it cannot finance the Iraq War as easily as it did the 1991 Persian Gulf War in which other countries offered substantial financial assistance.

Resource mobilization: The low cost of the Iraq war relative to the size of the entire U.S. economy means this war did not require a massive mobilization of physical resources. This situation is due in large part to the military becoming more technologically dependent. Specifically, advances in technology have three effects on physical resource mobilization.

First, the military requires fewer armaments. With better technology, the military requires fewer munitions. For example, in the 1991 Persian Gulf War, an aircraft carrier's air-wing (group of fighters, typically 70 to 80) could be expected to hit 200 targets. In 2003, the same air-wing could hit 700 targets.[32]

Second, armaments are less expensive. This lower cost is illustrated by the success of guided-missile technology. In the 1991 Persian Gulf War, a Tomahawk cruise missile could perform a precision bombing at a cost of $1 million. In the 2003 Iraq War, old "dumb" bombs could be converted into guided munitions using a JDAM package (Joint Direct Attack Munitions) at a cost of $20,000.[33]

Third, technological spillover is reversed. As will be discussed in Chapter 5, technology normally spills over from the military to the private sector with beneficial economic outcomes. However, in today's military, the technological spillover is from private to military. For example, the targeting system in an Abrams M1 tank runs on a laptop and operates similar to a video game.

Labor mobilization has also been limited. This limited mobilization is because the military is now more dependent on jobs that are low labor-intensive/high capital-intensive. Therefore, the military no longer requires as many active-duty troops. Additionally, at the end of the Cold War and throughout the 1990s, the U.S. Congress, for budgetary and security reasons, began to reduce the size of the active duty contingent of service members. However, the result of reducing the active-duty contingent has been a need to call up military reservists. This reliance on reservists is reflected by the decline in the Active/Reserve (A/R) ratio since 1990 (shown in Figure 2.15). In addition to reliance on more reserve personnel, the military also resorted to extending the tours of duty for many active and reserve service members beyond what was originally planned. The military also issued a "stop loss" measure. This measure concerns personnel who could leave the military when their volunteer commitment expires. According to the measure, these personnel must remain to the end of their overseas deployment.[34]

Result: The war had a comparatively low cost. It was located in an economically sensitive region and it hurt consumer confidence. However, based on the rise in real GDP growth seen in Figure 2.6, is it possible that the war did support the Iron Law? The war did in fact give the economy a boost, just not a sustained one. In the second quarter of 2003, real GDP growth reached 2.4 percent. Over a quarter of that growth was accounted for by a 25 percent annualized pace in the growth of government spending (meaning that government spending would increase by 25 percent for the year if the pace from that quarter continued for the rest of the year). The government spending was attributable to a 44.1 percent annual rate of increase in defense spending (the fastest pace in defense spending growth since a 110 percent rate in the third quarter of 1951).[35] However, this boost was not sustainable because the majority of expenditures were geared toward troop and hardware transportation and maintenance, not the replacement of munitions or the purchasing of additional weapons.[36]

Once the war began and the troops quickly converged on Baghdad, consumer sentiment rebounded quickly, rising to 92.1 in May of 2003 before eventually rising to103.8 in

Figure 2.15

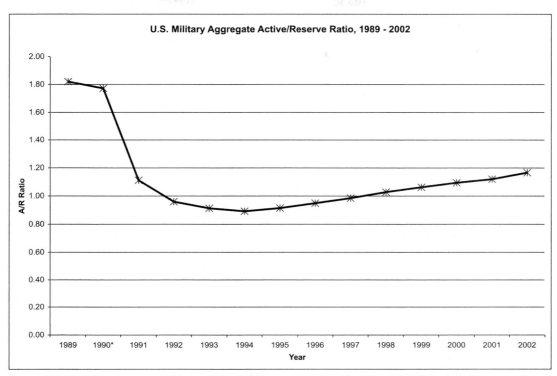

U.S. Military Aggregate Active/Reserve Ratio, 1989 - 2002

Source of data: U.S. Department of Defense. "Selected Manpower Statistics, Fiscal Year 2002." Table 2-11. Directorate for Information Operations and Reports. Available at http://web1.whs.osd.mil/mmid/pubs.htm.

January of 2004. Removing the shroud of uncertainty, rather than the military expenditures, probably played the primary role in the continued growth in the U.S. real GDP.

Finally, despite the mobilization not being large enough to have a macroeconomic impact, the mobilization has had a dramatic microeconomic impact. Many communities have experienced one of the negative consequences of the lower A/R ratio. Because the military is forced to call up more reservist and National Guard units, communities have lost police officers, nurses, teachers, mechanics, and other vital occupations from the private sector. At the same time, other communities, particularly those located in Washington, Mississippi's Gulf Coast, and Southern California, have benefited greatly from the increase in expenditures. Metropolitan Washington, D.C., with its numerous government contractors, gained 42,000 jobs in 2002 and had an unemployment rate of only 3.5 percent. Corporations such as Virginia-based Unisys Corp. hired about 900 new workers. Los Angeles-based Northrop Grumman Corp. increased employment by nearly 6,000 employees. General Dynamics Corp. added 250 jobs to fulfill increased orders for the Stryker assault vehicle.[37]

Unfortunately, this argument should not be overplayed. Many defense contractors witnessed the price of their stock rise rapidly after September 11, 2001 only to return to normal levels (and, in the case of Boeing, fall below the September 2001 level). The inability of these stocks to continue growing is because, as was mentioned previously, many defense-contracting experts consider the Iraq War as marking a move away from massed warfare toward smarter, computerized fighting. Consequently, Cold War-style programs such as the

F-22 warplane (Boeing), the Comanche helicopter (Boeing-Sikorsky), and the Crusader cannon (United Defense-General-Dynamics) have been canceled (or will be). Other Cold War-era equipment that proved its usefulness in Iraq, such as the General-Dynamics M1 Abrams tank, may survive such military revamping.

2.4   KEY POINTS

Key Macroeconomic Points:

- Earlier 20th century wars—World War I, World War II, and Korea—appear to unequivocally support the Iron Law of War.
- Under certain conditions war is beneficial for the economy. These conditions are slow economic growth entering the war; low use of resources entering the war; large sustained expenditures during war; a conflict of moderate duration; a war not fought on the homeland territory; and a war that is financed responsibly.
- Later wars, starting particularly with Vietnam, have failed to meet many of the criteria necessary for war to be economically beneficial.
- Government spending still rises with the onset of war, but the rise in expenditures may simply represent a one-time increase spike in troop hazard pay, mobilization of existing troops and equipment to the war region, and additional orders of explosives (bullets and missiles).
- The Federal Reserve intentionally helped finance World War I, World War II, and Korea. A misunderstanding concerning the long-run operation of the Phillips Curve contributed to the Fed's unintentional financing of the Vietnam War.

Key Microeconomic Points:

- Recent wars have benefited individual firms who receive government contracts.
- As the Active/Reserve ratio declines, recent wars have harmed communities when reservists are placed on active duty.

Key Terms

Consumer Price Index	Economic sanctions
Trade balance	Containment
Exports	Monetizing debt
Imports	Loanable funds market
Federal Reserve System	Crowding out effect
Cash and Carry policy	Phillips Curve
Lend-Lease Act	Friedman-Phelps Phillips Curve
Truman Doctrine	Long-run Phillips Curve
Fed-Treasury Accord of 1951	Short-run Phillips Curve

Key Questions

1. From an economic perspective, what similarities are there between the Vietnam War and the 2003 Iraq War (and subsequent occupation of Iraq)?
2. How did location benefit the United States during World War I and World War II, but harm the United States during the 1991 Persian Gulf War?
3. How is the financing of the 1991 Persian Gulf War different from other wars?
4. Why did the Vietnam War generate large budget deficits, but the Korean War did not?
5. Based on the evidence found in these case studies, what, in your opinion, is the ideal manner in which to finance a war?

Endnotes

1. See Chapter 6 for a discussion of the impact of war on developing economies.
2. National Bureau of Economic Research (NBER), "U.S. Business Cycle Expansions and Contractions," Available at www.nber.org/cycles/.
3. See Mitchell (2003), p. 468 for data on the increase in imports from Mexico, and p. 504 for the rise in U.S. iron, steel, and coal exports to Europe.
4. Source of data: Chapter 1, Table 1.2.
5. Schwartz, Jordan, in Higgs (1990), pp. 4–5.
6. See Meltzer (2003), p. 89, for a discussion on the Fed's role in financing WWI.
7. Schwartz, Jordan, in Higgs (1990), p. 6.
8. Information for this section comes from Labonte (2001), pp. 5–7 (unless otherwise cited).
9. Source of data: Chapter 1, Table 1.2.
10. *The Fiftieth Anniversary of the Treasury-Federal Reserve Accord,* Federal Reserve Bank of Richmond, 2001. At http://www.rich.frb.org/research/specialtopics/treasury/index.html.
11. Information in this paragraph from Harrison (1998), pp. 94–95.
12. Gropman (1996), Chapter 9.
13. Primary source is Labonte (2001), pp. 7-8.
14. Source of data: Chapter 1, Table 1.2.
15. Primary sources include McCormick (1995), Labonte (2001), and information from the University of Illinois's MAPS journal. Discussion of the Friedman-Phelps Phillips Curve from Virginia Postrel's "Rethinking Milton Friedman," in *The New York Times,* November 6, 2003; also from Gordon (1998), p. 574.
16. Source of data: Chapter 1, Table 1.2.
17. Riedl, Brian. "Most New Spending Since 2001 Unrelated to the War on Terrorism." Heritage Foundation (2003). Available at www.heritage.org/research/budget/bg1703.cfm.
18. Bowen, William. "The Vietnam War: A Cost Accounting." *Fortune,* April 1966; as cited in Kapstein (1992), p. 77.
19. Kapstein (1992), pp. 77–78.
20. See Taylor (1992) and Sargent (1999) for further discussion of the Phillips Curve explanation. Nelson (2004) argues against this explanation, but for pedagogic purposes it is appropriate to present the Phillips Curve here.
21. The term *Great Inflation* is used widely by economists to describe the 1970s. For examples, see Virginia Postrel's "Rethinking Milton Friedman" in *The New York Times,* November 6, 2003. In addition: Taylor (1992), and Nelson (2004).
22. Source: Energy Information Administration (EIA). *Petroleum Supply Annual,* Vol. 1. U.S. Department of Energy, 2003. Table 21. Available at http://www.eia.doe.gov/pub/oil_gas/petroleum/analysis_publications/oil_market_basics/Trade_Links.htm.
23. Primary source for cost and financing is the introduction in Neal (1994).
24. Source of data: Chapter 1, Table 1.2.
25. Source: "Economic Growth Revised Up." *CNN/Money,* February 27, 2004. Available at money.cnn.com/2004/02/27/news/economy/gdp/.
26. Source: "World Oil Market and Oil Price Chronologies: 1970–2003," Energy Information Administration, U.S. Department of Energy. Available at www.eia.doe.gov/emeu/cabs/chron.html#a1997.
27. Main sources: "Cost of War," *Economists Allied for Arms Reduction.* Available at www.ecaar.org. For estimates of Iraq War's cost by the end of Fiscal Year 2004 and Fiscal Year

2005, also see *Congressional Budget Office,* "Estimated Costs of Continuing Operations in Iraq and Other Operations of the Global War on Terrorism," June 25, 2004, available at www.cbo.gov/ftpdoc.cfm?index=5587&type=1.

28. Source of data: Chapter 1, Table 1.2.
29. Source: "How Much Will War Cost?" *CNN/Money,* March 19, 2003. Available at money.cnn.com/2003/03/17/news/economy/war_cost/.
30. Primary Source: Davis et al. (2003). Available at gsbwww.uchicago.edu/fac/steven.davis/research.
31. From Hufbauer (1998).
32. Hettena, Seth. "Nimitz deployment brings unprecedented firepower to Middle East." *The Associated Press* news dispatch. March 1, 2003. Available at www.globalsecurity.org/org/news/2003/030301-nimitz01.htm.
33. "Military-industrial Complexities." *The Economist,* March 19, 2003, p. 55.
34. "Army Expanding 'Stop Loss' to Keep Soldiers from Leaving." *USATODAY.* January 5, 2004.
35. "GDP Growth Accelerates," *CNN/Money,* July 31, 2003.
"Rise in Defense Spending Gives Economic Boost in Some Areas," *The Wall Street Journal*, April 15, 2003 1;1
"GDP Data Spark Hopes Recovery Is Strengthening." *The Wall Street Journal,* August 1, 2003.
36. "Military-industrial Complexities," *The Economist,* March 19, 2003, p. 55.
37. "Rise in Defense Spending Gives Economic Boost in Some Areas." *The Wall Street Journal,* April 15, 2003.

■ UNIT TWO ■

Military Economics

Chapter 3

Defense Spending and the Economy

3.1 INTRODUCTION

Politics in the United States can be a divisive issue. Because members of the Democratic and Republican parties vehemently argue to fund their favored programs, votes to approve such funds often split down party lines. However, in late June 2004, both the U.S. House of Representatives and Senate accomplished a rare feat—both passed near unanimous spending bills (403 to 17 vote in the House, and 98 to 0 vote in the Senate). This bipartisan support is easily explained. The bills were to authorize over $400 billion in defense spending; because the United States was at war during an election year, no politician of either party wanted to be accused of failing to support U.S. troops.[1]

Because the United States is the wealthiest nation in the world (in 2000 the U.S. economy was equal in size to that of the next four largest national economies—Japan, Germany, France, and Britain—combined), it can afford to spend $400 billion on defense. As of 2004, the U.S. accounted for 38 percent of all military spending worldwide, as much as the next 11 countries combined. The rest of the North Atlantic Treaty Organization (NATO) countries and Japan, taken together, account for only about 27 percent of global military expenditures. Based on 2004 estimates, by 2006 the U.S. defense budget would equal that of all the other countries in the world together. In 2003, the *increase* in U.S. defense spending was nearly as large as Britain's entire defense budget and three-quarters of China's defense budget. Yet, despite this impressive level of defense spending, U.S. military expenditures as a percentage of Gross Domestic Product (GDP) are less than in the early 1990s and only half of that spent at any given year during the Cold War.[2]

Section 2 offers a brief discussion on the growth and composition of U.S. military expenditures over the past 50 years. Sections 3 and 4 consider the macroeconomic costs and benefits of these expenditures. Section 5 compares U.S. defense expenditures to those of other countries. Section 6 explores why countries militarize and how this can result in an economically detrimental arms race.

3.2 U.S. MILITARY EXPENDITURES

3.2.1 Military Expenditures Compared to Other Government Expenditures

Figures 3.1 through 3.3 tell an interesting story. Since World War II there has been a noticeable upward trend in both U.S. military expenditures and nonmilitary expenditures, though military expenditures have been more volatile (Figure 3.1). To gain some insight into why military expenditures have continually increased, take a look at the discussion of the military-industrial complex, found in Box 3.1.

Even though military expenditures are large in terms of dollars, they are rather small when compared to the size of the U.S. economy (as measured by GDP). In fact, as a percentage of GDP, military expenditures have fallen steadily (Figure 3.2). Additionally,

Box 3.1
Historical Perspective
Eisenhower and the Creation of the Military-Industrial Complex

The entrenched relationship between government and military firms is captured in the phrase **Military Industrial Complex** (MIC). This phrase was famously coined by U.S. President Dwight Eisenhower in his January 1961 farewell address. In his address he attributes the MIC's creation and persistence to a multitude of factors.[1]

National security: First, Eisenhower mentions national security:

> "A vital element in keeping the peace is our military establishment....Until the latest of our world conflicts, the United States had no armaments industry. American makers of plowshares could, with time and as required, make swords as well. But now we can no longer risk emergency improvisation of national defense; we have been compelled to create a permanent armaments industry of vast proportions."

This concept was embodied in the National Security Council policy position document NSC-68.[2] After the Communist coup in Czechoslovakia, the Berlin blockade of 1948, the first Soviet nuclear weapons test in August 1949, and the Communist takeover of China in 1949, the Truman administration exercised the militarization option of NSC-68. This policy entailed rearming America and its allies through an increase in military spending and aid.[3]

Economics: Second, Eisenhower highlights the economic motives underlying the MIC:

> "Added to this, three and a half million men and women are directly engaged in the defense establishment. We annually spend on military security more than the net income of all United State corporations. . . . Our toil, resources and livelihood are all involved; so is the very structure of our society."

Sustaining high military expenditures during peacetime offered the short-term positives of pulling the United States out of the 1949/1950 recession and revitalizing the industrial sector that had been hampered by post-war overcapacity. Additionally, military expenditures could maintain full employment until trade agreements could be reached.

Scientific research: Third, Eisenhower indicates that the new relationship between research scientists and the government motivated the creation and continuance of the MIC:

> "Akin to, and largely responsible for the sweeping changes in our industrial-military posture, has been the technological revolution during recent decades. In this revolution, research has become central; it also becomes more formalized, complex, and costly. A steadily increasing share is conducted for, by, or at the direction of, the federal government."

The essence of Eisenhower's reasoning is found in the July 1945 report to President Roosevelt by director of the Office of Science Research and Development (OSRD), Vannevar Bush. Upon the urging of Bush, President Roosevelt began the National Defense Research Committee in 1940—the precursor to the OSRD—as a civilian-controlled body to oversee the progress of U.S. military research projects. That scientific research played an important role in winning World War II was not lost on Roosevelt. In a letter to Vannevar Bush dated November 17, 1944, Roosevelt writes:

> "The Office of Scientific Research and Development represents a unique experiment of cooperation in coordinating scientific research and in applying existing scientific knowledge to the solution of the technical problems paramount in war.... There is no reason why the lesson to be found in this experiment cannot be profitably employed in times of peace. The proper roles of public and of private research, and their interrelation, should be carefully considered."[4]

Hence, the success of scientific research prompted the government to continue adopting Bush's philosophy of government-supported civilian scientific research. For example, the Navy was dubbed by *Newsweek* as "the Santa Claus of basic physical science."[5]

Political motivations: Throughout, Eisenhower mentions potential political motives, though it is only near the end of the address that he refers specifically to their corrupting influence:

> "As we peer into society's future, we—you and I, and our government—must avoid the impulse to live only for today, plundering, for our own ease and convenience, the precious resources of tomorrow. We cannot mortgage the material assets of our grandchildren without risking the loss also

(continued)

Box 3.1 *(concluded)*

of their political and spiritual heritage. We want democracy to survive for all generations to come, not to become the insolvent phantom of tomorrow."

Specifically, embedded political incentives contribute to the MIC's continuance. World War II witnessed the proliferation of new government agencies. They included the War Production Board, the Office of Price Administration, the War Manpower Commission, the War Food Administration, the OSRD, the War Shipping Board, the War Labor Board, Office of Strategic Services (precursor to CIA), as well as numerous new bases. As a result,

federal employment grew dramatically in the early 1940s and, despite declining after the war, would never again fall to pre-war levels (Table I).

As this enlarged bureaucratic structure sought a new mission after World War II, politicians began to exploit it as a form of patronage. Hence, the MIC exists, in part, because it generates privately appropriable benefits— profits for corporations, union wages, bureaucratic jobs, Congressional votes, research grants, and so forth. These benefits, in turn, enable a politician to stay in office or make his or her job easier.[6]

Table I: Federal Government Employment (in thousands), 1935–1950

Year	Total Employment	Department of Defense
1935	766	147
1936	850	148
1937	878	161
1938	865	163
1939	936	196
1940	699	256
1941	1081	556
1942	1934	1291
1943	2935	2200
1944	2930	2246
1945	3370	2635
1946	2212	1416
1947	1637	859
1948	1569	871
1949	1573	880
1950	1439	753

Source of data: U.S. Census Bureau. Statistical Abstract of the United States 2003. Available at www.census.gov/statab/hist/HS-50.pdf.

[1]See citation in Chapter 1, endnote 10.
[2]NSC-68: United States Objectives and Programs for National Security. National Security Council Report to the President. April 14, 1950. Available at www.fas.org/irp/offdocs/nsc-hst/nsc-68.htm.
[3]McCormick (1995), pp. 88–98.

[4]FDR to VB, November 17, 1944. National Science Foundation archives. Available at www.nsf.gov/od/lpa/nsf50/vbush1945htm.
[5]Zachary (1997), p. 329.
[6]Lee "Public Goods, Politics, and Two Cheers for the Military-Industrial Complex" in Higgs (1990) pp. 22–36.

military expenditures have continually comprised less and less of total government expenditures (Figure 3.3). In contrast, nonmilitary expenditures have increased as a percentage of GDP (Figure 3.2).

3.2.2 Composition of the Defense Budget

On what (and for what) are military expenditures directed? Figure 3.4 offers a snapshot of the distribution of U.S. Department of Defense expenditures over the past 50 years. Figure 3.5 shows the categories of defense expenditures as a percentage of the entire defense

Figure 3.1
U.S. Federal Government Expenditures (1947–2003)

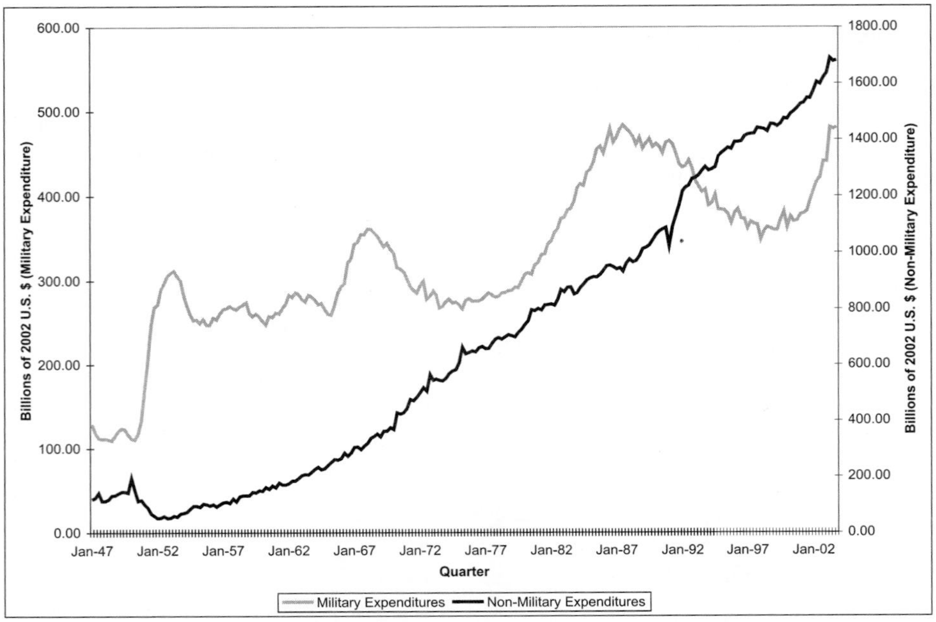

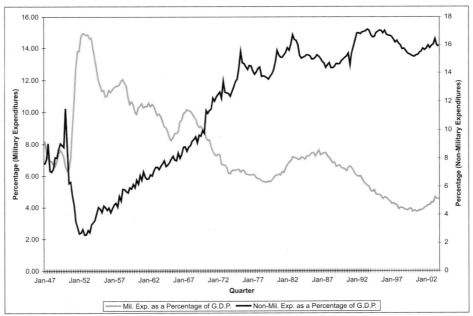

Source of data: Federal Reserve Economic Database (FRED). Federal Reserve Bank of St. Louis. Available at http://research.stlouisfed.org/fred2.

Figure 3.2
U.S. Federal Government Expenditures as a Percentage of GDP (1947–2003)

Source of data: Federal Reserve Economic Database (FRED). Federal Reserve Bank of St. Louis. Available at http://research.stlouisfed.org/fred2.

Figure 3.3
U.S. Military Expenditures as a Percentage of Federal Government Expenditures
(1947–2003)

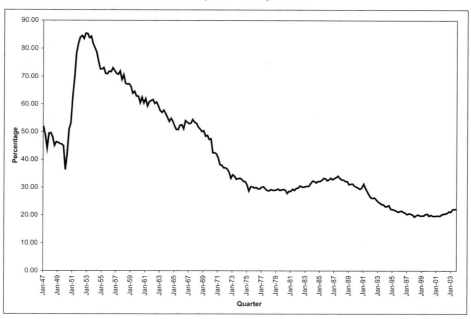

Source of data: Federal Reserve Economic Database (FRED). Federal Reserve Bank of St. Louis. Available at http://research.stlouisfed.org/fred2.

budget for each year. Note that the defense budget is primarily geared toward two functions: paying for personnel and paying for equipment. Historically, of the categories directed toward personnel, pay towards Department of Defense (DoD) civilians (such as the people who assisted me in creating these charts), has not been as large as the compensation directed toward military service members in uniform (in terms of pay and benefits such as housing and food). But this gap has been closing since the 1980s. It is clear, too, that as pay to military personnel has declined as a percentage of the defense budget, benefits ("Other Pay") have increased.

Because the "Total Military Personnel Pay" category includes all service members in uniform (active, reserve, and National Guard), it is worth looking at Figure 3.6. It shows the distribution of total military personnel pay from 1996 through 2005. As can be seen, pay towards Reservists and National Guard members comprise a very small portion of pay toward military personnel. As the final column shows, pay to active duty service members constitutes over 80 percent of total military personnel pay.

Overall, 60 percent of the total DoD budget is dedicated toward support and logistics units. This focus is because the majority of active-duty service members conduct tasks that assist the combat-directed units. This focus is known as the **tooth-to-tail** ratio. "Tooth" refers to the combat-directed units (fighter pilots, infantry, artillery), while "tail" refers to the support troops (medics, air-traffic controllers, truck drivers). For example, in 2002 there were 470,000 Army support personnel for 60,000 combat soldiers. In the Air Force, there were 360,000 support personnel for just 16,000 pilots and navigators.[3]

Figure 3.4

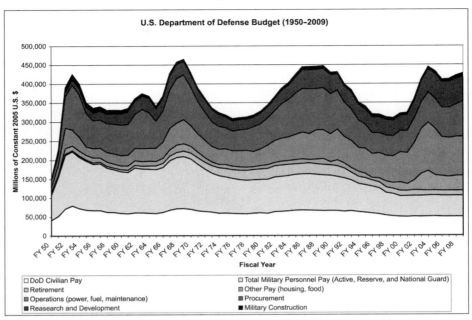

Source of data: *National Defense Budget Estimates for the FY 2005 (Green Book).* U.S. Department of Defense. Office of the Comptroller. Tables 6-12 and 6-11. Available at www.defenselink.mil/comptroller/ defbudget/fy2005/index.html. Note: Figures for fiscal years 2006 through 2009 are estimates.

Figure 3.5

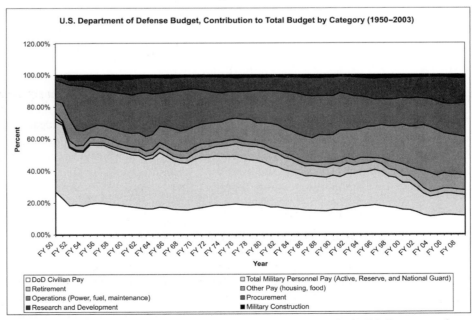

Source of data: *National Defense Budget Estimates for the FY 2005 (Green Book).* U.S. Department of Defense. Office of the Comptroller. Tables 6-12 and 6-11. Available at www.defenselink.mil/comptroller/ defbudget/fy2005/index.html. Note: Figures for fiscal years 2006 through 2009 are estimates.

Figure 3.6

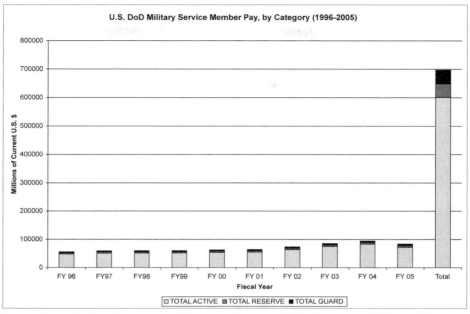

Source of data: *National Defense Budget Estimates (Green Book).* U.S. Department of Defense. Office of the Comptroller. (Various years.) Tables 6-12 and 6-11. Available at www.defenselink.mil/comptroller/ defbudget/fy2005/index.html.

In summary, U.S. defense expenditures are quite large in dollar terms but are shrinking as a percentage of U.S. GDP. Has the smaller size of U.S. military expenditures (relative to the U.S. economy) helped or hindered the economic performance of the United States? How do U.S. military expenditures compare to those of other countries? The next three sections will address these questions.

3.3 U.S. MILITARY EXPENDITURES AND MACROECONOMIC PERFORMANCE: THE COSTS OF DISARMAMENT

How do military expenditures impact the U.S. economy? This question centers on a debate surrounding the merits of **disarmament.** Disarmament is the process of converting from war production to peacetime production.

3.3.1 Disarmament's Costs in Theory

The impact of disarmament on the U.S. economy is illustrated in Figure 3.7. It shows a **production possibilities frontier** with butter (peacetime goods) on the vertical axis and guns (wartime goods) on the horizontal axis. Assuming these are the only two goods that can be produced in this economy, if the country is using all its productive resources, then it can produce a bundle of butter and guns somewhere along the curve. The curve is outward bowing to illustrate increasing opportunity costs. **Increasing opportunity costs** is the idea that as a country (or firm or person) switches more and more resources from producing one item to producing a second item, the country will eventually have to use resources that are

Figure 3.7
The Economic Impact of Disarmament

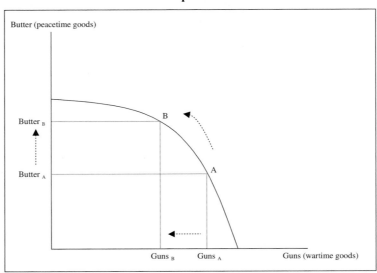

not very well suited for producing the second item (but were ideally suited for producing the first item). For example, some people and industries are good at producing butter, but not very good at making guns. If a government decides that its country needs to produce more guns, but still wants butter, it would initially keep the best butter producers making butter while it found other people and industries to make guns. However, if the government needs even more guns, then it will have to convert some of the best butter producing people and industries over to guns production. The result will be a small increase in the quantity of guns relative to the large decrease in the quantity of butter. Consequently, the "cost" (measured in terms of the butter that can no longer be produced) becomes greater as more and more guns are produced.

In general, there exists a short-run tradeoff between guns and butter. If the economy wishes to produce more guns, it must sacrifice butter. If the economy wishes to produce more butter, it must sacrifice guns. This tradeoff is illustrated by the movement from point *A* to point *B*.

Unfortunately, the tradeoff is not instantaneous. The machines must be converted to peacetime production and the private sector may not be ready to immediately substitute the government expenditures. Therefore, the movement from point *A* to *B* can be slow and may have to be supported by government policies to stimulate demand and facilitate the transfer of resources among industrial sectors.[4] In short, the movement can be, as in the case of World War II, painful in the short run.

3.3.2 Evidence of Disarmament's Cost

During the 1990s, as the military sought to save money, there began much discussion regarding the economic impact on communities from military base closures (see Box 3.2). Yet, to gain perspective on the impact declining military expenditures can have on the economy as a whole, consider the experience of the U.S. economy just after World War II. Because the wartime industrialization was of such great magnitude, the costs of the postwar overhang

Box 3.2
Civilian Employment and Base Closures

The impact of defense spending on labor is not limited to military personnel and their families. It also impacts communities. Specifically, the presence of a military base (and the removal of that base) can have a profound impact on the economic vitality of surrounding communities. For example, Kelly Air Force Base had created 11,000 civilian jobs, making it the largest employer in the San Antonio region in 1995 and a primary engine of economic mobility for the local Mexican-American community.[1]

The reasons for base closures: After the Cold War, the U.S. Department of Defense deemed many bases to be surplus and, therefore, needed to close them. As a response to this need, the U.S. Congress enacted Base Realignment and Closure (BRAC) legislation that authorized base closures in 1988, 1991, 1993, and 1995. These first four rounds of BRAC closed 97 bases, realigned 55 others (remodeled them to accommodate troops from the closing bases), and resulted in $16 billion in cost savings through 2001 and an additional $6 billion annually in savings.[2]

In 2001, Defense Secretary Donald Rumsfeld and Army General Henry H. Shelton, chairman of the Joint Chiefs of Staff, told the U.S. House Armed Services Committee that the military still maintained 25 percent more facilities than it needed and that the these excess bases annually cost taxpayers an estimated $3.5 billion.[3] Therefore, a new round of closures was scheduled to begin in 2005.

Impact on communities: Though such closures may be strategically necessary and fiscally responsible, they are not without costs. In particular, the closings can result in large job losses (as the first four BRAC rounds impacted nearly 324,000 military and civilian jobs).

Fortunately, the overall data suggest that the removal of a military base need not be an economic death knell to surrounding communities. According to a 2001 Government

Accounting Office analysis of year 2000 unemployment rates, the rates of 69 percent of the BRAC-affected communities were at or below the national average for the United States. This figure compares to 68 percent of BRAC-affected communities being at or below the U.S. national unemployment rate in 1998. As a 1996 Rand Corporation study found, the burden of base closures tends to fall more on individual households and companies, rather than on the communities as a whole.[4] There are four factors that explain why base closings did not have dire economic costs to the surrounding communities.

(1) The bases are usually economically isolated from the neighboring communities.[5] For example, Schweinfurt, Germany, a city of 55,000 German residents, is also home to 12,000 U.S. military personnel. According to estimates from Schweinfurt officials, the American military personnel spend approximately $31 million per year in the community's various restaurants, bars, discos, public transport, and car dealerships. This figure is equivalent to only 5 percent of the town's total annual retail sales.

(2) Communities, through government assistance, find ways to redevelop the land and replace the lost jobs. This process can take time as the community must close the base, identify promising alternative businesses to attract, persuade these businesses to locate on the base, find a suitable site on the base, negotiate an acceptable lease or sale, recruit qualified workers, and find jobs that match the workers' skills and expectations. For example, in Fort Ord, California, California State University opened a new campus in a collection of former Army buildings. The University of California Santa Cruz opened a high-tech center and local community colleges planned to construct a regional police training facility on the base.[6] Table III shows that the majority of those installations closed by April 1999 (31 of 56) had replaced at least 51 percent of the lost jobs with new civilian jobs.

Table I: Job Replacements by BRAC Round

	Job Replacement by BRAC Round			
	1988	1991	1993	1995
New Jobs as Percent of Job Losses	76%	60%	42%	14%

Source: Frieden, B. and Baxter, C. *From Barracks to Business: The M.I.T. Report on Base Development.* Economic Development Administration. U.S. Department of Commerce. March 2000. Table 5.4, p. 131.

(continued)

Box 3.2 *(concluded)*

However, the process is lengthy. Consequently, by 1999 the facilities closed in 1988 had replaced, on average, 76 percent of civilian jobs; while facilities closed in 1995 had replaced only 14.2 percent. Overall, Table I shows the status of new civilian job creation at installations closed through April 1999.

Table II: Status of New Civilian Jobs at Closed Installations

Number of Installations	New Jobs as a Percent of Lost Jobs
2	0 percent
15	up to 25 percent
8	26 to 50 percent
10	51 to 75 percent
5	76 to 99 percent
16	100 percent or more

Source: Frieden, B. and Baxter, C. *From Barracks to Business: The M.I.T. Report on Base Development*. Economic Development Administration. U.S. Department of Commerce. March 2000. Table 1.7, p. 8.

(3) Most communities were economically healthy prior to the base closing. For example, of the 89 counties impacted by the first four rounds of base closings, only 16 had per capita incomes less than 80 percent of the national average. These poor counties tended to be rural and located in remote areas. It was these communities that were hit hardest by the base closures.

(4) There is a small percentage of civilian employment as a share of total county employment located at the military installation. According to Table III, only two of the 89 counties with military installations closed in the first four BRAC rounds had greater than 10 percent of the civilian labor force dedicated to the base. The vast majority (60 of 89) had less than 1 percent of civilian employment dedicated to the base.

Table III: Civilian Base Jobs as a Share of County Employment

	Total Civilian Employment as a Share of County Employment			
	< 1 Percent	1–5 Percent	5–10 Percent	> 10 Percent
Number of Installations	60	22	5	2

Source: Frieden, B. and Baxter, C. *From Barracks to Business: The M.I.T. Report on Base Development*. Economic Development Administration. U.S. Department of Commerce. March 2000. Table 1.2, p. 4.

[1]Frieden and Baxter (2000), p. 61.
[2]Globalsecurity.org . "Base Realignment and Closure." Available at www.globalsecurity.org/military/facility/brac.htm.
[3]Ibid.
[4]*The Effects of Military Base Closures on Local Communities: A Short Term Perspective,* RAND National Defense Research

Institute, 1996; as cited in U.S. General Accounting Office (2001), p. 9.
[5]Frieden and Baxter (2000), p. 1.
[6]Weintraub, Daniel. "Base Closings Can Benefit Communities." *The Sacramento Bee,* March 23, 2004.

were substantial. Industrial production declined by 10 percent between the first quarter of 1948 and the last quarter of 1949, and by approximately one-fourth between 1944 and 1949. In March 1950, there were approximately 4,750,000 unemployed, as compared to 1,070,000 in 1943 and 670,000 in 1944. The gross national product declined in terms of constant prices by about 20 percent between 1944 and 1948.[5] Furthermore, the wartime industrialization was unevenly distributed throughout the country (as the need for production uninterrupted by concerns of climate led the U.S. government to locate defense plants and shipyards in warm areas of the country not normally associated with heavy industry). As such, small towns and communities in the southern and western portions of the United States that had suddenly found themselves manufacturing and assembling war parts and machines faced the prospect of steep unemployment.[6]

3.4 U.S. MILITARY EXPENDITURES AND MACROECONOMIC PERFORMANCE: THE BENEFITS OF DISARMAMENT

3.4.1 Disarmament's Benefits in Theory

In the long run, the process of converting from wartime production to peacetime production should, in theory, be beneficial. This is because military expenditures have the ability, in theory, to reduce private sector spending (private consumption and private investment). The macroeconomic identity introduced in Chapter 1, $Y = C + I + G + (X - M)$, and the concept of **Disposable Income** can be used to illustrate how and why government expenditures can reduce private-sector spending.

Disposable income is the income earned by households after removing taxes and adding government subsidies (such as social security benefits). In turn, households can either consume or save disposable income. The equation, $Y - T = C + S$, represents disposable income. Y is income, T is taxes, C is private household consumption, and S is private household savings.

How much disposable income do households consume and how much do they save? This is determined by the **Marginal Propensity to Consume** (MPC) and the **Marginal Propensity to Save** (MPS). Stated simply, the MPC is the fraction of each additional dollar of disposable income a household consumes, while the MPS is the fraction of each additional dollar of disposable income a household saves. Since households only consume or save their disposable income, then the MPC and the MPS added together must always equal 1. For example, if a household receives an additional dollar and consumes 80 cents of it, that leaves only 20 cents for additional savings. In this example, the household's MPC is 0.80 and its MPS is 0.20. Together, 0.80 plus 0.20 equal 1.

Before going on, one should take note of Box 3.3. This box shows a few simple algebraic operations using the basic macroeconomic identity, $Y = C + I + G + (X - M)$, and disposable income equation, $Y - T = C + S$. These operations generate results that are needed in order to illustrate how government expenditure can reduce private-sector spending.

Box 3.3
Algebraic Proofs Necessary for Understanding the
Impact of Government Expenditures on the Private Sector

The following algebraic formulations are needed in order to illustrate how government spending can impact private spending.

I. Derivations of the Disposable Income equation:

$Y - T = C + S$ (the Disposable Income equation)

$Y = C + S + T$ (the Disposable Income equation solved for Y)

$C = Y - T - S$ (the Disposable Income equation solved for C)

$S = Y - T - C$ (the Disposable Income equation solved for S)

II. Substitute the Disposable Income equation solved for Y, $Y = C + S + T$, into the basic macroeconomic identity, $Y = C + I + G = (X - M)$. Note: Assume a **Closed Economy.** This means no external trade. Therefore, $(X - M) = 0$

$C + S + T = C + I + G$

$S + T = I + G$ (cancel out the C)

$S + (T - G) = I$ (solve for I)

III. The relationship between savings, S, and investment, I, if $(T - G) = 0$.

$S = I$

Equipped with the algebraic results from Box 3.3, assume that government expenditures, G, increase. There are two possible scenarios through which the rise in G could reduce private-sector spending. The first scenario assumes that taxes, T, are raised in order to pay for the rise in G. Notice from Box 3.3 that $S + (T - G) = I$. If the rise in G is offset by an equal rise in T, then the rise in G does not alter the value of the left-hand side of $S + (T - G) = I$. Hence, the right-hand side (private investment), I, does not change. However, that's not the whole story. Notice Box 3.3 also shows that $C = Y - T - S$ and $S = Y - T - C$. If T increases, then C and S must decrease. Additionally, Box 3.3 shows that $S = I$ when $(T - G) = 0$. Since S is falling, then I must also decrease. Therefore, this scenario generates two possible outcomes for I. I could stay the same or I could fall. In short, if G and T increase, then C falls and I may or may not fall.

The second scenario assumes that taxes, T, do not rise in order to pay for the increase in G. Instead, taxes are held constant and the government borrows in order to pay for the increase in G. In this instance, a rise in G will cause $(T - G) < 0$. As a result the entire left-hand side of $S + (T - G) = I$ will decrease in value. Because the right-hand side must be equal in value to the left-hand side, I must also fall. This illustrates the **Crowding out effect.** Recall from Chapter 2 that the crowding out effect is when government borrowing takes away loanable funds that could have been used for private investment. Furthermore, since T does not change, then C does not change. Therefore, in this scenario, the rise in government expenditures clearly causes private investment, I, to decrease, but leaves C unchanged.

What is important to understand is that these two scenarios show how private-sector spending may or may not decrease when government expenditures increase. If government expenditures do cause private-sector consumption and investment to decline, then such "crowding out" of private investment and consumption can be avoided by decreasing government expenditures. In the context of defense economics, the expansion of the private sector due to a reduction in military expenditures is known as the **peace dividend.**

The idea of a peace dividend (which is believed to be a major contributor to the U.S. economic prosperity during the 1990s), explains why the famous economists William Nordhaus and James Tobin (1973) labeled defense expenditures as a "regrettable" but necessary outlay. They offer several rationales supporting their argument. First, they point out that no reasonable country buys national defense for its own sake. Without the risk of war, defense expenditures would (should) become extraneous and no one would be worse without them. This situation is primarily because such expenditures divert productive capacity away from wealth-generating activities (crowding out). Second, defense expenditures are an *input* into an elusively measurable *output*. Spending massive amounts of money on defense does not necessarily make a country more secure, which, in the end, is supposed to be the ultimate objective of defense expenditures. Switzerland, for example, is one of the most secure countries in the world due primarily to its policy of neutrality, not high levels of military expenditure. In short, defense expenditures are not a measure of national security, which is arguably not measurable.[7]

In an attempt to reevaluate the argument of Nordhaus and Tobin, Aizeman and Glick (2003) acknowledge that defense expenditures typically have a non-significant and negative impact on economic growth (as measured by GDP growth). However, they qualify this statement by arguing that military expenditures in the presence of sufficiently large external threats actually increase growth. It is only military expenditure without threats and threats without military expenditure that reduce growth.[8]

3.4.2 Evidence of Disarmament's Benefit

Does increasing government expenditure actually have a tendency to reduce private-sector spending? More directly related to this chapter's topic, how do military expenditures impact private consumption and private investment?

These questions can be explored using a **scatter-plot diagram.** In a scatter-plot diagram, each observation (for example, the year) is represented by a single point. The horizontal axis measures the value of one variable (for example, the level of military expenditures in that year) and the vertical axis measures the value of another variable (for example, the level of private investment in that year). Such a diagram allows one to see the overall relationship between the two variables. When looking at a scatter-plot, it is most useful to look for the trend in the data. In other words, do the data points have a tendency to move down, or move up? To determine this, a scatter-plot will commonly include a trend line. This is a line that indicates the general direction in which all of the data points are moving. If the trend line is pointing downward, this situation means that one variable increases in value (the variable on the horizontal axis) as the other variable decreases in value (the variable on the vertical axis). This result is known as a **negative relationship** or **negative correlation.** The term "negative" is used because if one were to write the equation that represents the trend line, the slope of the line would be a negative number.

Conversely, if the trend line is pointing upward, this means that one variable increases in value (the variable on the horizontal axis) as the other variable also increases in value (the variable on the vertical axis). This result is known as a **positive relationship** or **positive correlation.** Again, this is because the slope of the trend line's equation is a positive number.

Figures 3.8 through 3.13 present scatter-plot diagrams using quarterly data from 1947 through 2003 for the United States. Notice that each diagram includes the trend line and, in the lower right-hand corner, the trend line's equation (which, by providing the numerical

Figure 3.8
United States Federal Government Expenditures and Private Investment, (1947–2003)

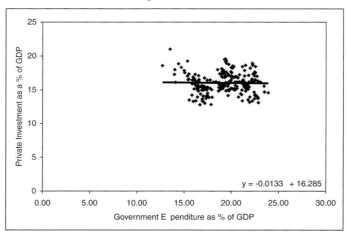

Source of data: Federal Reserve Economic Database (FRED). Federal Reserve Bank of St. Louis. Available at http://research.stlouisfed.org/fred2. Real GDP is "Current Gross Domestic Product," adjusted for inflation using the current quarter's "Gross Domestic Product: Chain-type index" divided by 100 (index in year 2000). Government expenditures is "Federal Government: Current Expenditures," adjusted for inflation using the current quarter's "Gross Domestic Product: Chain-type index" divided by 100 (index in year 2000). Private investment is "Gross Private Domestic Investment," adjusted for inflation using the current quarter's "Gross Domestic Product: Chain-type index" divided by 100 (index in year 2000). All data are quarterly. 228 observations.

Figure 3.9
United States Federal Government Expenditures and Private Consumption, (1947–2003)

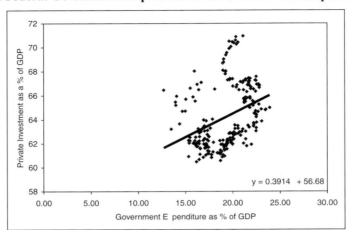

Source of data: Federal Reserve Economic Database (FRED). Federal Reserve Bank of St. Louis. Available at http://research.stlouisfed. org/fred2. Real GDP is "Current Gross Domestic Product," adjusted for inflation using the current quarter's "Gross Domestic Product: Chain-type index" divided by 100 (index in year 2000). Government expenditures is "Federal Government: Current Expenditures," adjusted for inflation using the current quarter's "Gross Domestic Product: Chain-type index" divided by 100 (index in year 2000). Private consumption is "Personal Consumption Expenditures," adjusted for inflation using the current quarter's "Gross Domestic Product: Chain-type index" divided by 100 (index in year 2000). All data are quarterly. 228 observations.

value of the slope, will make it easier to tell whether the trend line is showing a negative or positive relationship).

Look first at Figures 3.8 and 3.9. These show the relationship between overall federal government expenditures and private investment (Figure 3.8) and overall federal government expenditures and private consumption (Figure 3.9). Government expenditures appear to have a slight negative relationship (-0.0133) with private investment, but quite a large positive (0.3914) relationship with private consumption. Next, Figures 3.10 and 3.11 show how federal government nonmilitary expenditures relate to private investment (Figure 3.10) and private consumption (Figure 3.11). Nonmilitary government expenditures have a small positive relationship with private investment (0.0569), but a relatively large positive relationship with private consumption (0.3477). Overall, these first four diagrams suggest that government expenditures and private investment are weakly related, while the relationship between government expenditures and private consumption is stronger. Moreover, private consumption and government expenditures appear to be positively correlated, not negatively correlated as the theory predicted.

Turn finally to Figures 3.12 and 3.13. These two figures are at the heart of the analysis since both illustrate the impact of military expenditures on the private sector. Figure 3.12 shows that private investment is negatively correlated with military expenditures (-0.1691). Figure 3.13 also shows a negative relationship between private consumption and military expenditures (-0.6549). The negative relationship in these figures suggests that rising military expenditures do reduce private sector spending.

However, one must be careful not to confuse *correlation* with *causation*. Just because one variable rises while the other falls, does not mean the rise of the one variable *causes* the fall of the other. For example, the economy may slow down and the private sector may stop investing because of fear caused by geopolitical tensions. These same tensions cause

Figure 3.10
United States Federal Government Non-Military Expenditure and Private Investment, (1947–2003)

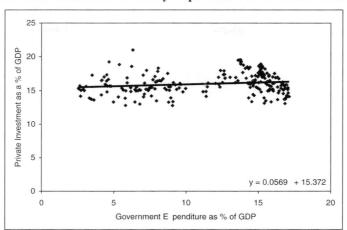

Source of data: Federal Reserve Economic Database (FRED). Federal Reserve Bank of St. Louis. Available at http://research.stlouisfed. org/fred2. Real GDP is "Current Gross Domestic Product," adjusted for inflation using the current quarter's "Gross Domestic Product: Chain-type index" divided by 100 (index in year 2000). Government expenditures is "Federal Government: Current Expenditures," adjusted for inflation using the current quarter's "Gross Domestic Product: Chain-type index" divided by 100 (index in year 2000). Military expenditures is "National Defense Consumption Expenditures & Gross Investment," adjusted for inflation using the current quarter's "Gross Domestic Product: Chain-type index" divided by 100 (index in year 2000). Private investment is "Gross Private Domestic Investment," adjusted for inflation using the current quarter's "Gross Domestic Product: Chain-type index" divided by 100 (index in year 2000). **All data are quarterly. 228 observations.**

Figure 3.11
United States Federal Government Non-Military Expenditures and Private Consumption, (1947–2003)

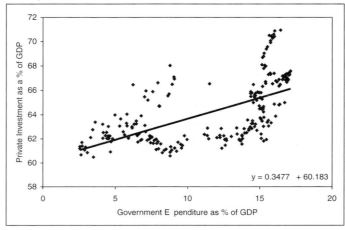

Source of data: Federal Reserve Economic Database (FRED). Federal Reserve Bank of St. Louis. Available from http://research.stlouisfed. org/fred2. Real GDP is "Current Gross Domestic Product," adjusted for inflation using the current quarter's "Gross Domestic Product: Chain-type index" divided by 100 (index in year 2000). Government expenditures is "Federal Government: Current Expenditures," adjusted for inflation using the current quarter's "Gross Domestic Product: Chain-type index" divided by 100 (index in year 2000). Military expenditures is "National Defense Consumption Expenditures & Gross Investment," adjusted for inflation using the current quarter's "Gross Domestic Product: Chain-type index" divided by 100 (index in year 2000). Private consumption is "Personal Consumption Expenditures," adjusted for inflation using the current quarter's "Gross Domestic Product: Chain-type index" divided by 100 (index in year 2000). All data are quarterly. 228 observations.

Figure 3.12
United States Federal Government Military Expenditures and Private Investment, (1947–2003)

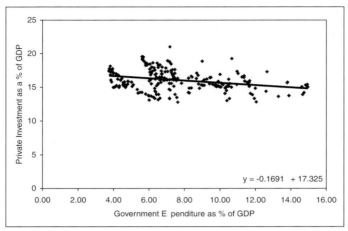

Source of data: Federal Reserve Economic Database (FRED). Federal Reserve Bank of St. Louis. Available at http://research.stlouisfed.org/ fred2. Real GDP is "Current Gross Domestic Product," adjusted for inflation by using the current quarter's "Gross Domestic Product: Chain-type index" divided by 100 (index in year 2000). Military expenditures is "National Defense Consumption Expenditures & Gross Investment," adjusted for inflation using the current quarter's "Gross Domestic Product: Chain-type index" divided by 100 (index in year 2000). Private investment is "Gross Private Domestic Investment," adjusted for inflation using the current quarter's "Gross Domestic Product: Chain-type index" divided by 100 (index in year 2000). All data are quarterly. 228 observations.

Figure 3.13
United States Federal Government Military Expenditures and Private Consumption, (1947–2003)

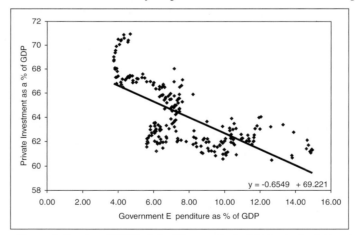

Source of data: Federal Reserve Economic Database (FRED). Federal Reserve Bank of St. Louis. Available at http://research.stlouisfed. org/fred2. Real GDP is "Current Gross Domestic Product," adjusted for inflation using the current quarter's "Gross Domestic Product: Chain-type index" divided by 100 (index in year 2000). Military expenditures is "National Defense Consumption Expenditures & Gross Investment," adjusted for inflation using the current quarter's "Gross Domestic Product: Chain-type index" divided by 100 (index in year 2000). Private consumption is "Personal Consumption Expenditures," adjusted for inflation using the current quarter's "Gross Domestic Product: Chain-type index" divided by 100 (index in year 2000). All data are quarterly. 228 observations.

Table 3.1
World and Regional Military Expenditure Estimates (1993–2002)
(in billions of U.S. $)

Region	YEAR										
	1993	1994	1995	1996	1997	1998	1999	2000	2001	2002	2003
Africa	7.4	7.7	7.2	6.9	7.1	7.6	8.4	8.8	8.9	9.6	11.4
North	2.5	2.9	2.7	2.8	3	3.1	3.3	3.6	..	..	5.5
Sub-Saharan	5	4.8	4.5	4.1	4.1	4.4	5.1	5.2	..	..	5.9
Americas	385	365	347	328	328	321	322	333	338	368	451
North	365	344	324	306	304	298	299	310	313	344	426
Central	2.8	3.4	3	3.1	3.2	3.2	3.4	3.4	3.5	3.3	3.3
South	17.6	17.4	20	18.3	20.9	20.1	19.6	19.5	21.5	21.1	21.8
Asia & Oceania	120	121	123	128	128	127	129	134	140	147	151
Central Asia	..	0.4	0.4	0.4	0.5	..	0.5	..	..	..	..
East Asia	99.8	101	103	107	107	105	106	111	116	122	125
South Asia	12	12	12.6	12.8	13.4	13.5	14.6	15.2	16.2	17.3	16.9
Oceania	7.7	7.7	7.4	7.4	7.4	7.7	7.5	7.3	7.4	7.4	8.5
Europe	196	192	178	177	177	175	177	180	181	181	195
CEE	25.6	25.9	20.1	18.8	19.6	16.9	17.8	18.9	20.1	21.4	24.5
Western	171	166	158	158	157	158	159	161	161	160	171
Middle East	53.5	54.1	50.9	51.7	56.5	60.7	60	67.3	73.8	78.4	70
World	762	740	707	691	696	690	696	723	741	784	879

Source of data: 1993–2002 data from Stockholm International Peace and Research Institute (SIPRI). *Year Book 2003: Armaments, Disarmament and International Security.* New York: Humanities Press. Appendix 10A, Table 10A.1 and Table 10A.3. 2003 data from Stockholm International Peace and Research Institute (SIPRI). *Year Book 2004: Armaments, Disarmament and International Security.* New York: Humanities Press. Appendix 10A, Table 10A.1 and Table 10A.3. 2004. Available at http://projects.sipri.org/milex/mex_wnr_table.html.

an increase in military expenditures. Therefore, military expenditures rise while private investment simultaneously declines, but one did not necessarily cause the other.

Is this negative relationship between military spending and private sector spending unique to the United States? This idea is an important question to now keep in mind. The next section compares the level of U.S. military expenditures to those of other countries.

3.5 GLOBAL MILITARY EXPENDITURES

3.5.1 International Comparisons

It is useful to have a general picture of global military expenditures and their geographic distribution. As Table 3.1 shows, world military expenditures, after declining throughout much of the 1990s, are now higher than they were a decade ago. Also, with the exception of Central and Eastern Europe (CEE), military expenditures are higher (or the same) in every region of the world. However, one should consider that despite the increase in global military expenditures, these expenditures are still drastically lower than the peak level of $1.7 trillion reached in 1986.[9]

Table 3.2
Top 15 Countries in Military Expenditure Levels, 2002
(billions of constant year 2000 U.S. dollars)

Country	2002 (SIPRI Yearbook)	Country	2002 (Military Balance)
United States	335.7	United States	329.6
Japan	46.7	China	48.4
U.K.	36.0	Russia	48
France	33.6	France	38
China	31.1	Japan	37.7
Germany	27.7	UK	35.2
Saudi Arabia	21.6	Germany	31.5
Italy	21.1	Italy	24.2
Iran	17.5	Saudi Arabia	20.9
South Korea	13.5	India	13.1
India	12.9	South Korea	12.6
Russia	11.4	Brazil	9.6
Turkey	10.1	Israel	9.4
Brazil	10.0	Turkey	8.7
Israel	9.8	Spain	8.2

Source of data: Stockholm International Peace Research Institute. *SIPRI Yearbook 2003—Armaments, Disarmament, and International Security.* Oxford, UK: Oxford University Press. Table 10.4. p. 312. The International Institute for Strategic Studies. *The Military Balance 2003–2004.* Oxford, UK: Oxford University Press. Table 33. pp. 335–339.

One should also consider the expenditure levels of specific countries. There are numerous sources that provide regularly updated military expenditure data. Two that provide on-line access include the U.S. Central Intelligence Agency's *CIA World Fact Book* and the Stockholm International Peace Research Institute's *SIPRI Yearbook*.[10] Other sources include the International Institute for Strategic Studies' *Military Balance* yearly publication and The U.S. State Department's *World Military Expenditures and Arms Transfers.*

Look at Table 3.2. It provides two rankings of the top 15 countries according to military expenditures in the year 2002. One list is from the *SIPRI Yearbook 2003* and the other list is from *The Military Balance 2003–2004.* Notice that many of the same countries are on both lists, but the level of military expenditure for these countries varies.

Why do measures of military expenditure vary? There are several reasons. First, there can be a lack of credible government data collection, such as for Iran and Russia. Second, some studies will include expenditures on paramilitary (group of civilians trained in a military fashion) and police in the figures, depending on the extent to which the central government controls these entities. Third, some studies may be using a different base year upon which to adjust for inflation (the same level of expenditures can appear as a higher figure if prices from a later year are used).

Regardless of the figures used, the United States spends an extraordinary amount of money on defense. However, it ranked only 47th in the world in 2002 when military expenditures are measured as a percentage of a country's GDP (U.S. military expenditures were 3.1 percent of U.S. GDP).[11] The same can also be said of the number two country in the SIPRI rankings, Japan, whose high level of military expenditure was only about 1 percent of GDP (*see* Box 3.4).

Military expenditure as a percentage of GDP is important because it illustrates a country's level of **militarization**—how much of a country's economy is dedicated to the

Box 3.4
Historical Perspective
Japan's Constitution and its Military Expenditures

During the later stages of World War II, the leaders of the United States, the United Kingdom, and the Soviet Union held a series of conferences to discuss the composition of the world system after the war and the conditions for Japanese and German surrender. In Potsdam, Germany, in July 16, 1945, the terms for Japanese surrender were specified. After the conference, U.S. President Truman and British Prime Minister Atlee issued the Potsdam Declaration, which specified that after Japan's defeat "the occupying forces of the Allies shall be withdrawn from Japan as soon as these objectives have been accomplished and there has been established in accordance with the freely expressed will of the Japanese people a peacefully inclined and responsible government."[1]

The Potsdam Declaration led to the incorporation of Article 9, the Renunciation of War article, into Japan's postwar constitution. Article 9 states:

"Aspiring sincerely to an international peace based on justice and order, the Japanese people forever renounce war as a sovereign right of the nation and the threat or use of force as means of settling international disputes.

"In order to accomplish the aim of the preceding paragraph, land, sea, and air forces, as well as other war potential, will never be maintained. The right of belligerency of the state will not be recognized."[2]

However, how can Article 9 be rectified with the fact that Japan is one of the largest military spenders in the world? Since World War II the Japanese government has continually interpreted the article as suggesting that it cannot become a military *power*. For Japan, this means it cannot possess military capability strong enough to pose a military threat to other countries or maintain defense capability beyond the minimum necessary for self-defense.[3] Therefore, Japan does not have 'armed forces.' Instead, it has "Self Defense Forces" (SDF). The SDF is not allowed to fight outside the country and cannot engage in mutual defense pacts (i.e., cannot defend an ally under attack).[4]

Furthermore, though Japan has high military expenditures, it only spends approximately 1 percent of its GDP on military expenditures, significantly less (as a percentage of GDP) than many European countries. Hence, Japan's large expenditures are simply the result of the fact that it has a large economy (second largest in the world, behind the United States), rather than a concerted effort on the part of the Japanese government to create a heavily militarized country.

However, Japan's military policy has begun a gradual shift over the past decade. Ever since Japan was criticized during the 1991 Gulf War for not actively participating, Japan has allowed troops to take part in United Nations sanctioned peacekeeping operations. The threshold for preventing Japan from using its military outside the country was further lowered in 2004 when Japanese Prime Minister Junichiro Koizumi authorized the deployment of approximately 1,000 peacekeeping troops to Iraq (Japan's first non-UN authorized military mission).

---

[1] *Potsdam Declaration*. July 26, 1945. East Asian Studies Documents. UCLA Asia Institute. Available at www.isop.ucla.edu/eas/documents/potsdam.htm.
[2] *The Constitution of Japan. Chapter II. Article 9*. November 3, 1946. Prime Minister of Japan and His Cabinet. Available at www.kantei.go.jp/foreign/constitution_and_government_of_japan/constitution_e.html.
[3] "Basic Policies of National Defense" in *Overview of Japan's Defense Policy 2002*. Japanese Defense Agency. Available at www.jda.go.jp/e/index_.htm.
[4] Pilling, David. "Japan Searches for a Role on the World Stage." *Financial Times*. April 13, 2004.

military. Hence, countries with a higher percentage of GDP devoted to military expenditures are considered to be more militarized than countries with lower percentages. Table 3.3 shows what are considered the most militarized countries in the world (in terms of military expenditures as a percentage of GDP). It is interesting to note that of the top 25 military spenders (in terms of percentage of GDP), six rank 200 or below in terms of GDP per capita (out of 231), 15 rank 100 or below, and 20 rank 50 or below. The relationship between military expenditures and global poverty will be explored more in Chapter 6.

Table 3.3
World's 25 Most Militarized Countries, 2002

Country	Military expenditures - percent of GDP (%)—2002	GDP per capita Rank	GDP—per capita
North Korea	25	206	$1,000
Democractic Republic of Congo	21.7	223	$600
Eritrea	16	220	$700
Oman	13.4	90	$8,300
Saudi Arabia	12	64	$11,400
Kuwait	10.7	50	$17,500
Qatar	10.6	36	$20,100
Syria	10.3	142	$3,700
Angola	9.8	179	$1,700
Israel	9.7	40	$19,500
Jordan	9.3	132	$4,300
Ethiopia	8	221	$700
Vietnam	7.1	163	$2,300
Bahrain	6.7	55	$15,100
Armenia	6.4	143	$3,600
Burundi	5.9	229	$500
Algeria	5.9	114	$5,400
Yemen	5.7	214	$800
Serbia & Montenegro	5.3	118	$5,100
Brunei	5.2	46	$18,600
Singapore	5.2	25	$25,200
Turkey	5.1	97	$7,300
Myanmar	5	183	$1,700
Sudan	4.9	189	$1,400
Russia	4.8	77	$9,700

Source of data: GDP per capita rank from CIA World Fact Book 2002. Available at http://www.cia.gov/cia/publications/factbook/docs/rankorderguide.html.
Military expenditures as a percent of GDP from the International Institute for Strategic Studies *2003-2004. Military Balance* data cited in Chamberlin, Jeffrey. "Comparisons of U.S. and Foreign Military Spending: Data from Selected Public Sources." Congressional Research Service Report for Congress. January 28, 2004. Table 1 available at http://fas.org/man/crs/RL32209.pdf.

Not surprisingly, many heavily militarized countries are involved in international disputes. These countries include Turkey and Greece (dispute over Cyprus), India and Pakistan (dispute over Kashmir), and Israel and Syria (who have no formal peace treaty after a war between them in 1973).

However, being involved in an international dispute does not mean a country will be heavily militarized, as some countries involved in international disputes spend surprisingly little of their GDP on the military. Examples include Taiwan, China, and South Korea. China and Taiwan are embroiled in a dispute over how much autonomy the island of Taiwan should be given from the mainland, while South Korea is still officially in a state of war with North Korea (the most heavily militarized country in the world). The low level of militarization for these three countries (as measured by the military expenditure to GDP ratio) can be easily explained. Despite its low level of militarization, its massive population allows China to compile the largest number of troops in the world (see Chapter 4). For decades

South Korea has been reliant on a direct U.S. military presence in the country, while Taiwan has been reliant on U.S. diplomacy. It is also worth noting that despite Europe being on the front lines of the Cold War standoff between the United States and the Soviet Union and instability in Bosnia and Kosovo during the 1990s, reliance on U.S. defense support through NATO also explains why many European countries (with perhaps the exception of France and the United Kingdom) do not spend as much of their GDP on defense as the United States.[12]

3.5.2 Macroeconomic Impact of Military Expenditures: International Comparisons

Section 3.4 showed a negative relationship between military expenditures and private investment in the United States. What about the rest of the major military spenders? Using data from 1979–1999, Figures 3.14 and 3.15 compare military expenditures as a percentage of GDP to private investment as a percentage of GDP (Figure 3.14) and military expenditures as a percentage of GDP to private consumption as a percentage of GDP (Figure 3.15), for the 25 largest military spenders. Right away, one should notice that, much like the U.S.-only data in Figures 3.12 and 3.13, Figures 3.14 and 3.15 also show a negative relationship between military expenditures and private-sector spending.

However, one should again keep in mind that correlation does not mean causation. The relationships shown in Figures 3.12 and 3.13, or in Figures 3.14 and 3.15 do not account

Figure 3.14
Military Expenditures and Private Investment
The Top 25 Military Spenders (1979–1999)

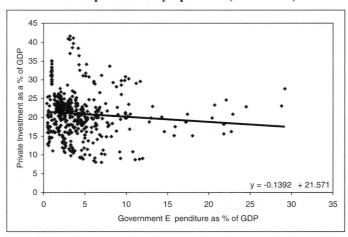

Source of data: Military exp./GDP from the U.S. Department of State's World Military Expenditures and Arms Transfers (WMEAT) 1979–1989 and 1999–1989. Data are from the Inter-University Consortium for Political and Sociela Research (ICPSR). I/GDP from Penn World Tables (Investment Share of RGDPL).
Countries included are the United States, Russia, China, France, Japan, United Kingdom, Germany, Italy, India, South Korea, Brazil, Israel, Turkey, Spain, Canada, Australia, Taiwan, Netherlands, Indonesia, Mexico, Greece, Poland, Iran, and Syria.

Notes: Only 24 of the top 25 used, because private investment data is not available for Saudi Arabia. Only years 1990 to 1999 were used for Russia (for 1979 through 1989, private investment data are not available). Military expenditures for Iran from 1983–1988 are not available. 486 total observations.

Figure 3.15
Military Expenditures and Private Consumption
The Top 25 Military Spenders (1979–1999)

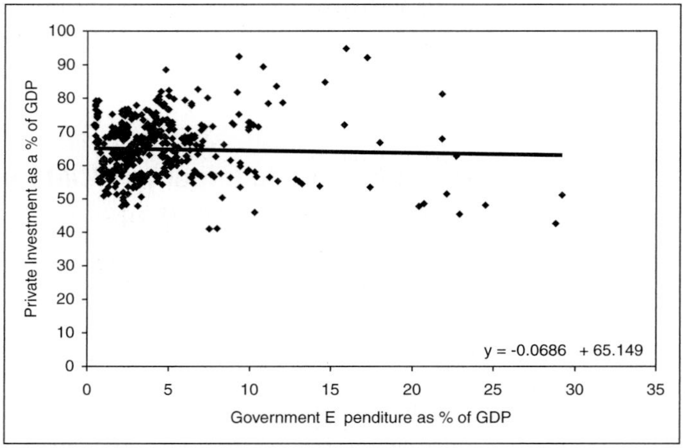

Source of data: Military Exp./GDP from the U.S. Department of State's World Military Expenditures and Arms Transfers (WMEAT) 1979–1989 and 1999–1989. Data from the Inter-University Consortium for Political and Sociela Research (ICPSR). C/GDP from Penn World Tables (Consumption Share of RGDPL).

Countries included are the United States, Russia, China, France, Japan, United Kingdom, Germany, Italy, India, South Korea, Brazil, Israel, Turkey, Spain, Canada, Australia, Taiwan, Netherlands, Indonesia, Mexico, Greece, Poland, Iran, and Syria.

Notes: Only 24 of the top 25 used, because private consumption data are not available for Saudi Arabia. Only the years 1990 to 1999 are used for Russia (for 1979 through 1989, private consumption data are not available). Consumption estimated at 64.5 for Taiwan in 1999. Military expenditures for Iran from 1983–1988 are not available. 486 total observations.

for other factors that, when taken into consideration, may render military expenditures and private investment as having, in reality, no relationship (such as the onset of war impacting both separately).

3.6 EXPLORING THE CAUSES OF MILITARIZATION

International disputes lead countries to spend a higher proportion of their GDP on military expenditures because of what is called the **security dilemma.** When two countries each perceive the other as a threat, both countries will buy and construct weapons in an attempt to have more than the other. Because both sides are obtaining weapons, neither side will be able to stop obtaining weapons. This situation results in an **arms race.**

3.6.1 Modeling the Security Dilemma

Figure 3.16 illustrates the security dilemma using **game theory** (a theory designed to understand how individuals behave when they expect their actions to influence the behavior of others). In game theory, there are two actors, for example, the United States and the Soviet Union (U.S.S.R.). Each side can choose one of two courses of action (to arm or disarm). The action one actor chooses will have implications for the action taken by the other. For example, if the U.S. chooses to arm and the U.S.S.R. chooses to disarm, then

Figure 3.16
Game Theory Depiction of an Arms Race

	U.S.S.R.	
	Arm	Disarm
U.S. Arm	Arm /Arm	Arm /Disarm
Disarm	Disarm /Arm	Disarm /Disarm

the U.S.S.R., because it disarmed, will feel threatened. Because neither side knows the intentions of the other, then both sides will choose to arm rather than disarm because neither side will want to risk being threatened by the other. Hence, we call arming the **dominant strategy** for each side. This situation means, regardless of what the other side does, each side will choose this strategy. Because both sides choose to arm, the game ends in the upper left-hand corner of Figure 3.16. This outcome is called the **Nash equilibrium** (an outcome resulting from both players executing the strategy that best responds to the strategy executed by their opponent).

This result actually occurred during the 1980s between the United States and the Soviet Union. As Figure 3.17 shows, the Soviet Union's military spending in constant 1989 dollars was significantly higher than that of the United States in 1979. Soviet military expenditures stood at $284 billion, while U.S. military expenditures were $196 billion. However, after the Soviets invaded Afghanistan in late 1979, the U.S. began a program of massive military spending. Both adversaries continued to raise expenditures. The U.S. military expenditures grew faster (at an average of 6.9 percent per year from 1980 to 1986, compared to only 1.6 percent for the Soviets), so their expenditure levels quickly converged.

Yet, even though both sides began to increase military expenditures, military expenditures as a percentage of economic output were significantly less for the United States during this period. As can be seen in Figure 3.18, throughout the 1980s, the United States spent between 5 and 7 percent of GDP on military expenditures, while the Soviets spent approximately 13 percent of GDP on military expenditures.[13]

3.6.2 Modeling the Economic Impact of an Arms Race

How did the higher level of military expenditures as a percentage of GDP impact the Soviet economy? Figure 3.19 provides an illustration.[14] Quadrant [b] uses a production possibilities frontier (PPF) to demonstrate the production limits of the Soviet economy for a set level of technology, scarce resources, capital, and human capital. It is assumed that

Figure 3.17

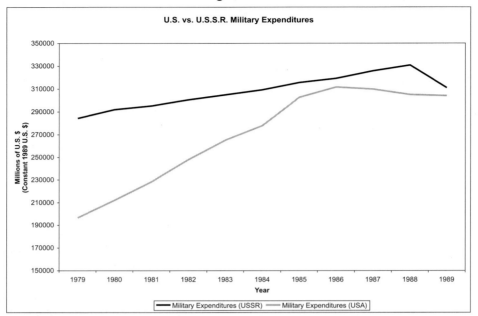

Source of data: U.S. Department of State. World Military Expenditures and Arms Transfers (WMEAT) 1979–1989; data from the Inter-University Consortium for Political and Social Research (ICPSR).

Figure 3.18

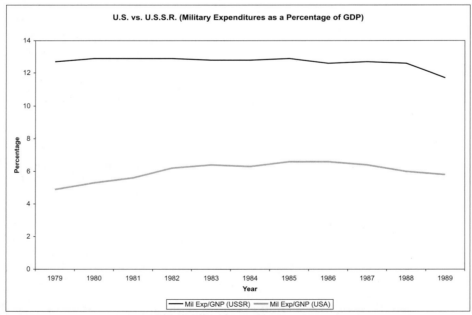

Source of data: U.S. Department of State. World Military Expenditures and Arms Transfers (WMEAT) 1979–1989; data from the Inter-University Consortium for Political and Social Research (ICPSR).

only two goods can be produced—guns (weapons) or butter (civilian goods). Quadrant [c] shows the weapons stock flow line for the Soviet Union. Specifically, it shows the total number of weapons possessed by the Soviet Union including this year's weapons production (taken from quadrant [b]) and adding this to last year's weapons stocks that are still usable. This value is then transferred over to quadrant [d]. Quadrant [d] presents the **national security function** of the Soviet Union. The national security function shows the relationship between the Soviet Union's weapons stock and its perceived level of security. The more weapons the Soviet Union has, the more it perceives itself to be secure. However, the slope of the national security function illustrates that there are diminishing marginal returns to having more weapons. For example, one nuclear weapon may improve the Soviet Union's perceived security greatly. However, once the Soviet Union has enough nuclear warheads to destroy its adversary, having an additional nuclear warhead will not greatly increase its level of security.

Assuming diminishing marginal returns to security means that quadrant [a] of Figure 3.19 represents the resulting bundle of civilian goods and security that can be obtained by the Soviet Union. The PPF in quadrant [a] illustrates all the bundles of perceived security and civilian goods that are possible given the guns produced and the size of the economy. The indifference curve, IC_1, represents the Soviet Union's preference for particular bundles of civilian goods and national security. IC_1 tells us that the Soviet Union's **utility** (the benefit it perceives itself as obtaining from a particular bundle) will not change if it has less security (as long as the Soviet Union is compensated with additional civilian goods). However, the Soviet Union, like any country, will always want some civilian goods and some security (hence the indifference curve never touches either axis).

Point A in quadrant [a] shows the location in which the indifference curve is tangent to the security-butter PPF. This point shows the bundle of security and butter that the Soviet Union thinks is best. To understand why this is so, consider the following.

The space created by the butter and perceived security axes is full of indifference curves. For now, IC_1 is the only important indifference curve, so we ignore the indifference curves above and below IC_1 (as represented by the dotted IC curves above and below IC_1). We ignore the indifference curves below IC_1, because they represent bundles of goods that are not as good as those offered by IC_1. Conversely, we ignore the indifference curves above IC_1 because they represent bundles that, given the butter-security PPF, are unobtainable. Therefore, a rational country would want to be on the highest indifference curve possible, while still touching the PPF.

Next, assume the United States (the Soviet Union's rival during the Cold War) increases its stock of weapons. To understand how this increase impacts the Soviet Union, observe Figure 3.20. First, because the United States now has more weapons, the same level of weapons for the Soviet Union will no longer produce as much security. Therefore, the national security function in quadrant [d] will shift down. Because this downward shift also alters the potential bundles of security and civilian goods that are available to the Soviet Union, the Soviet Union's butter-security PPF in quadrant [a] will shift inward. This shift shows that some levels of perceived security that used to be obtainable are no longer obtainable. Consequently, the Soviet Union also falls to the lower indifference curve, IC_2.

Notice in quadrant [b] that this result forces the Soviet Union to produce more guns rather than butter. One should now be able to guess the eventual outcome. If the United States continues to increase its weapons stock, the Soviet Union will have to follow suit. Eventually, the Soviets will reach the end of their PPF, with all resources directed toward weapons and none toward the civilian sector. As a consequence, this result will place severe strains on the Soviet Union's society and economy.

Figure 3.19
Economic Impact of an Arms Race Model
(U.S.S.R. Initial Setup)

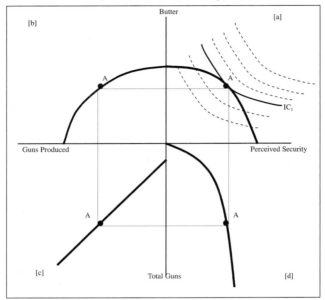

Source: Based on Anderton (1990).

Figure 3.20
Economic Impact of an Arms Race Model
(U.S.S.R. Response to Increase in U.S. Weapons Stock)

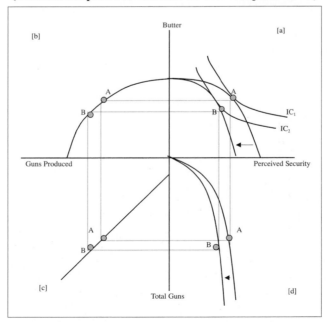

Source: Based on Anderton (1990).

3.7 KEY POINTS

Key Macroeconomic Points:

- Theory suggests that military expenditures can harm an economy by crowding out the private sector. However, the empirical evidence presents only a weak negative relationship between U.S. military expenditures and U.S. private investment.
- Though the United States spends significantly more on defense than any other country in the world, it spends only a moderate amount relative to the size of its economy. Countries that are involved in major international disputes are commonly highly militarized, unless they have military support from the United States (such as South Korea, Taiwan, and Europe).
- The ability of weapons to produce national security is constrained by diminishing marginal returns—each additional weapon fails to add as much to a country's national security as the previous weapon.

Key Microeconomic Points:

- The short-term costs of moving along a country's Production Possibilities Frontier (trading "guns" for "butter") means that disarming can, in the short run, be economically harmful.
- Game theory can illustrate the security dilemma (that states will continue to amass weapons in an effort to have more weapons than their rival, so as to prevent their rival from defeating them in a military confrontation).
- Because arming a country can take resources away from the civilian sector, arms races can be detrimental to economies with small production possibilities frontiers.

Key Terms

Disarmament

Production possibilities frontier

Increasing opportunity costs

Crowding out effect

Disposable income

Marginal propensity to consume

Marginal propensity to save

Closed economy

Peace dividend

Scatter-plot diagram

Negative relationship/Negative correlation

Positive relationship/Positive correlation

Militarization

Security dilemma

Game theory

Dominant strategy

Nash Equilibrium

National security function

Utility

Key Questions:

1. Why do you think U.S. military expenditures have fluctuated more over the past 50 years than U.S. nonmilitary government expenditures?
2. Using the macroeconomic identity $Y = C + I + G + (X - M)$, illustrate why government expenditures may crowd out private investment.
3. Which do you think is a better measure of how "militarized" a country has become: its level of military expenditures, or its level of military expenditures relative to its GDP? Why?
4. For years, India and Pakistan have disputed who controls the region of Kashmir. Because this dispute has led to war on three occasions over the past 50 years, both countries feel threatened by the other. Use game theory to illustrate how this will lead to an arms race.
5. Continuing from the previous question, if Pakistan has a smaller economy than India, illustrate why an arms race will be more harmful to Pakistan than to India.

Endnotes

1. Morgan, Dan and Dewar, Helen. "House Approves Defense Spending." *The Washington Post,* June 23, 2004, p. A4; and Morgan, Dan. "Senate Unanimously Approves $417 Billion Defense Bill." *The Washington Post,* June 25, 2004, p. A5.
2. Bobbit, Philip. "Better than Empire." *Financial Times,* March 12, 2004.
3. Falconer (2003), pp. 50–52.
4. Kapstein (1992), p. 82.
5. Mosley (1985), p. 8.
6. Schwartz in Higgs (1990), p. 17.
7. Nordhaus and Tobin (1973), pp. 515–517.
8. Aizenman and Glick (2003), p. 2.
9. In 2003 dollars. Current Value Expenditures available in Main Statistical Table 1. U.S. Department of the State. *World Military Expenditures and Arms Transfers (WMEAT).* 1996. Available through the Federation of American Scientists at http://www.fas.org/man/docs/wmeat96/.

   The CPI data is from the Federal Reserve Bank of Minneapolis—Consumer Price Index (Estimate) 1800–2000. Available at minneapolisfed.org/Research/data/us/calc/hist1800.cfm.
10. For those wishing to quickly obtain the most up-to-date military expenditure data available, both the *CIA World Fact Book* and *SIPRI Yearbook* have data available on-line *CIA World Fact Book* data available at www.odci.gov/cia/publications/factbook/docs/rankorderguide.html and *SIPRI Yearbook* data available at www.sipri.org.
11. CIA World Fact Book 2003. "Rank Order—Military Expenditures—Percent of GDP." Available at www.cia.gov/cia/publications/factbook/rankorderguide.html.
12. See, for example, Alesina, Alberto. "More Military Spending in Europe is Needed." May 2002. Available at http://post.economics.havard.edu/faculty/alesina/columns.html.
13. WMEAT data is actually using GNP, not GDP. However, the difference between GNP and GDP is very small, as indicated by observing the Penn World Tables' GNP as a percentage of GDP for the United States:

1979	99.89	1985	100.33
1980	100.05	1986	99.36
1981	100.23	1987	100.22
1982	101.05	1988	101.2
1983	99.71	1989	100.07
1984	100.43	1990	99.97

14. Model taken from Anderton (1990).

Chapter 4

Military Labor

4.1 INTRODUCTION

After U.S. Secretary of Defense Donald Rumsfeld was informed that Representative Charles Rangel of New York had proposed a bill to reinstate the military draft, Rumsfeld quickly dismissed the proposal: "We're not going to re-implement a draft. There is no need for it at all. . . .The disadvantages of using compulsion to bring into the armed forces the men and women needed are notable."[1] Understanding the basis of Secretary Rumsfeld's remarks is a critical issue surrounding military manpower. In fact, because labor constitutes a large expense for defense departments and ministries, it is a logical place to begin an evaluation of the markets for defense resources.

Section 2 overviews worldwide military manpower, comparing personnel levels in various countries according to a variety of measures. Next, the chapter dives into the contentious issue of volunteer versus conscripted forces. Section 3 analyzes the differences between a conscripted military force and an all-volunteer military, while Section 4 offers a case study into the post-Vietnam War U.S. transition from a conscripted military to an all-volunteer military. Section 5 explores particular facets of the U.S. military's current compensation system and whether it is at a level appropriate to induce qualified personnel to voluntarily choose to serve in the military (given the alternatives they might have in the private sector), yet not so large as to waste taxpayer money. Section 6 ends with a discussion and analysis of a new form of voluntary military personnel—the private military company (PMC).

4.2 COMPARING MILITARY MANPOWER

Figures 4.1 and 4.2 tell an interesting story. Figure 4.1 shows the 25 countries with the largest levels of active military personnel in the world. China has the largest contingent of active military personnel; the Chinese level is nearly 50 percent more than that of the next closest country, the United States. These two countries are then followed by India, North Korea, and Russia (all with 1 million or more active personnel). Yet, in comparing Figure 4.1 to Figure 4.2, one notices that 19 of the 25 largest active military forces are also in the top 25 of country population (the exceptions being Israel, North Korea, Myanmar, Switzerland, Taiwan, and Syria). Therefore, even though military size is surely important from a security standpoint, from an economic point of view, the number of troops a country has does not tell the full story.

Instead, it is more useful to consider the active military force in relation to the total population. As it turns out, this ratio generates a much different grouping of countries (Figure 4.3). Regional conflicts, security concerns, and dominance of the military over the domestic political process can all explain why many countries in this set have such high ratios of active duty military personnel to population.

For example, notice that Greece and Cyprus are the only two European nations on the list. Even if one were to expand the list to the top 35 countries, Bulgaria, Belarus, and Turkey would be the only other European nations to make the list. For these countries, security explanations play a major role in explaining their high ratios of active duty military personnel

Figure 4.1

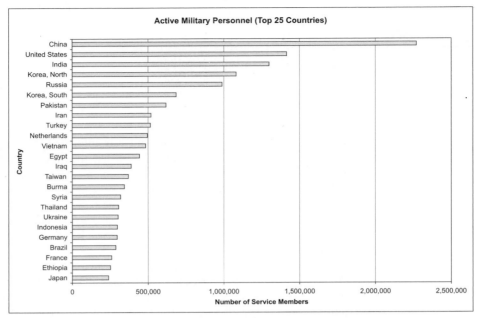

Active Military Personnel (Top 25 Countries)

Source of data: International Institute for Strategic Studies, *Military Balance.* 2002–2003. London, England: Oxford Press. 2002–2003.

Figure 4.2

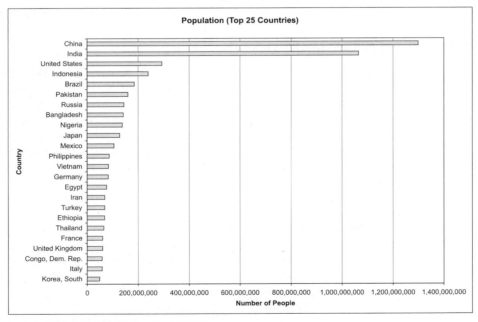

Population (Top 25 Countries)

Source of data: CIA. *World Fact Book* (2004).

Figure 4.3

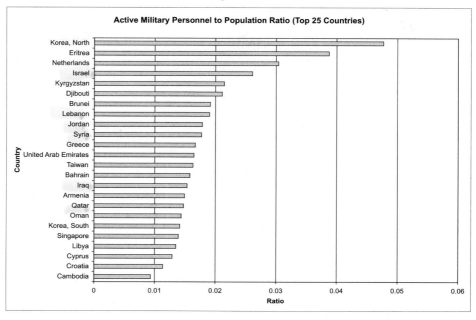

Source of data: Facts from both the CIA's *World Fact Book* and also the International Institute for Strategic Studies, *Military Balance*. 2002–2003. Oxford, UK: Oxford University Press. 2002–2003.

to population. First, as mentioned in Chapter 3, Greece and Turkey's long-standing dispute over Cyprus potentially forces each country to maintain as large a military as is economically practical. Also, Turkey's military has historically been politically influential in Turkey and, therefore, has been able to court a large number of recruits.

As for Bulgaria, it is located between Greece and Turkey, to the east of the volatile Balkans and was historically a military stalwart for the Soviet Union. More recently, because Bulgaria made gaining membership into the North Atlantic Treaty Alliance (NATO) a top foreign policy priority (which was achieved in 2004), maintaining a relatively large military was an important demonstration of its ability to make a significant military contribution to NATO. Finally, North Korea has the highest ratio of active-duty military personnel to population. This is for the same reason why North Korea has the highest military expenditures as a percentage of GDP—it is a communist state that is still at a state of war with its southern neighbor.

4.3 ALL-VOLUNTEER FORCE (AVF) VS. CONSCRIPTION

Table 4.1 shows that many of the countries listed in Figure 4.3 have **conscription** (a form of government-mandated, obligatory military service; also called the draft) rather than an **all-volunteer force** (AVF). An AVF is a recruitment system in which the military must use pay and benefit incentives to induce people to serve (AVF is the current system of the United States).[2] Table 4.1 lists those countries with an AVF.

As Donald Rumsfeld implied, the system of military recruitment adopted by a government is a vital and controversial issue, not just today, but also historically. In fact, some

Table 4.1
Countries without Conscription (as of 2004)

Antigua and Barbuda	Iceland	Pakistan
Australia	India	Panama
Bahamas	Ireland	Papua New Guinea
Bahrain	Italy*	Portugal
Bangladesh	Jamaica	Qatar
Barbados	Japan	Rwanda
Belgium	Jordan	San Marino
Belize	Kenya	Saudi Arabia
Botswana	Kyrgyzstan	Sierra Leone
Brunei Darussalam	Latvia*	Slovenia
Burkina Faso	Lesotho	South Africa
Burundi	Luxembourg	Spain
Cameroon	Malawi	Sri Lanka
Canada	Malaysia	Suriname
Costa Rica	Maldives	Swaziland
Czech Republic*	Malta	Tonga
Djibouti	Mauritania	Trinidad and Tobago
Fiji	Mauritius	Uganda
France	Monaco	United Arab Emirates
Gabon	Myanmar	United Kingdom of Great
Gambia	Nepal	Britain and Northern
Ghana	Netherlands	Ireland
Grenada	New Zealand	United States of America
Haiti	Nicaragua	Uruguay
Hong Kong	Nigeria	Vanuatu
Hungary	Oman	Zambia
		Zimbabwe

Source of countries: Information about most countries listed is from "The Question of Conscientious Objection to Military Service," in *Office of the United Nations High Commission for Human Rights,* 53rd Session. Report of the Secretary-General prepared pursuant to commission resolution 1995/83. Published January 16, 1997. Further information is from "table of the situation of military service and conscientious objection in the EU countries" at the European Bureau for Conscientious Objection. Available at www.ebco-beoc.org/country_reports.htm.
* Plans to eliminate conscription by 2008.

scholars argue that the method of military recruitment employed by the Roman Republic played a critical role in the Republic's eventual collapse (see Box 4.1).

4.3.1 Graphing the Military Labor Market

The two major systems of military recruitment are AVF and conscription. Determining which system is ideal requires consideration of the costs/benefits of AVF versus conscription. Figure 4.4 illustrates the economic workings of both systems. The vertical axis shows the wages paid to service members and the horizontal axis is the number of service members. The downward sloping **labor demand curve,** L_d, represents the government's demand for service members and the tendency for the government, all thing being equal, to hire fewer service members when the average wage for a service member is higher, than when it is lower.

Box 4.1
Historical Perspective
Military Recruitment and the Collapse of the Roman Republic[1]

During much of the Roman Republic's existence (c. 500 B.C.E.–24 B.C.E.), military service was voluntary. Because the government did not take responsibility for arming soldiers, membership in the Roman army was limited only to those who possessed the minimum census qualifications of 10,000 sesterces (about $420), later reduced to 3500 sesterces (about $145).[2] Typically, the number of volunteers would be limited, with the exception of lucrative campaigns that offered ample opportunities for plunder.

By the late 2nd century B.C.E., finding recruits from this small group of landowners became increasingly difficult. In 105 B.C.E. the system of recruitment was changed to conscripting *proletarii* (those Romans who failed to meet the minimum census qualifications). In this system, an 18-year-old draftee could spend 16 to 20 years outside Italy.[3] Since the *proletarii* were paid primarily through the reward of land on which to farm and because many of these troops were dispatched to lands far away from Rome, only their commanding general could be counted on to provide the land. Consequently, the *proletarii*'s loyalty turned to their general, not Rome. This result is a primary contributor to the civil wars that plagued Rome starting in 133 B.C.E. and ending in 27 B.C.E. with the rise of Caesar Augustus as the first Roman Emperor.

_____

[1] Information for this section comes primarily from Mackay, Christopher. Classics 378 "Roman Military" Lecture. University of Alberta. 2002. Available at www.ualberta.ca/~csmackay/CLASS_378/Military.html.

[2] Conversion of Sesterces to denarii at 4 Sesterces /denarii is extrapolated from figures in Starr (1982), p. 88. Conversion of denarii to U.S. dollars at 6 denarii/dollar is from "Monarchians" entry in the *Catholic Encyclopedia*. 1997. Available online at Bowdoin College at www.bowdoin.edu/~samato/IRA/reviews/issues/dec97/cath.html.

[3] From Rauh, Nicholas. History 102 "Fall of the Roman Republic" Lecture. Purdue University. 2004. Available at web.ics.purdue.edu/~rauhn/fall_of_republic.htm.

$L_{s\,AVF}$ is the **labor supply curve** that represents the behavior of the labor pool for troops when an AVF recruitment system is used. $L_{s\,AVF}$ is depicted as an upward sloping curve because of what is called the **opportunity cost effect.** Specifically, if people are free to choose whether or not to join the military, then as the wage offered by the military rises, so will the number of people who will join. This result happens because as the wages paid by the military rises, the potential wages and non-monetary benefits associated with civilian life begin to look less and less attractive, compared to military pay.

$L_{s\,Draft}$ represents the behavior of the labor pool for service members when a conscription recruitment system is used. The $L_{s\,Draft}$ curve is vertical to indicate that, under conscription, the government can set the level of service members employed regardless of what wage it pays. In short, the populace has no choice but to serve. Notice that the wage corresponding to the draft, W_{DRAFT}, hits the AVF labor supply curve, $L_{s\,AVF}$, at point Z. In turn, point Z corresponds with L_1. L_1 represents the number of people willing to voluntarily join the military at W_{DRAFT}. Therefore, even with conscription, the military will still have some volunteers. However, since L_1 falls well short of the number of troops desired by the military, the difference between L_{DRAFT} and L_1 represents the number of troops who will have to be drafted.

4.3.2 Budgetary Cost and Capital Intensity

One implication of these two systems is immediately clear. Under AVF, the military must pay wages that are sufficient to allow it to compete as an employer with the private sector and the military is unable to recruit as many troops for the same total budgetary cost. To illustrate the total cost of each system, Figure 4.4 is reproduced in Figure 4.5 except with shaded boxes, whose area measures total cost (wages paid, multiplied by the number of

Figure 4.4
All-Volunteer Force vs. Conscription

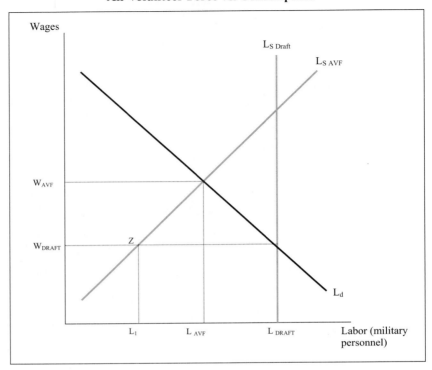

service members paid). Assuming that the area for conscription (box *GFEC*) is the same as the area for AVF (box *ABCD*), one can see that for the same total cost, conscription will enable the government to hire more service members.

The second implication of the two systems relates to the price of labor relative to other resources. Specifically, labor and **capital** (physical equipment) are the two resources that governments use to equip a military. Because an AVF raises the cost of labor, then a government switching to an AVF will consider labor to now be more expensive relative to capital. Therefore, the government will turn to developing a more capital-intensive military.

What evidence is there that an AVF does lead to higher personnel costs and a more capital-intensive military? Consider the United Kingdom and Germany, two European countries that, according to Table 3.2 in Chapter 3, have similarly sized defense budgets. However, since 1960, the United Kingdom has used an AVF, while Germany still employs conscription (and has no plans to end the system, see Box 4.2). Table 4.2 provides details on the composition of these two countries' military expenditures. France is included in the table as a comparison point (it only recently ended conscription in 2001).

One should immediately notice that the United Kingdom, as expected for an AVF country, has fewer troops. Second, the United Kingdom has a level of military expenditures per service member that is 27 percent higher than that of Germany. Again, this fact is consistent with the expectation that the United Kingdom, with an AVF, would spend

Figure 4.5
Conscription Allows More Troops for Same Total Cost

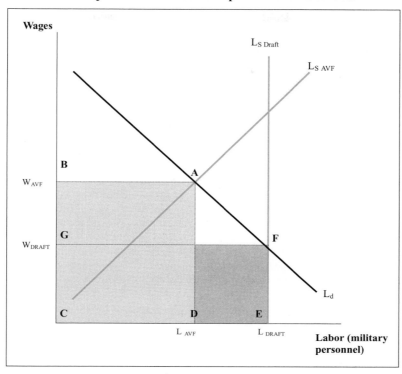

Table 4.2
Comparison of U.K., German, and French Military Budgets and Personnel (2003)

Country	Active Military Service members (2002)	Military Expenditures on Personnel (Constant 2000 U.S. $)	Personnel Exp./Act. Service Member (Constant 2000 U.S. $)	Military Expenditures on Equipment
United Kingdom	210,450	$14,739,000,000	$70,035.64	$8,710,000,000
Germany	296,000	$16,422,000,000	$55,479.73	$3,807,000,000
France	260,000	$20,595,000,000	$79,211.54	$7,229,000,000

Source of data: Numbers of active military service members are from International Institute for Strategic Studies, *Military Balance.* 2002–2003. London, England: Oxford Press. 2002–2003.
Figures on expenditure on personnel and expenditure on equipment are from Appendix 10B of the Stockholm International Peace and Research Institute. *SIPRI Yearbook 2004—Armaments, Disarmament and International Security.* New York: Humanities Press. Appendix 10B contains tables of NATO military expenditure by category, 1994–2003.

more per soldier than Germany. Most importantly, the military expenditures on equipment for the United Kingdom are 128 percent higher than that of Germany. This fact suggests that the United Kingdom, with its AVF system, has become a more capital-intensive military.

Box 4.2
Conscription in Europe

During the Cold War, conscription was in wide use throughout Europe. In 1990, the United Kingdom was virtually the only European country to not have conscription (which it had ended in 1960). By 2000, seven European nations had already eliminated or decided to eliminate conscription and in many other European countries ending conscription is being actively discussed.[1] For instance, the Czech Republic, Italy, Latvia, Romania, and Slovenia all plan to end conscription by 2008. Of course, some European countries such as Germany, Sweden, and Norway still use the system and have no plans to end it.

Why did so many European countries have conscription and why are several moving away from the system? Answering this question highlights both the economic and strategic reasons for a country to use conscription.

Economically, conscription reduces the cost of manning a military. For instance, it was estimated in 1992 that the 1987 defense budgets of European members of NATO were, on average, 6 percent lower because of conscription.[2] These government funds can, in turn, be put to use in other public welfare programs. Hence, it should come as no surprise that the Scandinavian countries (Sweden, Norway, and Finland), which all have extensive welfare systems, also have conscription.

Strategically, conscription was the result of Europe's Cold War security situation. During the Cold War, most European militaries were designed for territorial defense. Territorial defense requires a large number of soldiers to maintain territory. Because the European nations (both NATO and Warsaw Pact) required a large number of soldiers, universal or near-universal conscription is an efficient way to acquire them. It is less costly from a budgetary standpoint and, because everyone is involved, its fairness makes it more politically tolerable to the citizenship. However, after the Cold War, many of the European countries switched their security strategy from territorial defense to peacekeeping and expeditionary missions (that commonly take troops outside of Europe). Without a challenging territorial defense mission, it is no longer economically nor politically wise for the government to maintain a large military full of conscripts. Therefore, conscription has become nonuniversal and should eventually be eliminated altogether. Hence, it should come as no surprise that the trend has been for more European countries to end conscription in favor of an AVF.

---

[1] Jehn and Selden (2002), p. 98.
[2] Sandler and Hartley (1999), pp. 173–174.

4.3.3 The Labor Demand Curve as the Marginal Productivity of Labor

However, budgetary cost is only one cost that economists must consider. In order to discuss the other cost considerations, one must first understand that the labor demand curve represents the **Marginal Productivity of Labor** (MPL). MPL is the level of output each additional worker is able to generate for the military. In this case, the output would be national security. Therefore, each additional service member adds a little more to the ability of the military to produce security. However, the ability of additional service members to add to a country's security is subject to the **law of diminishing returns.** According to this law, each additional service member, all things being equal, adds less and less to the country's security. This result was illustrated in Chapter 3 with the national security function. For example, a country with no service members gains greatly (with regard to its protection) when it recruits its first few service members. However, once it has, for instance, a million service members (like China), one more service member will not add greatly (if at all) to the country's ability to protect itself.

Because the labor demand curve illustrates the productivity of each additional service member hired, it can also be thought of as representing the benefit of each additional unit of labor (**Marginal Benefit**). Because one could reasonably expect more productive service members to be paid higher wages, the first workers hired should be paid the highest wages. This expectation provides an alternative explanation for why the labor demand curve is downward sloping.

4.3.4　The Labor Supply Curve as the Willingness to Join

If the labor demand curve can be thought of as depicting the benefit each service member gives to the military, then the labor supply curve can be thought of as the cost of these service members to the military. In particular, look at the $L_{S\,AVF}$ curve. It shows the behavior of civilians when left to make their own decisions. Because the labor supply curve is upward sloping, it shows that individuals who are highly motivated to become service members will not require a very high wage in order to join the military. However, people who are not as motivated to join the military will require very high wages. Therefore, whereas the labor demand curve illustrates the marginal productivity of the service member, the labor supply curve illustrates the **willingness to join** the military. Service members who are paid lower wages have a higher willingness to join; while service members who require higher wages have a lower willingness to join.

4.3.5　Conscription and Opportunity Cost

The concepts of *diminishing MPL* and *willingness to join* make it possible to see that conscription has a tendency to generate inefficiencies. First, because the willingness to join (as depicted by the $L_{S\,AVF}$ curve) of some people hired under conscription is less than the wages those people are paid, those people are likely to be unmotivated.

Second, and perhaps more importantly, because the MPL (as depicted by the L_d curve) of many of the conscripted service members is low, then many of the conscripted service members will tend to be less skilled. This result is primarily because conscription refutes the idea of **comparative advantage.** Comparative advantage is the ability of a person to perform an activity or produce a good or service at a lower **opportunity cost** than someone else. Opportunity cost is the "next-best thing" someone must give up in order gain something else.

For example, consider Joe and Jane. Jane is an expert shooter, speaks four languages, and is a black belt in karate. Joe is the poet laureate of his home state and has never fired a weapon in his life. The country would be far safer if Jane became a Special Forces soldier than Joe. At the same time, the country would probably gain quite a bit having Joe write poetry. Unfortunately, under conscription, Joe, assuming he could not gain an exemption, would become a soldier. Though Jane would excel at the task, Joe would flounder. Besides frustrating his superior officer, Joe would also not have time to reflect and write poetry. Therefore, being a soldier has a high opportunity cost; not just for Joe (he can't do what he likes best), but for the country (the country isn't very safe with Joe as a soldier and the country misses out on Joe's poetry).

In short, some people have the physical and mental traits necessary to be a good service member, while others would be better off doing something else. But conscription can force someone to be in the armed forces and perform a task for which they are ill suited. Therefore, even though conscription has a *low budgetary cost,* it has a *high opportunity cost.*

4.3.6　The Inefficiencies of Conscription

A **universal draft** means anyone, barring medical disqualifications, must serve. A **non-universal draft** means exemptions can be granted for various family, educational, or work requirements. Both systems impose opportunity costs on society.

Universal drafts have produced numerous real-life examples of people forced to forgo promising civilian employment and life opportunities because of military service. Consider the very prominent example of Major League Baseball. During the 1950s, Hall of Fame baseball players such as Ted Williams and Willie Mays were drafted and forced to miss two seasons each. They are two among many well-known (and not so well-known) players that the military draft removed from the sports field, thereby eliminating the ability of people around the country to enjoy watching them play.[3]

Non-universal drafts can discriminate against low-income, low-educated, and under-privileged members of society who lack the ability to qualify for deferments (such as entering college). Additionally, people will begin spending time in **avoidance activities** rather than productive activities. Avoidance activities are actions taken for the sole purpose of gaining a military service exemption. These activities include early marriages, emigration, unnecessary schooling, and employment in exempted fields even if the person is not well suited to that line of work.[4] Overall, these various inefficiencies have led economists to estimate that the social cost of a non-universal draft can be twice its budgetary cost.[5]

4.4 CASE STUDY: THE VIETNAM TRANSITION FROM CONSCRIPTION TO AN AVF

The U.S. experience with military recruitment during and at the end of the Vietnam War offers an excellent illustration of the conclusions drawn from the military-labor market model.

4.4.1 Background

From November 1940 through July 1973, the United States employed a conscription-based recruitment system. Only during a brief period from January 1947 to March 1948 was conscription not used. However, not everyone had to serve. Individuals could gain exemptions from service if they were conscientious objectors (who would not fight for religious reasons and who was verified by a religious official), enrolled in college, medically disqualified, or married.

Yet, by 1969, public anger over the Vietnam War and resentment of the exemptions that appeared to favor the privileged led the Nixon administration to reform the draft system by ending such exemptions, particularly those for college students, and initiate a **selective service lottery**.[6] The lottery was held each year from 1969 through 1972. The 1969 lottery was intended to set the draft order for all male 18- to 26-year-olds in the country (born any year between 1944 and 1950). The lotteries in 1970, 1971, and 1972 determined the draft order for men born in 1951, 1952, and 1953 respectively.

Here's how the lottery worked. In the 1969 lottery, an individual reached into a container with 366 blue plastic capsules (one for each day of the year and one for February 29), removed a capsule and opened it (the first capsule was pulled by Rep. Alexander Pine of New York). The people born on the day specified in that first capsule would receive a draft number of 1. This date was September 14, which meant men born on that date between 1944 and 1950 could soon expect a letter in the mail ordering them to report for active military duty (unless they volunteered). People born on the date of the next capsule removed would be assigned the number 2, and so on. Table 4.3 provides the lottery numbers, by birth date, for the 1969 selective service lottery. Next, throughout 1970, the selective service would continue, in order, calling numbers on the list until all draft boards filled their quotas (keep in mind that some persons called were not physically able to serve). Individuals holding numbers that were not called in 1970 would then be free of all draft liability. The highest number called from the 1969 lottery was 195.

Table 4.3
1969 Draft Lottery Results***

DAY**	MONTH*											
	Jan	Feb	Mar	Apr	May	Jun	Jul	Aug	Sep	Oct	Nov	Dec
1	305	86	108	32	330	249	93	111	225	359	19	129
2	159	144	29	271	298	228	350	45	161	125	34	328
3	251	297	267	83	40	301	115	261	49	244	348	157
4	215	210	275	81	276	20	279	145	232	202	266	165
5	101	214	293	269	364	28	188	54	82	24	310	56
6	224	347	139	253	155	110	327	114	6	87	76	10
7	306	91	122	147	35	85	50	168	8	234	51	12
8	199	181	213	312	321	366	13	48	184	283	97	105
9	194	338	317	219	197	335	277	106	263	342	80	43
10	325	216	323	218	65	206	284	21	71	220	282	41
11	329	150	136	14	37	134	248	324	158	237	46	39
12	221	68	300	346	133	272	15	142	242	72	66	314
13	318	152	259	124	295	69	42	307	175	138	126	163
14	238	4	354	231	178	356	331	198	1	294	127	26
15	17	89	169	273	130	180	322	102	113	171	131	320
16	121	212	166	148	55	274	120	44	207	254	107	96
17	235	189	33	260	112	73	98	154	255	288	143	304
18	140	292	332	90	278	341	190	141	246	5	146	128
19	58	25	200	336	75	104	227	311	177	241	203	240
20	280	302	239	345	183	360	187	344	63	192	185	135
21	186	363	334	62	250	60	27	291	204	243	156	70
22	337	290	265	316	326	247	153	339	160	117	9	53
23	118	57	256	252	319	109	172	116	119	201	182	162
24	59	236	258	2	31	358	23	36	195	196	230	95
25	52	179	343	351	361	137	67	286	149	176	132	84
26	92	365	170	340	357	22	303	245	18	7	309	173
27	355	205	268	74	296	64	289	352	233	264	47	78
28	77	299	223	262	308	222	88	167	257	94	281	123
29	349	285	362	191	226	353	270	61	151	229	99	16
30	164	--	217	208	103	209	287	333	315	38	174	3
31	211	--	30	--	313	--	193	11	--	79	--	100

Source: Data are from the Selective Service System's "History and Records," in *The Vietnam Lotteries*. Available at www.sss.gov/lotter1.htm.

* Month drawn during lottery.
** Day drawn during lottery.
*** Number specified by each combination of month and day is the draft number for all men aged 18–26 born on that day.

4.4.2 The Typical Vietnam War Service Member

Of the service members in Vietnam, 75 percent were volunteers. However, a large number of these volunteers (41 percent of enlistments in 1971) were **draft-induced volunteers** (people who voluntarily join one of the other services to avoid being drafted into the Army).[7]

If one was drafted, this did not guarantee deployment to Vietnam. Over the course of the Vietnam War, military draftees stood only a 38 percent chance of serving in Vietnam, though service members belonging to that 38 percent were statistically more likely to die in combat than service members who volunteered—principally because the overwhelming majority of draftees sent to Vietnam were assigned to Army ground forces conducting most of the fighting.[8] Specifically, though draftees accounted for just 25 percent of the fighting

Table 4.4
Estimate of Distribution of Incomes of Vietnam Casualties
among Deciles of 1970 U.S. Income Distribution

Decile	Percentage of Deaths
Lowest	9.6
2nd	13.1
3rd	11.2
4th	11.8
5th	9.4
6th	10.8
7th	9.1
8th	9.2
9th	8
Highest	7.8

Source of data: Barnett, Arnold; Stanley, Timothy; and Shore, Michael.
"America's Vietnam Casualties: Victims of a Class War?" *Operations Research.*
September–October 1992, Table VI, p. 864.

force in South Vietnam (compared to 66 percent during World War II), they accounted for 30.4 percent of the combat deaths (of which 71 percent were incurred by individuals from 18 to 22 years of age).[9]

Even though upper-class individuals were more likely to gain draft deferments prior to the draft reforms of 1969, the Vietnam draft itself does not appear to have discriminated disproportionately towards minorities and the uneducated. Because over 80 percent of the service members fighting in Vietnam were of white European descent, there was not a disproportionate number of American minorities serving in the war.[10] Fully 79 percent of draftees had attained a high school education or higher.

There is some evidence to suggest that the draft and draft-induced volunteerism may have compelled more middle- and lower-class individuals to join the military. The 1970 median income for the communities from which casualties lived in the United States was an estimated $9,582 or 1 percent less than the $9,696 median income for all Americans from communities with at least 2,500 residents.[11] Also, as Table 4.4 illustrates, families in the lowest three (out of 10, hence the term "deciles") income levels incurred death rates marginally above the national average.

4.4.3 Pressures to End the Draft

Because the war was unpopular domestically, President Lyndon Johnson refrained from raising taxes to finance the war (see the Vietnam case study in Chapter 2) and refused to mobilize or activate the National Guard and the Reserves—even though this method meant that he had to expand the active-duty services by nearly a million people solely through an increase in draft calls. Consequently, the main drawback of the Vietnam draft was not its discriminatory features, but that it forced the military to send individuals on a constantly rotating basis, rather than as cohesive units.[12]

After Richard Nixon promised to end the draft if elected to president in 1968, the selective service lottery was installed before switching to an AVF in 1973. How did the switch to an AVF impact the military? One should consider this question according to the criteria specified by the military-labor market model: higher pay, fewer troops, and a more capital-intensive military.

Table 4.5
Military Pay and Government Civilian Pay Increases (1960–1975)

Effective Date of Pay Increase	Military Pay Increase (percentage increase)	Government Civil Service Pay Increase (percentage increase)
1-Jul-60	-	7.7
14-Oct-62	-	5.5
1-Oct-63	8.4	-
5-Jan-64	-	4.1
1-Jul-64	-	4.2
1-Sep-64	1.4	-
1-Sep-65	6.4	-
1-Oct-65	3.6	-
1-Jul-66	2.8	2.9
1-Oct-67	4.5	4.5
1-Jul-68	4.9	4.9
1-Jul-69	9.1	9.1
1-Jan-70	6.0	6.0
1-Jan-71	6.0	6.0
14-Nov-71	13.1	-
1-Jan-72	5.5	5.5
1-Jan-73	5.1	5.1
1-Oct-73	4.8	4.8
1-Oct-74	5.5	5.5
1-Oct-75	5.0	5.0
1-Oct-76	4.8	4.8
1-Oct-77	7.0	7.0
1-Oct-78	5.5	5.5
1-Oct-79	7.0	7.0
1-Oct-80	11.7	9.1
1-Oct-81	14.3	4.8
1-Oct-82	4.0	4.0
1-Jan-84	4.0	4.0
1-Jan-85	4.0	3.5

Source of data: Department of Defense. *Fiscal Year 2005 Budget Green Book,* Table 12, p. 56. Available at http://www.defenselink.mil/comptroller/defbudget/fy2005/fy2005_greenbook.pdf.

AVF leads to higher pay and expenditures per service member: Table 4.5 shows that in 1971, military pay did rise 13.1 percent. The majority of this 1971 pay increase was concentrated on raising the basic entry pay of enlisted personnel from $133 per month in 1970 to $326 per month in 1973, so as to prepare the recruitment system for an AVF.[13] However, from 1966 to 1970—and (with the exception of 1980 and 1981) from 1972 to 1985—military pay increases matched that of civilian pay increases.

Next, take a moment to refer back to Figures 3.4 and 3.5 in Chapter 3. Notice that the initial pay increases did cause military expenditures on personnel to rise. However, one can see that these expenditures soon began to decline both in dollar terms (Figure 3.4) and as a percentage of the defense budget (Figure 3.5).

Finally, look at Table 4.6. With an AVF, one should expect the United States to spend more per service member. Table 4.6 shows that military personnel pay per active service member (the fourth column) did rise from a low of $38,131 in 1968 to a peak of $48,259 in 1972, before leveling off between $43,000 and $45,000. However, given the high inflation rates the U.S. economy experienced during the late 1960s and early 1970s (see the Vietnam

Table 4.6
U.S. Military Personnel, Personnel Expenditures, and Equipment Expenditures (1960–1985)

Year	Total Active Duty	Pay to Military Personnel (in constant FY 2005 U.S. $)	Pay / Active Personnel	Total Reserves	Pay / Reservist	Military Expenditure on Equipment (in millions of constant FY 2005 U.S. $)
1960	2,475,438	$110,364,000,000	$44,584	4,147,294	$26,611	$118,256
1961	2,482,905	$109,614,000,000	$44,147	3,756,246	$29,182	$122,252
1962	2,805,603	$119,052,000,000	$42,434	2,994,633	$39,755	$130,568
1963	2,698,927	$116,170,000,000	$43,043	2,435,532	$47,698	$143,585
1964	2,685,782	$116,256,000,000	$43,286	2,550,716	$45,578	$136,502
1965	2,653,926	$116,190,000,000	$43,780	2,576,405	$45,098	$109,551
1966	3,092,175	$118,654,000,000	$38,372	2,768,628	$42,857	$119,864
1967	3,375,485	$131,090,000,000	$38,836	2,757,614	$47,537	$143,583
1968	3,546,071	$135,216,000,000	$38,131	2,844,734	$47,532	$160,166
1969	3,458,072	$137,000,000,000	$39,617	3,259,467	$42,031	$158,658
1970	3,064,760	$133,072,000,000	$43,420	3,639,478	$36,563	$138,691
1971	2,713,044	$123,310,000,000	$45,451	3,904,062	$31,585	$120,306
1972	2,321,959	$112,055,000,000	$48,259	3,711,211	$30,194	$109,872
1973	2,251,936	$103,466,000,000	$45,945	3,412,337	$30,321	$100,620
1974	2,162,005	$99,397,000,000	$45,974	3,064,566	$32,434	$95,366
1975	2,128,120	$95,803,000,000	$45,018	2,655,816	$36,073	$88,308
1976	2,081,910	$92,335,000,000	$44,351	1,647,904	$56,032	$83,789
1977	2,074,543	$90,281,000,000	$43,519	1,457,196	$61,955	$86,171
1978	2,061,708	$88,954,000,000	$43,146	1,326,902	$67,039	$87,047
1979	2,026,892	$88,513,000,000	$43,669	1,306,063	$67,771	$95,020
1980	2,050,627	$88,444,000,000	$43,130	1,360,035	$65,031	$98,574
1981	2,082,560	$89,735,000,000	$43,089	1,392,088	$64,461	$104,772
1982	2,108,612	$91,760,000,000	$43,517	1,422,454	$64,508	$114,477
1983	2,123,349	$92,910,000,000	$43,756	1,464,497	$63,442	$131,243
1984	2,138,157	$93,780,000,000	$43,860	1,534,107	$61,130	$141,816
1985	2,151,032	$94,752,000,000	$44,050	1,610,082	$58,849	$157,299

Sources of data: Figures of active duty service member levels are from the Department of Defense's "Fiscal Year 2003," *Selected Manpower Statistics*. Washington Headquarters Services, Directorate for Information Operations and Reports. Table 2-11 is available at http://web1.whs.osd.mil/mmid/M01/fy03/m01fy03.pdf.

Figures of reserve service member levels are from two Department of Defense tables. First, from Table 315, "Reserve Strength Not on Active Duty," from the Department of Defense OASD (Comptroller), Directorate for Management Information and Operations and Control, 1977. Second, from Table 5-2, "Reserve Strength Trends by Reserve Component," From the Department of Defense OASD (Comptroller), Directorate for Management Information and Operations and Control. 1987 (provided to author by request).

Figures for pay for military personnel and military equipment expenditure are from the Department of Defense's *National Defense Budget Estimates for the FY 2005 (Green Book)*. Office of the Comptroller. Tables 6-12 and 6-11 are available at http://www.defenselink.mil/comptroller/defbudget/fy2005/index.html.
NOTE: Figures for fiscal years 2006 through 2009 are estimates.

War case study in Chapter 2), the real level of pay per active soldier was less than in the early 1960s. In fact, only military pay per reservist (which fell from $45,732 in 1968 to $30,194 in 1972) experienced a dramatic rise to an average level between $60,000 and $65,000 in the late 1970s and early 1980s.

AVF leads to fewer troops: Table 4.6 shows that the number of active duty troops and reservists began to decline in 1969 and 1972, respectively. This result seems consistent with the expected impact of an AVF. However, because the Gates Commission (a commission formed by Richard Nixon in 1969 to investigate the possibility of shifting to an AVF) did not make its unanimous recommendation to President Nixon to eliminate the draft until November 1970, the decline in active duty military forces was probably due more to the decision of the Nixon administration to pull out of Vietnam, rather than the implementation of an AVF.

AVF leads to a more capital-intensive military: The final column of Table 4.6 shows the level of U.S. military expenditure on equipment. This level declined from $160 billion in 1968 to only $83 billion in 1976. However, it soon began to rise and, unlike military expenditures on personnel, by 1985 it had returned to nearly the same level as in 1968. This finding would suggest that after the initial transition into an AVF, the U.S. military gradually became more capital intensive. However, the 1980 figures correspond to the time of the Reagan military buildup (see section 3.6 of Chapter 3). Therefore, the higher levels, though surely indicative of a more capital-intensive military, were more likely the result of the Soviet Union arms race, not the AVF.

4.4.4 Summary

The U.S. transition to an AVF from conscription provides a unique opportunity to contrast the economic impact of both recruitment systems. The societal cost of conscription and the unpopular nature of the Vietnam War appear to have contributed to conscription's downfall. However, the Vietnam-induced downsizing of the military, the inflation of the 1970s, and the Reagan-era arms race all serve to muddle our understanding of how the transition economically impacted the U.S. armed services.

4.5   U.S. MILITARY COMPENSATION: IS IT ENOUGH?

Military compensation—both direct-cash payments for service, as well as non-cash benefits such as medical care coverage, child care, retirement, life insurance, government-provided housing, and subsidized groceries—became an important topic once the United States switched to an AVF. The U.S. may spend more per active military personnel than most countries in the world, but does this expenditure mean the military's compensation is adequate? This question is a particularly important one because the private sector of the U.S. economy offers many attractive alternatives to military employment. Therefore, it is important to compare military compensation to private sector compensation to determine if the AVF wages and benefits create the incentives necessary for the United States military to attract qualified people.

4.5.1   Military Pay

Though a service member's compensation consists of much more than his or her paycheck, take-home pay is still a useful starting point. The first component of a service member's pay is his or her base pay. Base pay is determined solely by a service member's rank and years of service.[14] The average military enlistee with 12 years experience earns $30,747.60 in taxable base pay. Senior enlisted members of the Army Green Berets or Navy Seals (with 20 years or more experience) can now earn about $50,000 in base pay.[15] Table 4.7 provides the breakdown of base pay levels. If a service member knows his or her years of service (years in the military) and pay grade (rank), then he or she can find his or her base pay using this table. For example, a commissioned officer at a 0-6 pay grade (either, for example, an Army Colonel or a Navy Captain in rank), with 10 years experience, will receive $5,882.10 per month in taxable base pay.

Table 4.7
U.S. Military Pay Scale (effective January 2004)

PAY GRADE	<2	2	3	4	6	8	10	12	14	16	18
					YEARS OF SERVICE						
					COMMISSIONED OFFICER						
O-10	0	0	0	0	0	0	0	0	0	0	0
O-9	0	0	0	0	0	0	0	0	0	0	0
O-8	7751.1	8004.9	8173.2	8220.6	8430.3	8781.9	8863.5	9197.1	9292.8	9579.9	9995.7
O-7	6440.7	6739.8	6878.4	6988.5	7187.4	7384.2	7611.9	7839	8066.7	8781.9	9386.1
O-6	4773.6	5244.3	5588.4	5588.4	5609.7	5850	5882.1	5882.1	6216.3	6807.3	7154.1
O-5	3979.5	4482.9	4793.4	4851.6	5044.8	5161.2	5415.9	5602.8	5844	6213.6	6389.7
O-4	3433.5	3974.7	4239.9	4299	4545.3	4809.3	5137.8	5394	5571.6	5673.6	5733
O-3	3018.9	3422.4	3693.9	4027.2	4220.1	4431.6	4568.7	4794.3	4911.3	4911.3	4911.3
O-2	2608.2	2970.6	3421.5	3537	3609.9	3609.9	3609.9	3609.9	3609.9	3609.9	3609.9
O-1	2264.4	2356.5	2848.5	2848.5	2848.5	2848.5	2848.5	2848.5	2848.5	2848.5	2848.5
PAY GRADE	**<2**	**2**	**3**	**4**	**6**	**8**	**10**	**12**	**14**	**16**	**18**
					ENLISTED MEMBER						
E-9	0	0	0	0	0	0	3769.2	3854.7	3962.4	4089.3	4216.5
E-8	0	0	0	0	0	3085.5	3222	3306.3	3407.7	3517.5	3715.5
E-7	2145	2341.2	2430.6	2549.7	2642.1	2801.4	2891.1	2980.2	3139.8	3219.6	3295.5
E-6	1855.5	2041.2	2131.2	2218.8	2310	2516.1	2596.2	2685.3	2763.3	2790.9	2809.8
E-5	1700.1	1813.5	1901.1	1991.1	2130.6	2250.9	2339.7	2367.9	2367.9	2367.9	2367.9
E-4	1558.2	1638.3	1726.8	1814.1	1891.5	1891.5	1891.5	1891.5	1891.5	1891.5	1891.5
E-3	1407	1495.5	1585.5	1585.5	1585.5	1585.5	1585.5	1585.5	1585.5	1585.5	1585.5
E-2	1337.7	1337.7	1337.7	1337.7	1337.7	1337.7	1337.7	1337.7	1337.7	1337.7	1337.7
E-1>4	1193.4	1193.4	1193.4	1193.4	1193.4	1193.4	1193.4	1193.4	1193.4	1193.4	1193.4
E-1<4	1104	0	0	0	0	0	0	0	0	0	0

Source: Department of Defense. "Monthly Basic Pay Table." Available at http://www.dod.mil/militarypay/pay/index.html.

However, a service member's base pay is not the same as the service member's total pay. There are additional bonuses and allowances. For example, if the service member is not provided with housing, then he or she is given a BAH (Basic Allowance for Housing) housing allowance. This allowance formerly covered only 89 percent of the 'average' off-base housing cost, but as of 2005, out-of-pocket housing costs dropped to zero for military personnel living in private housing.[16] Another one-third of active-duty service members live in government-provided housing; a factor that should also be included in any consideration of the total compensation package. A service member is also given a food allowance that pays for chow-hall meals and off-base eating. Called the BAS (Basic Allowance for Subsistence), it is approximately $260 per month for enlisted personnel, but only $175 per month for officers (who receive significantly higher base pay).[17]

Both the food and housing allowances are nontaxable income. Basic pay plus BAH, BAS, and the tax advantage on the two allowances comprise what is called "Regular Military Compensation" (RMC). Figure 4.6 offers a visual breakdown of RMC.

Additionally, service members can receive numerous special and incentive pays, such as extra monetary compensation provided to service members in high-demand military occupations, on particular assignments, or in hazardous areas.

Yet, how does this pay compare to that offered in the private sector?[18] Unfortunately, this question is complex. First, the pay component of military compensation is much more complicated and composed of more elements (such as the various allowances or reenlistment bonuses) than civilian pay compensation. Second, it is extremely difficult to establish a solid comparison between military ranks and pay grades on the one hand, and private-sector job titles and pay levels on the other. Third, and perhaps most importantly,

Figure 4.6
Distribution of Regular Military Compensation
Among its Components (in percent)

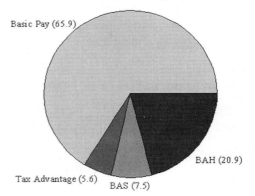

Source: Fernandez, Richard. "What Does the Military Pay Gap Mean?" *Congressional Budget Office.* June 1999. Chapter 1, Figure 1 is available at http://www.cbo.gov/showdoc.cfm?index=1354&sequence=0&from=1.

NOTES: BAH = basic allowance for housing (nontaxable). BAS = basic allowance for subsistence (nontaxable). An example of BAS is payments given for food purchase. The tax advantage is the amount of additional tax that typical personnel would pay if the subsistence and housing allowances were subject to federal income tax. Data are for 1998 and are averages for all personnel.

comparisons between different sets of compensation statistics can yield very different results. For example, comparing dollar amounts of pay received by various military pay grades with the *dollar amounts* received by comparable private-sector positions can lead to different conclusions than comparing the *annual increases* in pay for each position (which, in turn, can also vary according to the year chosen to begin the comparison).

Nevertheless, these limitations have not stopped efforts to estimate the pay gap between the military and the private sector.[19] For example, according to the RAND Corporation, since 1982, the overall pay increase in U.S. military base pay has been approximately 13 percent less than comparable civilian pay increases. In recent years, those estimates that support the presence of a pay gap often quote the cumulative pay raises for all military personnel as lagging behind the cumulative wage increases of private sector workers by some 7 to 15 percent. Yet, reducing the analysis to specific categories generates quite different results. Figure 4.7 illustrates such a comparison from 1982 until 2010 (using forecasted values for 2006 through 2010). Each year of Figure 4.7 shows the gap in accumulated pay raises between officers and their civilian counterparts (college graduates), and enlisted personnel and their civilian counterparts (high school graduates). Notice that all of the bars for the officers fall below zero, while all of the bars for the enlisted personnel are above zero. This result indicates that since 1982, military pay raises for enlisted personnel has kept pace or even outpaced civilian pay growth. However, officer pay raises have lagged behind that of comparable civilian sector employment (such as corporate managerial positions).

Figure 4.7
Defense Employment Cost Index pay gaps for officers and enlisted

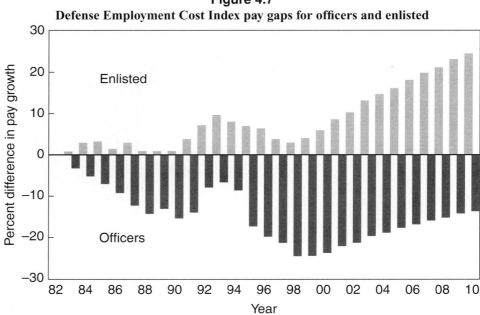

Source: Hosek, James, and Sharp, Jennifer. "Keeping Military Pay Competitive." *RAND Corporation Issue Paper 205,* Santa Monica, CA: RAND Corporation, 2001. Figure 5. Available at http://www.rand.org. Reprinted here with permission.

4.5.2 Military Benefits

Service members also take into consideration the benefits of staying in the armed forces. These benefits are wide ranging, including government subsidized child care, medical care, college education, subsidized groceries, and retirement pensions for those who stay in service for 20 years or more. In fact, as shown in Figure 4.8, **in-kind compensation** (payment made, not with cash but with tangible items) and non-cash benefits constitute 60 percent of the military pay package. Moreover, there is growing concern that such benefits will become an ever larger and potentially unsustainable burden on the U.S. defense budget.[20] However, because the benefits and economic issues surrounding them are simply too numerous to fully discuss in this section, focus will only be given to the recruitment issues surrounding two of the more controversial benefits: military retirement pensions and benefits to military families.

Retirement: After 20 years of service, military personnel can retire with an immediate pension that pays approximately 50 percent of their final base pay each year for the rest of their life. For example, a senior enlisted service member with 20 years of service earning about $50,000 per year in base pay can retire with a $25,000 per year pension.[21] Therefore, a military service member can begin to receive his or her pension as early as 38 years of age. However, if a military service member leaves prior to 20 years, he or she receives no pension at all.

This differs greatly with private sector pensions. Following the enactment of the 1986 Tax Reform Act, employees of all private-sector employers who offer a retirement benefit are considered fully vested after five years. This vestment policy means that if the employee leaves the company, he or she is allowed to transfer their accumulated retirement benefits

Figure 4.8
Cash and Non-cash Compensation per Active Duty Service Member (2002)

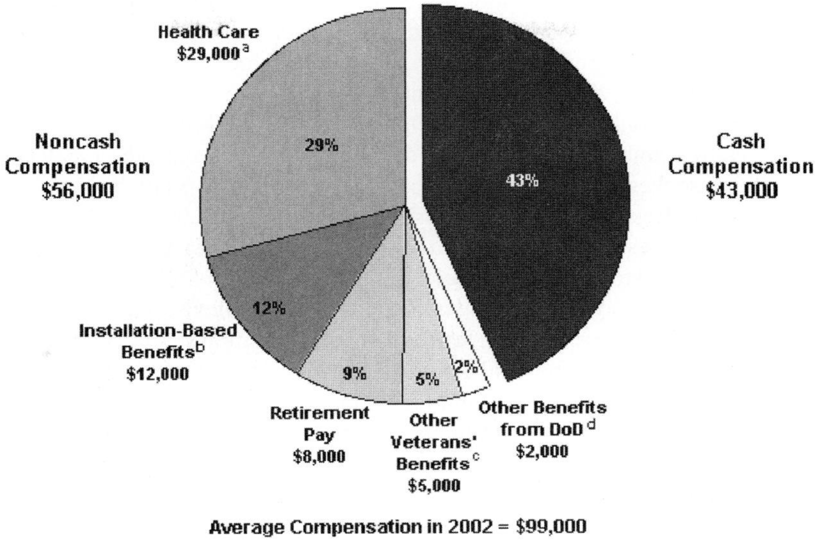

Health Care
$29,000[a]

Noncash
Compensation
$56,000

29%

Cash
Compensation
$43,000

43%

12%

Installation-Based
Benefits[b]
$12,000

9%

5%

2%

Retirement
Pay
$8,000

Other
Veterans'
Benefits[c]
$5,000

Other Benefits
from DoD[d]
$2,000

Average Compensation in 2002 = $99,000

Source: Murray, Carla Tighe. "Military Compensation: Balancing Cash and Non-Cash Benefits." *Congressional Budget Office.* Issue Brief. January 16, 2004. Available at http://www.cbo.gov/showdoc.cfm?index=4978&sequence=0.

NOTES:

a. Healthcare benefits include DoD's funding for active-duty service members and their dependents, as well as estimated accrual costs for current members who will retire and for those who may receive care from the Veterans Administration.

b. Installation-based benefits include subsidized in-kind goods and services found on military installations, such as commissaries, family and bachelor housing, and child care.

c. Other veterans' benefits include disability compensation, education benefits under the Montgomery G.I. Bill, home mortgage assistance and other loans, vocational rehabilitation and counseling, pension benefits, and burial benefits.

d. Other program benefits from the DoD include its contributions to Social Security's Old-Age and Survivors Insurance and Disability Insurance programs, Medicare's Hospital Insurance program, and the Unemployment Compensation for Ex-Servicemen program.

to their next employer. Yet, in the private sector, the typical retirement age is 65 and most people cannot begin receiving reduced payouts from their retirement account until 55.

Unfortunately, because the average military enlistment term is only four years, many members of the military do not reach the 20-year threshold. Though the 20-year threshold is considered an incentive that induces personnel to remain in the military, it also creates an incentive to retire shortly after reaching the 20-year mark. In 2000, Congress did create a Thrift Savings Plan, which allows military members to set aside tax-deferred dollars up to 7 percent of their income (meaning the government will not charge taxes on this income). However, this plan is still not comparable to many private sector plans, because the government—unlike many private employers—does not contribute matching funds.

Family support: There is a saying that "individuals join the military, but families stay."[22] Consequently, military compensation (as it pertains to the support services given to military families) is a critical issue, especially because nearly 60 percent of service members have families and military members at any given age are more likely to be married than their civilian peers. Additionally, military service members tend to start their families earlier, as 72 percent of all military children are under the age of 12.

Being young and having a family is a life choice that can create financial difficulties for any family. However, the financial difficulties appear to be greater for a military family. A 2002 RAND Corporation study found that approximately 27 percent of married junior-enlisted service members have serious problems paying bills, compared to only 13 percent of civilians of similar age, family, and demographic status. As many as 23 percent of military members in 1997 and 18 percent of military members in 1999 had creditor problems, in contrast to only 10 percent of comparable civilians.[23] Military families of Reserve or National Guard members during time of deployment face perhaps the greatest strains. Oftentimes, because these families are not located near a military installation where support services are located, Reservist families experience difficulties receiving such services. In contrast, support services appear to work fairly well for families located near or on military installations.[24] With regard to pay, another study found that 41 percent of Reservists report a loss of income, 29 percent report an increase of income, and 30 percent report no change in income.[25]

Nevertheless, a recent Kaiser Family Foundation survey reported that the vast majority of military personnel and families remain economically secure. The survey relied on a sample of over a thousand military spouses living at the 10 largest military bases (excluding those bases used for training only) in the United States. According to the survey, seven of every 10 military families experiencing extended deployment reported no trouble paying bills and nearly four in five did not require government food or family assistance (such as food stamps).[26]

The role of non-tangible benefits: Unfortunately, economists will always find it difficult to derive the optimal worker compensation for service members because, in the end, many people take on a military profession for non-tangible reasons. These reasons include patriotism, sense of duty and/or accomplishment, and a feeling of belonging. By creating job satisfaction that is independent of monetary or in-kind compensation, these reasons can relegate pay, benefits, and skills training to secondary importance.

In the end, even though differences between the conditions of employment and the structure of pay and benefits between the military and the private sector can make it impossible to compare pay and benefits, decision makers do have a way to tell how much pay is adequate: if enough quality volunteers come and stay, it is enough. If they don't, it's not.

4.6 PRIVATE MILITARY COMPANIES/FORCES (PMC/PMF)

There is a third option for acquiring military personnel, and this strategy has been growing since the late 1990s—privatization. Specifically, privatization of military operations pertains to what are called **Private Military Companies** (PMC) or **Private Military Forces** (PMF). Specifically, PMCs are private corporations that provide a range of military services. Services include noncombat tasks, such as building and guarding army bases, providing battlefield logistics, training local forces in places such as Bosnia and Iraq, gathering intelligence, analyzing strategy, instructing Reserve Officer Training Corps (ROTC) courses, serving as bodyguards (both to the former head of the U.S. Coalition Provisional Authority in Iraq, Paul Bremer, and to Afghanistan President Hamid Karzai), delivering mail, cooking, and even organizing troop entertainment.[27] Some PMCs, such as DynCorp, have assisted the United States and Columbian drug-fighting forces in Colombia (by leasing OV-10 Bronco jets from the U.S. military to spray the powerful herbicide glyphsate).[28] Besides DynCorp, other military PMCs offering support services include MPRI, Vinnell, the consultancies Control Risks and Global Risk Strategies, and the Halliburton subsidiary Kellogg, Brown, and Root (KBR).

Table 4.8
Notable PMC Contracts (1995–2004)

Year	Company	Task	Contract Value
1995	Executive Outcomes	Defend Sierra Leone's Capital/Repel rebels	$35 million
1998	Executive Outcomes	Lead attempt to overthrow Nigerian government	$100 million (offer declined by EO)
1998	Vinnell Corp	Supply and train Saudi Arabian forces	$831 million (over 5 years)
2000	Onix International	Rescue businessmen held hostage in East Timor	$220,000
2003	DynCorp	Provide security for Afghan President Hamid Karzai	$52 million
2003	DynCorp	Create new Iraqi police force	$50 million
2003	Vinnell Corp	Train new Iraqi army	$48 million
2003	Erinys International	Protect Iraq's oil pipeline	$39 million
2003	CACI Systems	Provide interrogation services in Iraq	$20 million
2004	Aegis Defense Systems	Provide security for monitors of Iraq reconstruction	$293 million

Source of data: Quirk, Matthew. "Private Military Contractors: A Buyer's Guide." *The Atlantic Monthly.* September 2004, p. 39.

A controversial minority, such as the British company Sandline International and the now-disbanded South African company Executive Outcomes (EO), perform direct combat duties. EO staff, for example, were hired by the governments of Sierra Leone and Papua New Guinea to fight rebel groups. In short, as Peter Singer of the Brookings Institute writes:

"The global trade in hired military services. . .runs the gamut from cooks whose services have been privatized through to the maintenance people on fighter jets, to communications technicians, to trainers and recruiters, to generals providing strategic expertise, to fighter pilots and commandos. The entire spectrum of military services has been privatized in some way or another." [29]

To illustrate the wide range of jobs fulfilled by PMCs, consider Table 4.8. It provides a listing of some notable PMC contracts since 1995, along with the cost of those contracts.

4.6.1 The Growth of PMCs

The PMC industry has witnessed enormous growth in the past decade. During the 1991 Persian Gulf War, estimates range from 1 contractor for every 50 service members,[30] to 1 contractor for every 100 service members.[31] In 2003, the U.S.-led military occupation in Iraq used 1 contractor for every 10 U.S. military personnel. Some pundits have gone as far as to label the Iraq War as the "first privatized war," because the more than 10,000 contractor personnel make private forces the second-largest military contingent.[32] Today the PMC industry is comprised of several hundred companies and over $100 billion in annual global revenue. Because PMCs are hired principally, though not exclusively, by the U.S. government, the industry's revenues are expected to increase 85 percent per year in industrial countries and 30 percent per year in developing countries.[33]

Four factors in the late 1980s and early 1990s help to explain the rapid growth of PMCs. First, the success of KBR, contracted to fix Kuwaiti oil fields after the 1991 Gulf War, illustrated the wealth to be earned in the industry. Though KBR had been serving the U.S. military since World War II, the wave of deregulation and privatization of government services that began in the 1980s created momentum toward further private-entity outsourcing of government functions. This momentum contributed to outsourcing expenditures doubling between 1998 and 2001.[34]

Second, in the 1990s the U.S. military continued to downsize the active military force (see the Iraq case study in Chapter 2). At the same time, the military's global operations expanded, creating a growing need for support services. For this reason, KBR's contract, known as LOGCAP, was renewed in 1993, 1997, and 2001. This work enabled KBR to provide logistics support to the military in Somalia, Haiti, Bosnia, and Kosovo during the 1990s.[35] Though only a handful of firms can provide the same level of logistics support as KBR, numerous smaller consultancy PMCs began to develop. For instance, the company MPRI was founded in 1987 by a group of former service members who believed that as the Army reduced its size it would beginning relying more on private contractors to fill the gap between what foreign policy requires and what the armed forces can provide. For this reason MPRI won a U.S. DoD contract in 1994 to train the Croatian army and then the Bosnian forces.

Third, as weapons systems became more complicated, private companies were needed to provide maintenance and training. For example, in Saudi Arabia, employees from Britain's defense contractor BAE Systems provide support and training for the Saudi Air Force and Navy, while private contractors maintain the U.S. B2 stealth bomber, F-117 stealth fighter, and operate the Predator unmanned drone.[36]

Fourth, PMCs are cost effective. Consider the experience of EO. In 1995, in the midst of a war against insurgents sponsored by Liberia, the Sierra Leone government hired EO to help end the civil war. The contract lasted 22 months and cost $35 million. EO helped to coordinate a plan that drove back the insurgents. Once the insurgents were driven back and a peace agreement was signed, EO was replaced by a UN-sponsored coalition of West African troops (ECOMOG) under the premise that, according to then UN secretary-general Kofi Annan, "the world may not be ready to privatize peace."[37] However, the UN observer force spent only eight months in Sierra Leone at a cost of $47 million before losing control of the country.[38]

4.6.2 PMCs and Efficiency Wages

What explains the effectiveness of PMCs? In a word, pay. PMCs offer large pay incentives to experienced military personnel. For example, consider Control Risks, a PMC that provides armed escorts and guards for various convoys and bases in Iraq. Former industrialized country service members working for Control Risks make approximately $15,000 per month, compared to only an average of $50,000 per year in active duty military base pay. Not surprisingly, this difference has raised concerns among many senior U.S. military officials that PMCs will poach the military's Special Forces recruits. In the words of Command Chief Master Sgt. Robert Martens Jr., "We can never compete dollar-for-dollar with outside firms."[39] As Ret. General Wayne Downing said, "They [U.S. Special Forces personnel] are not leaving out of disloyalty. The money is just so good, if they're going to be away from home that much, they may as well make top dollar."[40]

In essence, PMCs use what economists call an **efficiency wage.**[41] An efficiency wage is a wage rate that is set above the equilibrium wage in order to induce greater work effort. The idea is simple: if a firm only pays the equilibrium market wage, employees have no incentive to work hard because, quite frankly, they know that even if they are fired for poor job performance, they can find a job with another firm at a similar wage. But if a firm pays more than the equilibrium market wage, employees know that if they are fired, they cannot expect to find a job with another firm at a similar wage rate. Therefore, they will have an incentive to work hard. Further, by paying an efficiency wage, a firm can attract the most productive workers. In the case of the military, the most productive service members are Special Forces personnel. The efficiency wage would look like Wage, W_{PMC}, in Figure 4.9.

In fact, efficiency wages, though higher than the equilibrium market wage, allow the PMC to perform a task at a lower cost than normal military personnel. This result is for four reasons. First, when a service member is highly skilled and productive, he or she can typically finish a job in significantly less time. Second, when service members (like any other worker) are given very high pay, turnover is low. This low turnover saves the PMC money on recruiting costs. Third, because the service members receive their training

Figure 4.9
Efficiency Wages and PMCs

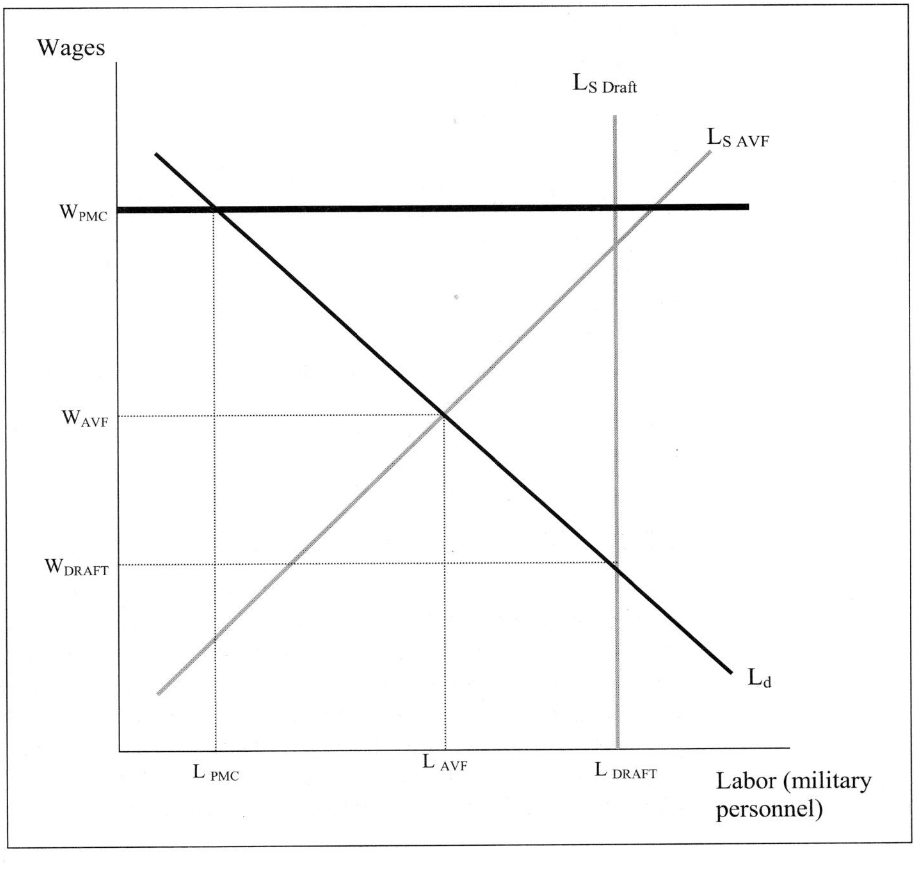

Figure 4.10
Cost Savings of PMC Relative to AVF

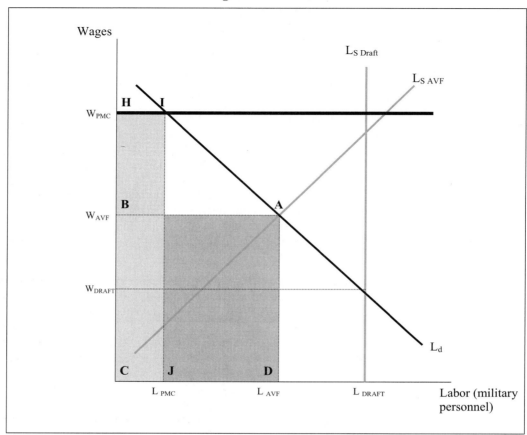

from the U.S. government, the PMC's own training costs are low. Fourth, the PMC is not responsible for the individual for the rest of his life, as the government is for a service member. The PMC can hire a pretrained individual for the length of a contract and then fire that person at will.

As Figure 4.10 shows, though W_{PMC} is greater than W_{AVF}, the area *HIJC* is less than the area *ABCD*. This result indicates that, overall, PMCs have lower costs than governments with AVF systems. Additionally, because the higher wage means PMCs receive service members near the top of the labor demand curve, a PMC service member has an MPL greater than the MPL of an AVF service member or a conscripted service member.

4.6.3 Controversies Surrounding PMCs

Though a growing phenomenon, the PMCs are by no means novel. Mercenaries (soldiers who would sell their services to the highest bidder) are as old as war itself.[42] In fact, the partial privatization of warfare and efficiency wages has been employed by such renowned forces as the Royal Navy of the British Empire (see Box 4.3).

Box 4.3
Historical Perspective
Efficiency Wages in the Royal Navy[1]

The Royal Navy awarded prize money for captured enemy vessels and personnel. The Navy paid the market value for the ship, £5 for each enemy sailor on board when the battle started, any cargo on board, and £60 per freed male slave. Typically, an admiral could receive 1/8 to 1/4 of all prizes taken by his squadron, a captain usually received another 1/4 of the prize, the officers sharing another 1/4 and the remaining crew sharing the rest. Therefore, the major source of wealth for the admiral and captains was the prize money and these prizes were generally higher than those necessary to induce a sufficient supply of naval officers.

By attracting a surplus of captains and admirals, the Navy's spoils system created an unemployment pool that actually served as a disciplining device. If a captain or admiral was not sailing, he was on 'half-pay,' a form of unemployment benefit. In order to ensure that the captain remained sailing or would sail again, he had to not only fight valiantly and capture ships, but also obey orders. Otherwise, there were more than enough captains to take his place. In short, the Royal Navy, much like modern PMCs, employed an efficiency wage to create an incentive for sailors to perform well and follow protocol.

_____
[1] See Allen (2002), pp. 211–215.

However, despite PMCs being highly productive, low in cost, and having a long history, they still pose a set of new problems. First, the ability of PMCs to recruit government service members creates four major costs to the government's military (and taxpayers). It costs the government an average of nearly $260,000 over 18 months to train a Special Forces personnel like an Army Green Beret. However, when one of these service members leave, the Army loses the investment and—because the government may very well have a contract with the company for which the soldier is now working—the Army is forced to pay for the service member's skills at a higher price. Additionally, the Army must incur the recruitment costs of acquiring another Green Beret.

Second, the presence of PMCs call into question the commonly held belief that national defense is a **public good.** A public good is a good in which the provider cannot exclude non-paying individuals from using it. A public good is also a good in which one person's use does not diminish the ability of another person to use it. Therefore, the private sector has no incentive to provide this good (See Section 6.6 for more on public goods). Though national defense is commonly considered the prime example of a public good, because PMCs seem to profit from providing security, does that mean national defense is not a public good? The answer appears to be "no."

Though the PMCs are private corporations, they work for governments, not private individuals. Yet, assume for a moment that a PMC was hired by your neighbor to protect the country. Would you still benefit from this protection, even though your friend is the one paying for it? Of course you would. The only way your friend could prevent you from benefiting from the protection she is paying for, is if you left the country. In other words, though governments use PMCs to lower costs and improve performance (maximize the use of taxpayer dollars), PMCs will remain reliant on governments as their primary, if not sole client.

4.7 KEY POINTS

Key Macroeconomic Points:

- There is a strong relationship between the size of a country's population and the size of its military.
- Countries with an AVF must spend more per service member than countries with conscription. Countries can use conscription as a means to reduce government military expenditures.

Key Microeconomic Points:

- A government's demand for military personnel (the labor demand curve) always exhibits a negative (downward sloping) relationship between wages and the quantity of personnel.
- The supply of military personnel (the labor supply curve) can show a positive (upward sloping) relationship between wages and the quantity of personnel when a country has an all volunteer force (AVF). This result is because, all things being equal, the higher the wages offered by the government for military service, the more citizens will voluntarily join the military.
- The supply of military personnel can show no relationship (vertical line) between wages and the quantity of personnel when a country has a conscripted force. This result is because the government will mandate that people join the military, regardless of the wages it pays.
- Conscription is inefficient because it violates comparative advantage. Specifically, it forces people to become service members who may not be very good service members and who would have been a greater benefit to the country and economy in an alternative form of employment. Therefore, the economic opportunity cost of an AVF is lower and the military effectiveness per dollar spent may be higher.
- An AVF induces a country's military to become capital intensive, rather than labor intensive.
- Though determining the optimal level of military compensation for service members is important, it can prove difficult because many people join the military for non-tangible reasons that are hard to quantify. The best way to set the optimal level may be to monitor recruitment and retention of high-quality people.
- An efficiency wage entices the most productive service members to work for Private Military Companies (PMCs). Additionally, the efficiency wage creates surplus employment for PMC jobs. This strategy ensures a large pool of quality candidates from which a PMC can hire. However, the efficiency wage offered by PMCs also generates many costs for the government, who originally trained the hired service member.

Key Terms:

All-volunteer force (AVF)	Opportunity cost
Conscription	Universal draft
Labor demand curve	Nonuniversal draft
Labor supply curve	Avoidance activities
Opportunity cost effect	Selective service lottery
Capital	Draft-induced volunteers
Marginal Productivity of Labor	In-kind compensation
Law of diminishing returns	Private military companies/forces
Willingness to join	Efficiency wage
Comparative advantage	Public good

Key Questions:

1. Why do many European nations have an active military personnel to population ratio that is higher than the United States?
2. You are an economist for the International Monetary Fund. You have been sent to a less-developed country where the national government can't seem to reduce its expenditures enough to balance its budget. If the country currently uses an AVF, why would you recommend that they adopt a conscription-based military? Illustrate your answer with a graph.
3. Based on the U.S. experience during the Vietnam War, does a draft discriminate against minorities and the poor?
4. Why did the government of Sierra Leone hire Executive Outcomes, rather than use a conscripted army?
5. Does the existence of PMCs mean that national defense is not a public good?
6. According to the United States Selective Service Agency, men given the number 195 from the 1969 draft lottery were the last group from that lottery called to serve (125 was the highest number called to serve from the 1970 lottery and 95 was the highest number called from the 1971 lottery). Therefore, if you had participated in the 1969 lottery, would you have been drafted?

Endnotes

1. "Rangel Introduces Bill to Reinstate Draft." *CNN.com,* January 8, 2003. Available at www.cnn.com/2003/ALLPOLITICS/01/07/rangel.draft/.
2. For a full and up-to-date listing of the recruitment system status of the various EU countries, see the "table of the situation of military service and conscientious objection in the EU countries" at the European Bureau for Conscientious Objection. Available at www.ebco-beoc.org/country_reports.htm.
3. Neyer, Rob. "Mays May Have Caught Ruth if Not for Army Stint." *ESPN.com,* May 28, 2004; and Pasquerelli, Len. "Patriotic Duty." *ESPN.com,* May 26, 2004. Available at http://espn.go.com/mlb/columns/neyer_rob/1387745.html.
4. Bandow (1999), p. 10.
5. Ibid.
6. Information on the Draft Lottery comes from Selective Service System's "History and Records," in *The Vietnam Lotteries.* Available at www.sss.gov/lotter1.htm.
7. Angrist (1991), p. 585.
8. CNN. Cold War Special website. Available at hwww.cnn.com/SPECIALS/cold.war/ episodes/13/the.draft/.
9. Goff and Tollison (1987), p. 317.
10. From *Vietnam War Statistics.* New Jersey State Council of the Vietnam Veterans of America, at http://www.njscvva.org/vietnam_war_stats.htm.
11. Barnett et al. (1992), p. 858.
12. Korb (2004), p. 2.
13. Warner and Asch (2001), p. 178.
14. For the latest information on military pay, refer to the "Pay and Allowances" section of the Department of Defense website: http://www.defenselink.mil/militarypay/pay/ index.html. Also, for an excellent discussion of U.S. military pay, benefits, as well as general questions regarding military life, see About.com's U.S. Military Feature articles available at http://usmilitary.about.com/library/weekly/aa092302e.
15. Schmitt, Eric and Shanker, Thom. "Big Pay Luring Military's Elite to Private Jobs." *The New York Times,* March 30, 2004.

16. Fiscal Year 2005 Defense Budget Slide Show. *Department of Defense,* January 30, 2004. Available at http://www.defenselink.mil/news/Feb2004/05brief.pdf.

17. See "Military Compensation: Pay and Allowances." *Office of the Secretary of Defense,* Available at http://www.dod.mil/militarypay/pay/bas/index.html.

18. Information for this paragraph taken from Goldich (2003), pp. 9–11.

19. Information for this paragraph from Hosek and Sharp (2001).

20. For example, see Jaffe, Greg. "As Benefits for Veterans Climb, Military Spending Feels Squeeze." *The Wall Street Journal,* January 25, 2005. p. A1.

21. Schmitt, Eric and Shanker, Thom. "Big Pay Luring Military's Elite to Private Jobs." *The New York Times.* March 30, 2004.

22. Information for this section comes from Raezer, Joyce W. "Transforming Support to Military Families and Communities" (2004) in Williams (2004), pp. 213–238, unless otherwise cited.

23. Buddin, Richard and Do, Phuong. *Assessing the Personal Financial Problems of Junior Enlisted Personnel.* RAND. 2002. Available at www.rand.org/publications/MR/MR1444/.

24. Also see the General Accounting Office's "Military Personnel: Preliminary Observations Related to Income, Benefits, and Employer Support for Reservists during Mobilization." March 19, 2003. Available at www.gao.gov/new.items/d03549t.pdf.

25. Ibid.

26. Altman, Drew and Blendon, Robert. "Perpetual War Hits Military Families Hard." *The Boston Globe,* June 13, 2004, p. H11. The survey itself is available at www.kff.org/kaiserpolls/7060.cfm.

27. Fidler, Stephen and Catlin, Thomas. "The Jobs of War." *Financial Times,* August 10, 2003; Yeoman, Barry. "Need an Army? Just Pick Up the Phone." *The New York Times,* April 2, 2004; and Singer (2004). p. 523.

28. Fidler, Stephen and Catlin, Thomas. "The Jobs of War." *Financial Times,* August 10, 2003.

29. Citation from *Corporate Warriors—The Rise of the Privatized Military Industry* by Peter Singer, as found in Fidler, Stephen and Catlin, Thomas. "The Jobs of War." *Financial Times,* August 10, 2003.

30. Fidler, Stephen and Catlin, Thomas. "The Jobs of War." *Financial Times,* August 10, 2003.

31. Singer (2004), p. 523.

32. "Military Industrial Complexities." *The Economist,* March 29, 2003, p. 56

33. Singer (2001/02), p. 15.

34. Ibid.

35. Fidler, Stephen and Catlin, Thomas. "The Jobs of War." *Financial Times,* August 10, 2003.

36. Ibid.

37. Fidler, Stephen and Catlin, Thomas. "Private Companies on the Frontline." *Financial Times,* August 11, 2003.

38. Brayton (2002), p. 313.

39. "The Baghdad Boom." *The Economist.* March 27, 2004, p. 55; and Schmitt, Eric and Shanker, Thom. "Big Pay Luring Military's Elite to Private Jobs." *The New York Times,* March 30, 2004.

40. Schmitt, Eric and Shanker, Thom. "Big Pay Luring Military's Elite to Private Jobs." *The New York Times,* March 30, 2004.

41. Definition and description of efficiency wage is taken from Bade and Parkin (2003), p. 201.

42. See Chapter 1 of the present text; also Josselin and Wallace (2001), p. 190; and Singer (2001/02) for a discussion of historical examples of war for profit.

Chapter 5

Weapons Procurement

5.1 INTRODUCTION

"This is by far and away the biggest plum to come along in a long time in a market where every little bit counts and the government pays on time."[1] These are the words of Richard Adoulafia, consultant with the Teal Group defense and aerospace consultancy corporation. His comments were in reference to a U.S. Department of Defense (DoD) contract to replace fifty U.S. Army and Navy reconnaissance aircraft. His comments also highlight the importance of such government business for defense contracting companies.

Government procurement is when the government makes a direct purchase of an item or service. The government can procure, for example, roads, buildings, or auditing services. This chapter focuses on the government's procurement of weapons. After providing an overview of the arms industry in Section 2, Section 3 explores the domestic arms market and how the government-firm relationship results in less competition and higher prices for weapons. Section 4 discusses key features of the global arms market, including how the market fails to exhibit traits of perfect competition. Finally, Section 5 illustrates the lessons learned in the chapter by providing a case study of the DoD purchase in 2001 of the Joint Strike Fighter.

5.2 OVERVIEW OF THE ARMS MARKET

In 2000, total arms sales (both domestic procurement and arms exports) for the top 100 defense companies in the world amounted to $157 billion; 60 percent of which originated from 43 major U.S. defense contractors.[2] For 2004, the DoD proposed a weapons procurement budget of $113.4 billion.[3] These amounts are both significant sums of money, but such numbers should not overstate the current economic significance of the global and domestic sale of weapon systems. In the mid-1980s global spending on military hardware was nearly double its present level at $290 to $300 billion per year.[4] Additionally, the global arms market today is smaller than the U.S. market for pharmaceuticals ($228 billion sales in 2001), automobiles (over $600 billion sales in 2001), new and used car dealers ($780.2 billion sales in 2001), food and beverage ($491 billion sales in 2001), general merchandising ($542 billion sales in 2001), life insurance (over $800 billion sales in 2001), and securities brokerage ($340 billion sales in 2001).[5] In short, business size does not make the arms industry a worthy study; many other industries are larger. Instead, the defense business is of interest because it operates in a fashion vastly different from the typical commercial enterprise.

Gansler and Weidenbaum (1990) catalogue the many unusual aspects of the defense market, highlighting seven primary features.[6] These features will serve as the basis for conducting our analysis of weapons procurement. First, the government is a **monopsony,** meaning it is the only buyer. Even in sales to foreign governments, the DoD plays the role of broker. Second, the market is **oligopolistic.** Usually only a few suppliers—sometimes only one—have the capability to supply the product. Third, price is a relatively unimportant aspect of the sale, whereas the technical attributes of the product are supremely important, almost regardless of cost.

Fourth, competition is limited to the initial technical and political rivalry to receive the beginning research and development contract. After the project starts, the initial supplier often becomes the sole source of the product and all subsequent spare parts, modifications, maintenance, and support. This ongoing connection means the supplier is a **monopoly** and, therefore, is able to extract relatively favorable terms from the government purchaser. Fifth, given the budget constraint and the huge size of major weapons programs, only a few programs can be financed at once. Therefore, the defense business is somewhat erratic, having a feast-or-famine quality for individual firms. Failure to obtain a single major contract may jeopardize the ability of a producer to remain in the industry. Sixth, to insure that major arms producers do not leave the industry, dispersing their technical teams and draining their reservoir of experience, the government uses various devices to subsidize their continuance in the business. The devices include subsidies to keep facilities open and to finance ongoing research and development, plus loans and loan guarantees, government-supplied plants and equipment, tax breaks, and perhaps even strategic placement of contracts. Finally, the seventh feature is that, as a consequence of the first six features, in no other industry are there more regulations and pervasive government involvement.

5.3 THE DOMESTIC WEAPONS MARKET

The government chronically underestimates production costs. For example, in 1997 the DoD announced that the development and production of the F-22 jet fighter would cost $80 billion, $15 billion higher than the previous estimate.[7] Economic analysis of the domestic weapons market shows how such cost overruns occur.

As a starting point, Figure 5.1 illustrates a perfectly competitive market for B-2 bombers. The market has a downward sloping **demand curve,** D_1. The demand curve slopes downward due to the **budget effect.** This effect holds that, for a fixed procurement budget, as the price of a B-2 rises, government purchasers will be unable to buy as many bombers.[8] The market also has an upward sloping **supply curve,** S_1. It slopes upward to show that as the price being paid for a bomber rises, firms have an incentive to sell more of

Figure 5.1
Perfectly Competitive Arms Market

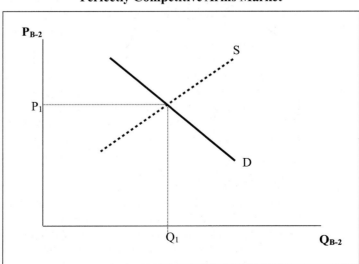

them so as to maximize revenue and, most importantly, make a profit. Where the demand and supply curves intersect is the **competitive equilibrium.** The equilibrium shows the quantity of bombers that will be sold in the market and the price at which these bombers will be sold, given the willingness of the buyers to purchase bombers and of the sellers to supply bombers.

5.3.1   Department of Defense as a Monopsony

In reality, the market for military hardware is anything but perfectly competitive. First, the Department of Defense (DoD) is the only buyer and it is buying a good for which there is no market outside itself. Clearly, when the government makes a request for a particular weapon, it is usually asking to buy something that does not yet exist. Second, as was mentioned previously, relative to other markets, only a handful of firms are in the defense industry to begin with, and of these only a few—sometimes only one—have the capability to supply the product. Therefore, instead of being a price taker, the DoD negotiates prices with firms as well as sets forth specifications of the goods to be produced.[9]

In addition, the DoD faces an upward sloping supply curve. To be able to convince a firm to produce additional bombers, the DoD must increase the price it pays. What is the result? Consider the following. If a perfectly competitive buyer (meaning the buyer is not the only buyer in the market) wants to purchase ten bombers instead of nine, the price of the additional bomber is equal to the market price set at the competitive equilibrium. If the DoD, as a monopsonist, buys ten bombers instead of nine, it must pay a higher price not just for the additional bomber, but for all of the bombers. This situation is because all the bombers are identical and, when agreeing to a price, any defense firm the DoD buys the bombers from will not accept different prices for the same item. Consequently, the **marginal cost** (the cost added to total cost) to the DoD for purchasing the bomber is greater than the price it pays for the bomber.

For clarification, consider this illustration. If the DoD pays $2 billion for one bomber, then the marginal cost to the DoD is $2 billion. If the DoD wishes to buy a second bomber, it must offer to pay more in order to entice the firm to sell the bomber. Assume this enticement makes the price for the second bomber $3 billion. However, because the DoD must pay $3 billion for the second bomber, it must also pay $3 billion for the first bomber. The total cost for the two bombers is now $6 billion (2 × $3 billion = $6 billion). This math means that the second bomber adds $4 billion to the total cost ($6 billion total cost for two bombers, minus the $2 billion total cost for just one bomber)! Therefore, *the marginal cost of each additional plane is greater than the price for that plane.*

Figure 5.2 shows the monopsony market for B-2 bombers. Notice that the marginal cost curve (*MC*) is above the supply curve. This illustrates how the additional cost for each additional bomber is greater than the price for that bomber. The DoD will only purchase a quantity of bombers where the cost of the bomber, MC, is equal to its willingness to pay for the bomber, D_{DoD}. Therefore, the quantity of bombers sold, Q_{DoD}, and the price, P_{DoD}, is lower than in a perfectly competitive market.

5.3.2   Simplifying the Analysis

Given that the DoD considers price relatively unimportant, then the key concept is that the quantity of bombers sold is lower than what would be sold in a competitive market. Therefore, let's consider an alternative model that illustrates this same concept, but does so more simply (at least until we bring in the monopoly firm).

Figure 5.2
Monopsony Market

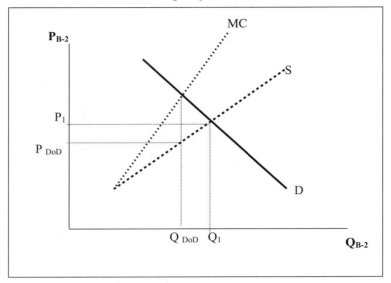

Figure 5.3
Arms Market with Monopsony

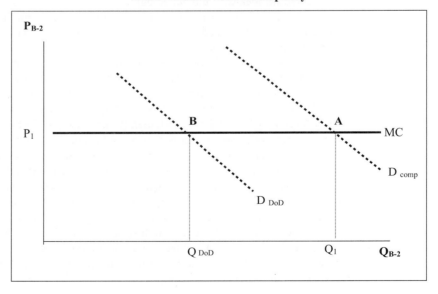

To begin, we will assume constant marginal cost. This term means the firm incurs the same additional cost for each unit it supplies to the market.[10] The firm still has fixed costs, but the amount by which total cost rises with each additional product is the same. Looking at Figure 5.3, the perfectly competitive arms market for B-2 stealth bombers is at point *A,* where the downward sloping competitive demand curve, D_{comp}, intersects the horizontal marginal cost curve, *MC*. This intersection generates an equilibrium price, P_1, and quantity, Q_1, for the B-2 bomber. Yet according to microeconomic theory, when there are fewer buyers in a market, the demand curve falls to a lower level. Because there is only one buyer in the market for B-2 bombers (the DoD), the DoD's demand curve, D_{DoD}, is drawn lower than the perfectly competitive demand curve. Notice that Q_{DoD} is lower than the competitive outcome, Q_1.

5.3.3   Bilateral Monopoly

The complication is that in a monopoly market, that outcome may not hold. Firms only compete in the initial phase of contract bidding. Once a firm receives a contract, it then becomes a monopoly. This honor gives the firm the ability to extract relatively favorable terms from the government purchaser (such as increasing the cost of the project once it is underway). Such a market, with a monopsony buyer and a monopoly supplier, is known as a **bilateral monopoly.** Understanding the implications of a bilateral monopoly first requires reviewing a bit of microeconomic theory. Specifically, let's review the difference between a price-discriminatory monopoly and a single-price monopoly. Then we'll see how this difference affects the marginal revenue earned by the firm.

The marginal revenue of a price discriminating monopoly: In addition to the *budget effect,* the demand curve slopes down because of **diminishing marginal benefit.** According to the idea of diminishing marginal benefit, the more a person believes he or she is benefiting from an item, the higher the price that person is willing to pay for the item. In an ideal monopoly, the monopolist would charge each consumer a price exactly equal to the "benefit" that consumer perceives to be gaining from the item. For example, suppose a buyer is in great need of a "stinger" Surface to Air Missile (SAM). Therefore, the buyer is willing to pay a lot for that SAM, say $50,000. However, once the buyer has the first SAM, the buyer will not value a second SAM as greatly. Therefore, the buyer will only be willing to pay $40,000 for the second SAM. The firm would like to be able to charge $50,000 for the first SAM and $40,000 for the second (because selling a second SAM for $40,000 is better than not selling a second SAM, assuming $40,000 will cover the firm's cost). Being able to charge different amounts for the same item according to the variance in a consumer's willingness to pay is known as **price discrimination.**

When a firm can price-discriminate, the additional revenue it earns on each additional item sold (marginal revenue) is equal to the price for which the item is sold. Consider Table 5.1. The second column shows the willingness of the buyer to pay for a particular quantity of SAMs (the price). For the first SAM, the buyer is willing to pay a lot, $50,000. For the second SAM, the buyer is still willing to pay quite a bit at $40,000; but this figure is not as high as for the first SAM. Because the firm is able to price-discriminate, it can sell the first SAM for $50,000 and the second for $40,000. So the **marginal revenue** (additional revenue earned on the additional item) for the first item was $50,000 and for the second item, it was $40,000.

Table 5.1
Price-Discriminatory Monopoly

Good	Price (willingness to pay)	Total Revenue	Marginal Revenue (change in revenue for the next item sold)
First SAM	$50,000	(1×$50,000) = $50,000	$50,000
Second SAM	$40,000	(1×$50,000 + 1×$40,000) = $90,000	$40,000

Table 5.2
Single-Price Monopoly

Good	Price (willingness to pay)	Total Revenue	Marginal Revenue (change in revenue for the next item sold)
First B-2	$3 billion	(1 × $3 billion) = $3 billion	$3 billion
Second B-2	$2 billion	(2 × $2 billion) = $4 billion	($4 billion - $3 billion) = $1 billion

The marginal revenue of a single-price monopoly: However, because the DoD and the monopolistic defense-contracting firm must agree on a price for the good being produced, the firm is a **single-price monopoly.** This term means that the firm, unlike in the previous example, cannot price discriminate. Therefore, the firm must charge the same price for each product it sells, rather than charge different prices. Consequently, if the firm, for example, wants to sell the government three items of the same product, it must charge the same price for each item. Because the government is receiving three items, the government will only pay a price equivalent to its willingness to pay for the third item.

How does this situation impact the firm? Whenever the firm decides to sell an additional unit of a product, it must not only charge a lower price for that unit, but it must also drop the price for the previous units. Therefore, the monopolistic firm forgoes the additional revenue that could have been earned on the other units.

For this example, let's return to the market for B-2 bombers. Assume the firm can sell one B-2 bomber for $3 billion, but the government will only pay $2 billion for a second bomber. Therefore, if the firm sells one B-2 bomber, its total revenue is $3 billion; but if the firm wants to sell two B-2 bombers, it will have to sell them for $2 billion each. Thus, selling the second B-2 bomber increases total revenue by $1 billion ($3 billion to $4 billion), even though the price for the second B-2 bomber was $2 billion. Table 5.2 summarizes this information. As you can see, the increase in total revenue for the additional bomber, $1 billion, is less than the bomber's price of $2 billion.

Because the marginal revenue earned for each item is less than the item's price, the monopolistic firm's marginal revenue (MR) curve is not the demand curve, but a curve drawn below the demand curve (Figure 5.4). Yet, even though the MR curve is below the demand curve, the price a monopoly charges still corresponds to the demand curve, not the MR curve (i.e., the firm charges the higher price, P_2, not P_1). The firm can charge the higher price for two reasons. First, in theory, the MR curve describes information that is only known by the firm, not the buyer. Second, the monopolistic firm is simply charging the price corresponding to the buyer's willingness to pay for that quantity of product. For the lower quantity of Q_3, buyers are willing to pay P_2. It is only for the higher quantity of Q_{DoD}, that buyers are only willing to pay the lower price of P_1. Since the buyer is willing to pay more, the monopolistic firm would be foolish to charge less.

5.3.4 The Contract Zone, Firm Diversification, and Higher Prices

However, the equilibrium of price P_2 and quantity Q_3 is not the end result in the domestic arms market. The government's monopsony position in the weapons market means that it, unlike a buyer in a perfectly competitive market (or, at least, a market without a monopsony buyer), knows the demand curve and will, as a result, also know the firm's marginal revenue curve. Therefore, the exact quantity produced and price paid will not necessarily correspond to point C of Figure 5.4. Instead, the price will be somewhere within what can be called the **contract zone** of area BCD (Figure 5.4).

Figure 5.4
Bilateral Monopoly

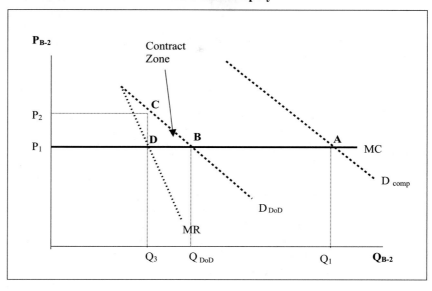

Whether the price is closer to P_2 or P_1 depends on the strength of the firm's bargaining position relative to the government. If the firm has viable alternative forms of production (i.e., civilian aircraft), then it can toe a harder line with the government and demand a more revenue-maximizing contract for producing weapons. This demand will move the price to P_2. Yet, if the firm is not as diversified, then it will not have leverage in a negotiation. In this case, the firm will have to settle for what the government offers. In this case, the price will be closer to P_1.

As can be seen from Table 5.3, the majority of the major contractors are highly diversified.[11] As of 2000, only nine of the top 20 companies (and 17 of the top 40) have more than 50 percent of their total sales originating from the defense industry.[12] Consequently, real-world prices are more likely to be higher than lower.

Notice how Table 5.3 verifies the fifth feature of the arms industry, that production is limited. Of the 10 smallest companies on the list (as measured by total sales), only one does not have at least 60 percent of its sales from the defense industry (Dyncorp). Of the 10 largest companies on the list (as measured by total sales), only two had over 25 percent of sales from the military sector (Lockheed and BAE Systems). Therefore, this correlation suggests that a company is more likely to grow large if it does not focus primarily on the defense industry.

5.3.5   Principal-Agent Model

Diversified production may give the firm an advantage when negotiating a contract, but what other economic explanations are there for high prices and cost overruns? **Principal-agent modeling** offers one alternative.[13]

The model's setup: According to the principal-agent model, the principal (meaning the DoD) signs a contract with the agent (the firm) to have the agent carry out a function (such

Table 5.3

The Forty Largest Arms-Producing Companies in the OECD and Developing Countries, 2000

Company	Country	Arms Sales (2000) (in millions of U.S. dollars)	Total Sales (2000) (in millions of U.S. dollars)	Arms/Total (2000) %
Lockheed Martin	USA	18610	25329	73
Boeing	USA	16900	51521	33
BAE Systems**	UK	14895	19054	78
Raytheon	USA	10100	16895	60
Northrop Grumman	USA	6660	7618	87
General Dynamics	USA	6520	10356	63
EADS	France/FRG/Spain	5340	22303	24
Thales****	France	5990	9306	64
Litton	USA	3950	5588	71
TRW*	USA	3370	17231	20
Finmeccania**	Italy	2935	6121	48
United Technologies	USA	2880	26583	11
Mitsubishi Heavy Industries	Japan	2850	28255	10
Rolls-Royce	UK	2130	8890	24
Newport News	USA	2030	2072	98
Science Applications	USA	1950	5896	33
GKN	UK	1740	7726	23
Computer Sciences Corp.	USA	1610	10524	15
DCN	France	1600	1603	100
General Electric	USA	1600	129853	1
Honeywell International	USA	1550	25023	6
Rheinmetall	FRG	1460	4137	35
Israel Aircraft Industries	Israel	1350	2180	62
L-3 Communications	USA	1340	1910	70
ITT Industries	USA	1330	4829	28
Saab***	Sweden	1210	1947	62
Textron	USA	1200	13090	9
United Defense	USA	1180	1184	100
Ordnance Factories	India	1130	1247	91
Mitsubishi Electric	Japan	1120	38318	3
CEA	France	1050	6329	17
SNECMA Groupe	France	970	5989	16
EDS	USA	950	19227	5
Dassault Aviation Groupe	France	930	3211	29
Kawasaki Heavy Industries	Japan	920	9840	9
Alliant Tech Systems	USA	900	1142	79
SAGEM	France	820	3934	21
Dyncorp †	USA	800	1809	44
Titan	USA	780	1033	76
Elbit Systems	Israel	700	700	100

Source of Data: Stockholm International Peace and Research Institute (SIPRI). "The 100 Largest Arms-producing Companies in the OECD and Developing Countries, 2000." *Year Book 2003: Armaments, Disarmament and International Security.* New York: Humanities Press.

* Merged with Northrop Grumman in 2002.

** Includes 50% of arms sales and total sales of Alenia Marconi Systems.

*** GM gained full ownership of Saab automotive division in 2000, but Saab's defense, aviation, and space division is still a separate company.

**** Includes arms sales and total sales of Thales Systémes Aéroportés.

† Merged with CSC consultancy in 2003.

as produce a weapon). The agent is interested in maximizing profits when agreeing to a contract. When signing the contract, the agent considers the pay it receives up front, the pay it receives for additional effort, and the cost it must incur for such effort. The ideal situation for the DoD is only to pay the firm for the work completed to the DoD's satisfaction. The ideal situation for the firm is to be **risk averse,** meaning it is unwilling to pursue projects with a high level of uncertainty (because such uncertainty could increase costs), or will only pursue such projects if it is guaranteed payment. Risk aversion can be a problem for the DoD because uncertainty is a common trait of weapons production, as exemplified by the U.S. plan to construct an Anti-Ballistic Missile System (see Box 5.1).

Moral hazard: The degree of uncertainty, like the high uncertainty associated with producing a National Missile Defense system, means the safest route for the agent is to demand high upfront pay. Therefore, cost overruns result from such firms requesting and then being granted large upfront payments. One problem with the payment of an upfront fee is that the firm now has little incentive to follow through with its project in a manner suitable to the buyer. This lack of incentive is known as **Moral Hazard** (when the agent behaves in a way that generates a benefit to the agent that is less than the cost it imposes on the principal). Moral hazard is seen in the defense industry in cases of under-investment in cost reduction, "scrimping" on quality improvements when the agent must incur some costs, and inadequate level of investment in innovations that are of social value.[14]

5.3.6   Contract Type

To avoid the moral hazard problem, the DoD uses a combination of three basic contract types. All three contracts help to account for the firm's apprehension of uncertainty; but by doing so, the contracts leave open the possibility of costs rising dramatically.

Box 5.1
National Missile Defense and Cost Uncertainty

The idea behind a national missile defense (NMD) system is to protect the U.S. against a nuclear missile attack.[1] In case an Inter-Continental Ballistic Missile (ICBM) tipped with a nuclear warhead was launched at the U.S., missile launchers in Alaska, North Dakota, and northern California could launch an interceptor rocket that would in turn release a kill vehicle. That kill vehicle (basically, a smaller missile) would rely on guidance from a variety of satellites and radar stations to seek out and ram into the ICBM, at speeds over 20,000 miles an hour.

   With all the system's various components in place, it would span nine time zones, use 13,000 miles of fiber optics, and have radar installations spanning the globe— from Australia, to Aegis cruisers off the shore of Japan, to the island of Shemya in the Aleutians, to Cheyenne Mountain, Colorado. It is such a complex system that it may never be fully tested until an attack occurs. Therefore, the DoD has instead relied on highly controlled tests, during which the interceptors scored hits five times in eight tries.

   The major contractors for this project are Boeing (for the radar and satellite systems), Bechtel (for the missile silos), and Raytheon (for the kill vehicles). It is estimated that the DoD has already spent $130 billion on the system and that these defense contractors are expected to benefit greatly from additional DoD expenditures of $10 billion per year over the next 5 years.[2] Of course, many experts acknowledge that the enormous complexity of this system renders such cost estimates virtually meaningless.

---

[1] Information from Glanz, James. "This Time It's Real: An Antimissile System Takes Shape." *The New York Times.* May 4, 2004.

[2] The $130 billion estimate is from "Accounting for the Cost of War." *The New York Times.* May 28, 2004. A1.

Fixed price contract: This contract operates like the upfront contract previously described. This contract type usually results in a very high price for the DoD, because the firm must set a fixed price while facing a great deal of uncertainty over the project. Therefore, the firm will ask for a higher price. This strategy is called incorporating a **risk premium** into the price.

Cost-plus contract: In this contract type, the DoD pays a fixed dollar fee, plus any costs incurred by the firm. Though this contract gives little incentive for the firm to keep costs down, it does provide the firm with an incentive to maintain quality.

Incentive contract: In this contract type, the DoD pays a fixed fee and agrees to pay only a set fraction of the project costs. In theory this contract should prevent the price from rising to point *C* of Figure 5.4.[15] However, if the firm is highly diversified, it still may be able to leverage the government into paying a large percentage of the production costs (though not all). Also, because the firm will have to pay for some of the costs, this contract type (as with the fixed price contract) creates the possibility that the firm will sacrifice on quality in order to keep costs low.

So what contract type does the DoD use most often? It is possible to visit the DoD contracts division webpage (www.defenselink.mil/contracts). At 5:00 p.m. each business day, this website posts a brief report detailing the contracts awarded that day. The report is organized by armed service branch. Each entry begins with the agent, the size of the contract in dollars, the type of contract, and what the contract entails. Figure 5.5 shows a contract report from April 28, 2004. Notice that on this particular day, the Army and Air Force used fixed-price contracts, while the Navy used a cost-plus contract.

5.3.7   Deadweight Loss and Externalities

Does it matter that these factors (leverage, uncertainty, and moral hazard) mean that the majority of firms are able to negotiate a higher price? Yes, as Figure 5.4 shows. You can see how being closer to point *C* results in a large amount of *revenues and money that is not earned by anybody.* This amount is called economic **Dead Weight Loss** (DWL) and is represented by the area *BDC*. But does economic DWL translate into societal DWL? In other words, is it necessarily a bad thing for the country as a whole that this DWL exists? Possibly not!

First, society may gain the benefit of the government providing defense with the latest technology. Second, this bilateral monopoly means fewer weapons are being created. Less weapons floating around may lessen the probability of provoking a resource-draining arms race (see Chapter 3).

Of course, if the new weapon is truly advanced, then there may be a **positive externality** for society, in the form of technological "spillover." An externality is when one person's actions impact a bystander.[16] Military history has many examples of technology converting from military to civilian use. Modifications and advancements in aircraft design and performance during the two world wars (the jet engine and rocket being just two) greatly drove forward commercial air travel. Nuclear energy is a product of the Manhattan Project during World War II. Microwave ovens use the same technology originally designed for radar. Most of all, the accelerated progress in medicine (from surgery and anatomy to microbiology) is due almost exclusively to the need to treat war casualties. Even "crisis intervention" and "group therapy" techniques arose towards the end of World War I to treat British troops suffering from shell shock and psychological trauma.[17] The best example of modern technological spillover from the military is the Internet (see Box 5.2) and it is expected that bioengineering will benefit greatly from homeland defense spending by the U.S. government.

Figure 5.5
Department of Defense Daily Contract Report

FOR RELEASE AT	No. 379-04
5 p.m. ET	April 28, 2004

CONTRACTS

MISSILE DEFENSE AGENCY

The Boeing Company of Huntsville, Alabama, is being issued a sole source modification to HQ0006-0209-0001 increasing the agreement value by $157,366,185 to perform system engineering and integration work for the Ballistic Missile Defense System (BMDS). The resulting engineering and integration products and support will be central to the definition, design, and test of the evolutionary, integrated BMDS. The period of performance for this work is April 1, 2004 through December 31, 2005. Funds will not expire at the end of the current fiscal year. The contracting activity is the Missile Defense Agency, 7100 Defense Pentagon, Washington, DC 20301-7100. The work under this modification will be funded using Fiscal Year 04, 05 and 06 RDT&E funds (HQ0006-02-9-0001).

ARMY

Radian Inc., Alexandria, Va., was awarded on April 26, 2004, a $10,572,079 modification to a firm-fixed-price contract for crew protection kits for the Medium Tactical Vehicle. Work will be performed in Alexandria, Va., and is expected to be completed by March 7, 2005. Contract funds will not expire at the end of the current fiscal year. This was a sole source contract initiated on March 5, 2004. The U.S. Army Tank-Automotive and Armaments Command, Warren, Mich., is the contracting activity (W56HZV-04-C-0321).

AIR FORCE

Northrop Grumman Systems Corp., Rolling Meadows, Ill., is being awarded a $21,023,149 firm fixed price contract modification to provide for LITENING pod upgrade kits and spares for use by the Air Force Reserve Corps and the Air National Guard. Locations of performance are Northrop Grumman, Rolling Meadows, Ill. (55 percent); and Rafael Missile Division, Haifa, Israel (45 percent). Total funds have been obligated. The Headquarters Aeronautical Systems Center, Wright-Patterson Air Force Base, Ohio, is the contracting activity (F33657-98-C-2020, P00053).

NAVY

BAE Systems Technologies, Inc., Rockville, Md., is being awarded a $22,318,876 estimated value modification to a previously awarded cost-plus-fixed-fee contract (N00421-03-C-0035) to provide engineering and technical support services for the Naval Air Systems Command Aircraft Control and Landing Systems Division. Work will be performed at the Naval Air Systems Command Aircraft Division, St. Inigoes, Md. (60 percent); and California, Md. (40 percent), and is expected to be completed in April 2005. Contract funds in the amount of $606,142 will expire at the end of the current fiscal year. The Naval Air Systems Command Aircraft Division, St. Inigoes, Md., is the contracting activity.

Source: Department of Defense Contracts Division contracts archive.

Box 5.2
Historical Perspective
The Internet

The central research and development organization of the DoD is DARPA (Defense Advanced Research Project Agency).[1] It was started in the 1950s as a way of furthering the technological development in the weapons industry started by the OSRD (see Box 3.1) and continued by the Office of Naval Research. Back in the 1950s, the military wished to create a decentralized communication system, which would function in the case that a nuclear attack destroyed a centralized communication hub. In 1969, DARPA created ARPANet (Advanced Research Projects Agency Network) when four computers (at UCLA, Stanford,

University of California at Santa Barbara, and the University of Utah) successfully linked through what is called an Interface Message Processor (IMPS)—the first Internet! When the Cold War ended in the early 1990s, this technology was allowed to enter the private sector.

_____
[1] For more information, see Michael Hauben's discussion of the Internet origins posted at the Instituto Superior de Engenharia do Porto (ISEP), Department de Egenharia Informática (DEI), at www.dei.isep.ipp.pt/docs/arpa.html.

So, one could say that society values the goods more than the individual. This concept suggests that the demand curve representing the societal demand for weapons, D_{soc}, is above that of the government's demand curve, D_{DoD}. The theoretical result is that society is actually willing to pay a higher price for the weapons and that the socially optimal quantity is greater than the quantity demanded by the government. Therefore, if weapons production generates positive externalities, then the price sold and quantity produced could move towards point E of Figure 5.6, which is actually outside the contract zone! However, recall that additional weapons can lead to an arms race, which removes resources from civilian production. This situation will make society demand fewer weapons. Due to the countervailing positive and

Figure 5.6
Arms Market with Positive Externality

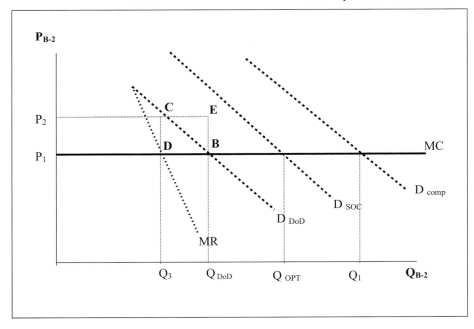

negative externalities, the final price and level of production will probably not go beyond point *E*; instead it lies somewhere within the box *CEBD* in Figure 5.6.

5.4 THE GLOBAL WEAPONS MARKET

The international weapons trade comprises a very small portion of the global military industry. In 2002, global military arms transfers amounted to $30 billion, with approximately $13 billion of the sales originating from the United States.[18] This amount was down from a peak of over $40 billion in 2000.[19] These sales figures pale in comparison to sales by defense firms to their home governments, and, given what we discussed in Chapter 4, are even substantially less than the revenue generated in the market for PMC personnel.

5.4.1 Growth of the Global Arms Market

Despite its relatively diminutive size, the global arms market has nevertheless become increasingly important for contractors. Total world-wide government military expenditures peaked in 1985, but as government military expenditures declined with the end of the Cold War, firms began to seek weapon markets outside their home country. Selling to foreign governments allowed firms to maintain high production levels, which in turn enabled the realization of lower average per unit costs. This process, known as **economies of scale,** is illustrated by Figure 5.7. The quantity of units produced, *Q*, is measured on the horizontal axis, while the average cost per unit, *AC*, is measured on the vertical axis. As firms produce a higher quantity of units (Q_1 to Q_2), **fixed costs** are distributed over more and more units. Fixed costs are costs that do not vary with the quantity of goods produced. A common example of a fixed cost is rent. As the fixed costs are distributed over more and more units, the average cost of production begins to decline. This is depicted by the downward sloping cost curve.

Figure 5.7
Economies of Scale

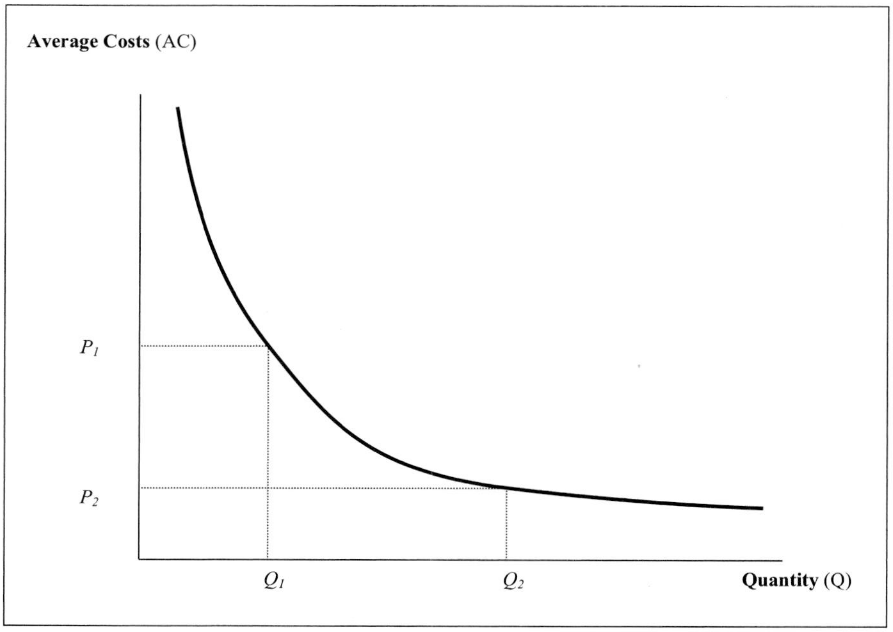

Table 5.4
World Arms Exporters (1995–2002)
(in millions of constant 2002 U.S. dollars)

Country	Worldwide Arms Transfer Agreements			Worldwide Arms Deliveries		
	1995–1998	1999–2002	2002	1995–1998	1999–2002	2002
USA	42,339	57,986	13,272	75,176	53,976	10,241
Russia	21,189	25,287	5,700	13,899	15,243	3,100
France	15,196	11,164	1,100	24,413	11,027	1,800
UK	10,198	3,415	800	26,314	21,953	4,700
China	3,835	5,103	300	3,746	2,838	800
Germany	7,075	8,076	1,100	8,006	4,963	500
Italy	2,591	3,014	1,500	1,050	1,597	400
All other European	11,640	18,088	3,800	17,108	10,230	1,800
All others	9,198	7,646	1,600	9,730	9,106	2,100
Total	**123,261**	**139,779**	**29,172**	**179,422**	**130,933**	**25,441**

Source of data: Grimmett, R. F. "Conventional Arms Transfers to Developing Nations, 1995–2002." Congressional Research Service Report for Congress. September 22, 2003, pp. 21, 33.

NOTE: The columns about arms transfer agreements indicate agreement to make sale. Arms deliveries columns measure items actually transferred.

Table 5.5
World Arms Importers (1997–1999)
(in billions of 2003 U.S. dollars)

Country	1997–1999	Country	1999
Saudi Arabia	27.5	Saudi Arabia	7.7
China-Taiwan	17.4	Turkey	3.2
Japan	7.9	Japan	3.0
United Kingdom	6.6	China-Taiwan	2.6
Turkey	6.2	United Kingdom	2.6
Israel	5.8	Israel	2.4
South Korea	5.3	South Korea	2.2
United States	5.1	Greece	1.9
Australia	4.0	United States	1.6
United Arab Emirates	3.7	Germany	1.3

Source of data: U.S. Department of State *World Military Expenditures and Arms Transfers. (WMEAT) 1999–2000.* February 6, 2003. Available at www.state.gov/t/vc/rls/rpt/wmeat/1999_2000/.

This situation is why the Clinton administration in 1995 added domestic economic considerations to the list of criteria for approving weapons exports.[20] The end result was for global arms sales to reach their highest levels in the late 1990s.

Table 5.4 shows the largest weapons exporters in the world. Given the United States' high level of military expenditures and extensive military-industrial base, it unsurprisingly was the largest exporter of military weapons in 2002, and has been the largest military exporter over the previous decade.

To where do these exports go? Table 5.5 shows the largest weapons importers in the world from 1997–1999 and in 1999. Developing and middle-income countries comprise a significant number of the top recipients, with Saudi Arabia, Turkey, and China-Taiwan in the top five. The propensity for weapons exports to concentrate in the developing world will be discussed in more detail in Chapter 6.

Figure 5.8
Perfectly Competitive International Arms Market

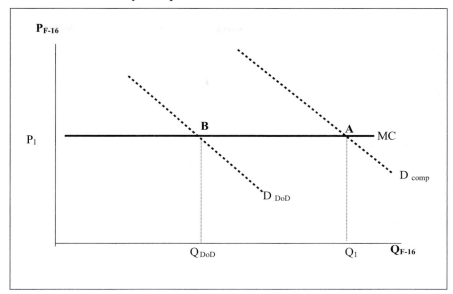

5.4.2 Analyzing the Global Arms Market

Because the most widely traded major weapon system is the Lockheed-Martin F-16 fighter (at a price of approximately $19 million), it will serve as an example for analyzing the international weapons market. Theoretically, free trade of arms means the arms market is a perfectly competitive market. In the theoretical scenario in Figure 5.8, Q_{DoD} is the level of F-16 fighters bought by the DoD; and $Q_1 - Q_{DoD}$ is the quantity of F-16 fighters exported to other countries.

However, this scenario is not how the market for F-16 fighters operates in reality. The international military weapons trade is different than other multinational and transnational commercial industries. Namely, few arms companies are truly private sector entities. For instance, nearly three-quarters of French arms exporters are state-owned, and of course U.S. arms companies receive public funds. Governments also exercise direct influence on the international sale of weapons produced in their countries. As a result of this governmental influence, international arms sales can be divided into two general categories: government-to-government and firm-to-foreign government/firm.[21]

Government-to-government arms transaction: Transactions between the DoD and another government are called **Foreign Military Sales** (FMS). The U.S. administration arranges the deal and is required to notify Congress of sales over $14 million for "major" defense articles (or $50 million for other defense items). In many instances, the DoD subsidizes the foreign government's purchase through a **direct grant of military aid.** In 1996, Turkey spent $4.3 billion on F-16s, but the U.S. gave $3.2 billion in grants and loans to seal the deal. Overall, the U.S. gives out $5 billion per year in military aid, the majority of which goes to Israel, about $2 billion, and Egypt (about $1 billion).

Figure 5.9
International Arms Market with DoD Quota

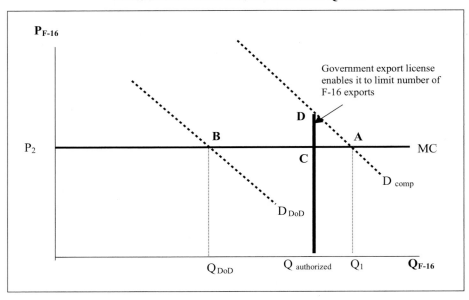

Firm-to-foreign government/foreign firm arms transaction: An arms transaction between a U.S. firm and a foreign government is called a **Direct Commercial Sale** (DCS). The transfer is negotiated between the U.S. manufacturing company and the foreign buyer, but it must be approved by the U.S. Department of State through the issuance of an **export license.** The U.S. government requires each sale to be licensed in order to remain the sole possessor of some technology.

The U.S. government's ability to control the quantity of weapons on the world market through an export license serves as a **quota** on the quantity of weapons exported. This quota creates economic DWL equal to the area *ACD* in Figure 5.9. However, this economic DWL may not necessarily be harmful for society. Specifically, though government restrictions are economically inefficient, it may benefit society that weapons are not sold to every entity with a willingness to buy. For instance, some organizations willing to purchase an F-16 are also willing to use it to harm the United States (such as transnational terrorist organizations). Other entities the U.S. will not sell to include oppressive regimes wishing to use such armaments against its own people.[22]

A DCS may also contain a "licensing agreement" that provides the purchasing state with access to newer arms technology and/or production jobs. Such provisions are typically called **offset arrangements.** Through this arrangement, the U.S. government grants compensatory economic measures to the foreign arms buyer so as to "offset" the heavy cost of the weapon. Offsets convert firm-to-foreign government transactions into firm-to-foreign firm transactions. U.S. firms will outsource production steps, as well as co-produce weapons and co-research with foreign firm.

Consider a few examples. Lockheed had to use British-made Rolls-Royce engines instead of General Electric engines to power Apache attack helicopters sold in Europe. In 1996, the U.S. allowed the parts for a sale of F-16 fighters to be shipped to Turkey and then assembled by 2,000 Turkish laborers. In 2002, Lockheed permitted Poland to build the engines for 40 F-16 fighters Poland had purchased.[23] In a $3.3 billion agreement for the sale of 40 F-15K Strike Eagle jets to South Korea, Boeing gave Korea avionic software, and design technology. The wings and front fuselage were made in Korea and then returned to Boeing's St. Louis plant for final assembly.

Controversies surrounding offsets: Offsets are not without controversy. First, several critics argue that these provisions, by shifting production overseas, eliminate U.S. jobs. Yet, this argument must be balanced with the recognition that many foreign sales would not have gone through in the first place without the offset. A 2001 presidential commission on offsets surveyed eight large U.S. defense contractors. Seven estimated that they would lose 50 to 90 percent of foreign sales without offsets.[24]

Second, critics contend that the required sharing of technology places the United States at a strategic disadvantage, because other countries are now able to produce as advanced, if not more advanced, weapons. On the other hand, the U.S. government controls the sale of weapons to foreign governments and many countries can purchase U.S. weaponry. Members of NATO and countries deemed important non-NATO allies (such as Australia, Japan, and Pakistan) face the lowest restrictions in obtaining DCS transactions, or the least U.S. government interference, when their companies engage in joint projects with U.S. weapons producers.

Modeling offsets and aid: Offset arrangements (and direct military aid used in FMS) serve as a **transfer payment** or government gift to the purchasing country. Looking at Figure 5.10, suppose that the NATO allies of the United States only wish to purchase Q_{NATO} of F-16 fighters. However, suppose that U.S. contractors would like for its allies to purchase $Q_{authorized}$ of F-16 fighters. The military aid or offset arrangement from the DoD increases NATO's demand for F-16s, represented by the shift of D_{NATO} from D_{NATO} to $D_{NATO + offsets/aid}$.

Figure 5.10
International Arms Market with DoD Subsidy

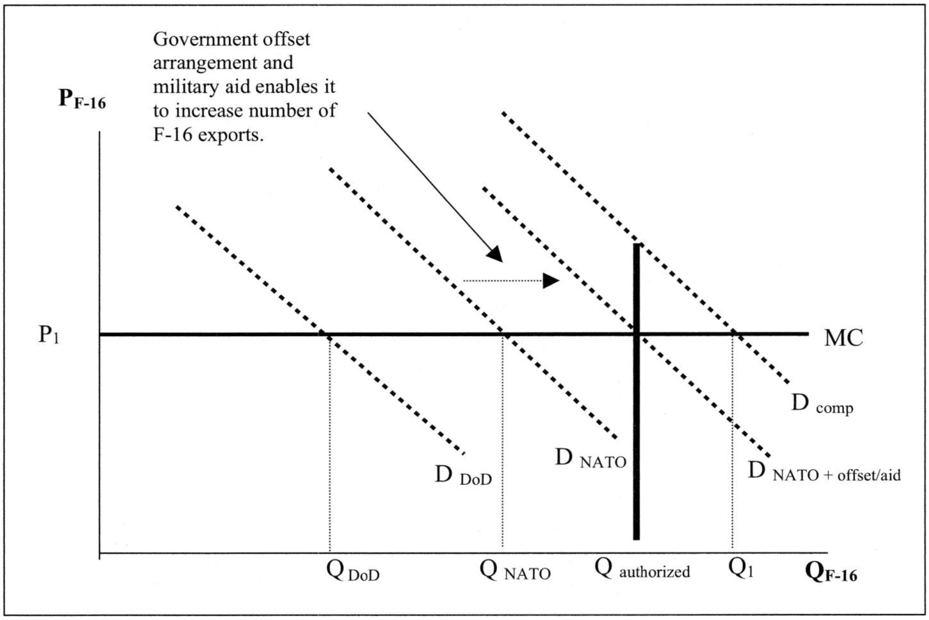

5.5 CASE STUDY: JOINT STRIKE FIGHTER

5.5.1 The Project

The Joint Strike Fighter (JSF) [25] was an ambitious project undertaken to achieve several goals. First, it was to create a family of closely related airplanes that could be different enough to meet the needs of each military branch (Navy, Air Force, and Marines) and yet similar enough to realize **economies of scope** (such as when the auto industry uses a similar chassis for pickups and SUVs).

Second, the JSF, unlike previous airplanes that were designed solely for U.S. purposes and then sold around the world, would be a world airplane with **interoperability** functions—airplanes from allied nations would have the same parts, the same software, and the same repair kits. Because the DoD wanted the JSF to have such interoperability features, it invited other countries (starting with Britain) to share the development costs of the airplane, and, in return, to have their companies become eligible for competition as suppliers. Consequently, the JSF project epitomized **coproduction.** Rather than purchasing the weapon directly off the shelf, some form of economic activity and production is conducted by *other* companies in *other* countries. For example, British Rolls-Royce was to make a propulsion-system part for the Lockheed design, and British BAE made part of the airframe.

Third, the JSF project sought to build a plane inexpensive enough to offset the steady decline in **force structure**—the number of aircraft held by the Air Force (which has declined steadily since World War II). Because the cost of aircraft had been continually rising faster than the defense budget, the DoD needed to contain costs so as to be able to buy enough aircraft to fill the aircraft requirements of the Navy, Air Force, and Marines. In the early to mid-1990s, this need led to the creation of the Joint Advanced Strike Technology (JAST) project, from which the JSF appeared. In short, the JSF would be the first fighter in which affordability was a requirement (rather than only factors like speed, performance, payload, and survivability).

As an initial step toward achieving these three goals, the JAST project required that the primary components (engine, radar and electronic systems, and avionic software), which comprise the vast majority of the plane's cost, be interchangeable between different versions of the same plane. Nevertheless, creating a plane that could meet the needs of all three branches would still prove challenging because all three services had different and contradictory requirements. The Navy wanted an airplane with two engines—in case one failed over the ocean. It needed two seats so that a navigator or a weapons operator could be onboard. It wanted enormous gas tanks—so that the plane could fly 1,000 miles inland from a carrier to launch an attack. The Air Force wanted an airplane with stealth technology; one seat; and one engine (to keep size and weight down). The Marines wanted a plane with one seat; one engine; and stealth technology. But the Marines also wanted the plane to be able to take off and land vertically. The Royal Navy had still different requirements. It needed a plane that could fit onto the smaller runway and elevators of its aircraft carriers. With cost as a primary concern, if one branch or service wanted to add something, something else would have to be taken out.

5.5.2 The Bidding Process

The JSF project started as $30 million grants to four companies that would produce designs of the new aircraft (Northrop Grumman, McDonnell Douglas, Boeing, and Lockheed). Northrop Grumman combined efforts with Lockheed early on in the process. This effectively limited the competition to three groups. The companies could only use the grant money to produce the designs. This restriction was to prevent Boeing, the largest company, from outspending the others.

By this time, the Navy had already acquiesced to having a single-engine craft. Therefore, the four companies began to focus on the Marine's desire for a vertical take-off/landing craft. The first design, that of McDonnell Douglas (who teamed up with Northrop Grumman), simply ignored the Marine's needs. They expected the DoD to not jeopardize a run of 3,000 jets on the 600 that the Marines needed. However, due to the Marine's Congressional connections and fervor in protecting its interests, the McDonnell Douglas plan was **downselected** (rejected) in 1996.

The second approach, Boeing's, focused on its existing Harrier jump-jet design, which diverted exhaust from the tail to downward-pointing nozzles under the wings and nose. However, this design suffered from a key engineering problem and environmental problems. Specifically, this plane, like the Harrier, would weigh approximately 30,000 pounds, thereby requiring slightly more than 30,000 pounds of thrust to ascend vertically. Too little thrust would not allow it to take off; but with slightly too much thrust, it would burn up the landing zone or carrier deck. The third approach, Lockheed's, relied on an untested lift-fan concept that, if successful, would avoid the thrust problems of the Boeing design.

The Principle Deputy Assistant Secretary of the Air Force oversaw the day-by-day operations of Boeing and Lockheed heading into the final downselect. In 1998 and 1999, each company received more than $1 billion each to build two flying demonstration models of its version of the JSF. Both companies experienced difficulties in keeping costs down, but the Pentagon—unlike with previous projects—refused to budge on its cost requirements. On June 24, 2001, both Lockheed and Boeing ran successful vertical takeoff and landing tests and both companies quickly covered a set of **test points** (that show the plane's ability to meet the program's goals).

Even as the technical and managerial aspects of the JSF progressed, its political support began to falter. Specifically, its goal of interoperability, though economically sensible, was proving a political liability. Most defense programs have automatic backing from the service to which the weapons will belong and political support from the Congress (the men and women representing districts in which the weapons will be built). Thus, most programs deliberately choose suppliers in as many congressional districts as possible so as to maximize support (the F-18, for example, had subcontractors in every state but Wyoming). Yet, because the project had extensive European ties, particularly the British, it would only have direct suppliers in about half the states. Additionally, there was concern that the new Bush administration would scrap the project in favor of "next-generation" weaponry. Nevertheless, the program continued and moved into the final selection process.

5.5.3 The Final Bid

The 200-plus civilian and military members of the selection panel judged the final two contestants on three criteria: affordability (both the initial cost of the plane and the long-term operating expenses); performance of the flying models; and each company's record in past programs. Some 500 aspects of each company's program were rated according to these criteria, and the complete ranking results totaled tens of thousands of pages.

Lockheed Martin was more desperate for the contract because it, unlike Boeing, was a less diversified company. Specifically, the F-16, its leading fighter since the 1970s, was nearing the end of its run (4,000 produced since the late 1970s, nearly half of which went to foreign buyers). Therefore, the officials at Lockheed feared that if it failed to secure this contract, it in all likelihood would be consigned to the business of parts supply.

Fortunately for Lockheed, it was announced as the winner in 2001. This award was primarily because its innovative lift-fan design enabled the plane to perform better. Boeing had the manufacturing advantage, but it could not overcome the design advantage of Lockheed. What did Lockheed win? With an estimated 6,000 aircraft for approximately $200 billion over a 25-year period, the JSF contract would be the largest military contract in history. About 3,000 planes would go to the U.S. Air Force, Navy, and Marine Corps, plus the Royal Air Force and Royal Navy in Britain (all of which shared in the cost of developing the plane). Another 3,000 would be set aside for other foreign customers.

As soon as Lockheed secured the contract, it began taking bids from suppliers and subcontractors, made presentations to foreign governments that might eventually buy the JSF, hired new employees at a rate of 250 a month, and began clearing room in its Fort Worth, Texas factory for production. In contrast, Boeing cancelled plans to build a new, modern factory for JSF production, began lobbying Congress to get the Air Force to lease Boeing civilian airliners for conversion to military tankers, tried to convince Lockheed to share some of the JSF production in St. Louis, and began to emphasize the need for more unmanned aircraft. As Gansler and Weidenbaum (1990) point out, such is the fate of a firm in the defense industry. Now, the JSF will attempt to be the first plane to go into service under budget. Is this likely to happen? The probability is low.

5.6   KEY POINTS

Key Macroeconomic Points:

- U.S. government spending on weapons programs, though large, is significantly lower than during the 1980s.
- The United States is the largest exporter of weapons in the world. Saudi Arabia is the largest importer of weapons in the world.

Key Microeconomic Points:

- Because the U.S. government is a monopsony buyer and the chosen firm is a monopoly, the domestic weapons market is a bilateral monopoly.
- Negotiating leverage, uncertainty, and moral hazard all contribute to weapons prices being exceptionally high.
- The global arms market is not perfectly competitive because governments still exercise control of the weapons trade, even a sale between a domestic firm and a firm of a different country.
- Government use of quotas and transfer payments in the global arms industry creates economic inefficiencies, but also prevents the onset of negative externalities.

Key Terms:

Government procurement	Cost-plus contract
Monopsony	Incentive contract
Oligopolistic	Dead Weight Loss
Monopoly	Positive externality
Demand curve	Economies of scale
Supply curve	Fixed costs
Competitive equilibrium	Foreign Military Sale (FMS)
Marginal cost	Direct grant of military aid
Bilateral monopoly	Direct Commercial Sale (DCS)
Diminishing marginal benefit	Export license

Price discrimination   Quota
Marginal revenue   Offset arrangement
Single-price monopoly   Transfer payments
Contract zone   Economies of scope
Principal-agent model   Interoperability
Risk averse   Coproduction
Moral Hazard   Force structure
Fixed-price contract   Downselect
Risk premium   Test points

Key Questions:

1. In the spring of 2004, Boeing signed a contract to sell the 7E7 civilian airliner to All Nippon Airways of Japan. How could this contract potentially result in higher prices for mid-air refueling planes that the U.S. Department of Defense purchases from Boeing?

2. Why it is optimal for society that the DoD uses licensing agreements and FMS to control the number of weapons exported from the United States?

3. While watching continual war coverage on CNN, you hear General State Theobvious (ret.) make the following comment: "There is perfect competition for defense contracts in the U.S. defense industry. The fact that prices for contracts are still very high indicates that weapon prices would be even higher if perfect competition were nonexistent." How is the general's statement wrong? Draw and describe what actually causes the price of defense contracts to rise in the domestic arms market.

4. What role does moral hazard play in the defense contracting process?

5. How does the weapons trade benefit domestic U.S. weapons producers?

6. When was the last time you had a birthday during the week? Go to the contract archives at the Department of Defense contracts website [www.defenselink.mil/contracts] and find your birthday during that year. What companies also received a special gift that day (in the form of a U.S. DoD contract)? What type of contract was used (cost-plus, fixed, etc.)?

Endnotes

1. Merle, Renae. "In Defense Bidding, Yankee Doodle Does It." *The Washington Post,* March 18, 2004. E1.

2. Stockholm International Peace and Research Institute. "The 100 Largest Arms-Producing Companies in the OECD and Developing Countries, 2000." SIPRI. Available at http://projects.sipri.org/milex/aprod/100largest2000.pdf.

3. Cahlink, George. "Making Sacrifices for the Future." *Government Executive,* August 2003, p. 32.

4. Held et al. (1999), p. 103.

5. Data about the size of U.S. markets by industry is from Bizstats.com (2003). At www.bizstats.com/marketsizes.htm.

6. From Higgs (1990), pp. xxv–xxvi.

7. Rosen (1999), p. 74. For a more recent account on the status of the F-22 fighter program and its financing, see Wayne, Leslie. "Air Force Campaigns to Save Jet Fighter." *The New York Times,* January 13, 2005.

8. The budget effect is more commonly referred to as the "income effect" in principles texts. See, for example, Parkin (2005), p. 59.

9. Description of monopsony adopted from Ehrenberg and Smith (2003), p. 73.

10. Such a simplification is also made by Bish and O'Donoghue (1970) when they discuss the role of monopsony in the provision of public goods.
11. Also see Sandler and Hartley (1999), pp. 128–130.
12. Stockholm International Peace and Research Institute "The 100 Largest Arms-Producing Companies in the OECD and Developing Countries, 2000." SIPRI. Available at http://projects.sipri.org/milex/aprod/100largest2000.pdf.
13. See Zhou (2002) for a formal pedagogical treatment of the Principle-Agent model.
14. Ergas (2003), p. 7.
15. Rosen (1999), pp. 73–76.
16. Mankiw (2001), p. 491.
17. See Cookson, Clive. "It Is Rocket Science, Then." *Financial Times,* April 4, 2003.
18. Grimmett (2003). p. 3.
19. Ibid, pp. 17, 73.
20. Stohl, Rachel. "Reflections on the Clinton Presidency: The Arms Trade." Center for Defense Information. 2001. Available at www.cdi.org/weekly/2001/armstrade.html.
21. The major piece of legislation that controls U.S. arms exports is the Arms Export Control Act and its amendments. Available through the Federation of American Scientists at http://www.fas.org/asmp/resources/govern/aeca01.pdf.
22. Such was the motivation for the U.S. government and the European Union to ban the export of arms to China after the Tiananmen Square massacre of 1989.
23. Wayne, Leslie. "Foreigners Exact Trade-Offs from U.S. Contractors." *The New York Times,* February 16, 2003.
24. Ibid.
25. Adopted from Fallows (2002), pp. 62–74.

■ UNIT THREE ■

The Economics of Security Issues

Chapter 6

Civil Wars in the Developing World

6.1 INTRODUCTION

In the late 1940s, Winston Churchill wrote: "Peace with Germany and Japan on our terms will not bring much rest. . . . As I observed last time, when the war of the giants is over, the wars of the pygmies will begin."[1] To what kind of war was Churchill referring? If *war* is defined as an armed conflict that results in at least 1,000 deaths, then over the past 200 years the incidents of international wars (war between two countries) has gradually declined, while the incidents of civil wars (war between factions within a country) has rapidly grown (particularly in just the past forty years). These trends are illustrated in Figure 6.1. Consequently, whereas a century ago conflicts were primarily between nations and 90 percent of casualties were soldiers, today almost all wars are civil and 90 percent of the victims are civilians.[2]

This chapter explores civil conflicts and their disparaging impact on the economies of less-developed countries. Sections 2, 3, and 4 consider the economic costs of civil wars

Figure 6.1

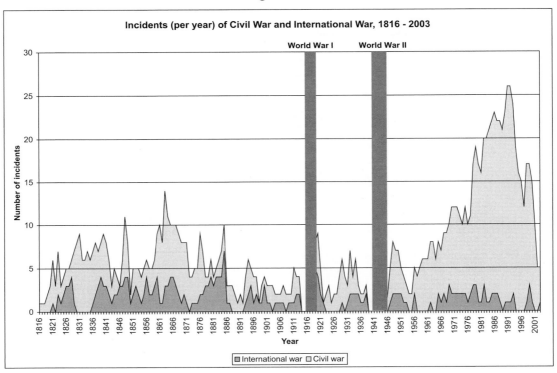

Source of data: See Gleditsch, K. "A Revised List of Wars between and within Independent States, 1816–2002." *International Interactions.* 30. 2004.pp. 231–262. available at http://weber.ucsd.edu/~kgledits/vita.html. Data used here by Permission.

Box 6.1
Historical Perspective
Does Trade Make International War Obsolete?

One prominent explanation for the decline in the regularity of international war is growing international economic integration through trade and finance. In 1996, Thomas Friedman of the *The New York Times* introduced what he called the "Golden Arches Theory." According to his theory, no two countries with a McDonald's restaurant have gone to war with each other once they opened their McDonald's.[1] His theory has since been "tested," but it still appears to be a useful rule of thumb. India (whose first McDonald's opened in 1995) and Pakistan (whose first McDonald's opened in 1998), were on the brink of all-out conventional war (if not nuclear war) in 2002; but the two soon pulled back. The 1999 NATO air strikes in the Yugoslavian territory of Kosovo also tested the theory; but because these strikes were an instance of international intervention in a civil war (and Yugoslavia was not able to fight back against the NATO alliance), the NATO action also appears to not disprove the theory.

More substantive is the evidence presented by Table I. This data reveals an interesting trend. Specifically, look at the two 50-year periods with the highest estimate of average yearly global trade (the measure of total imports and exports moving throughout the global economy) as a percentage of total world output (the measure of the combined GDP for all countries). These periods, 1901–1950 and 1951–2000, are also the two 50-year periods with the lowest average number of international wars started per year.

Of course one of those periods was the highly volatile and crisis-ridden period of 1901 through 1950, in which the world witnessed two World Wars, and the Great Depression. Even still, there is a noticeable relationship between higher trade in the global economy and the decreased prevalence of international war (military engagements between at least two countries in which at least 1,000 military personnel die).

Table I: Average International Wars Started per Year Compared to Average Global Impact of Trade per Year (1816–2000)

Time Period	Number of Years in Period	Number of Wars Started in Period	Average Wars Started/Year	Average Global Trade/Global Output for Period
1816-1850	35	55	1.57	0.03
1851-1900	50	105	2.1	0.13
1901-1950	50	46 (Not including WWI and WWII)	0.92	0.148 (During Great Depression ratio fell below 8%)
1951-2000	50	61	1.22	0.213

Note 1: The 1870–1940 trade data are from Estevadeordal, et al. (2002). Data provided by Estevadeordal by request. Author will make data available upon request.

Note 2: Figures for 1820–1849 are calculated by using the Maddison (2001) values of 0.02 for 1820, and the Estevadeordal et al. (2002) estimate of 0.11122832 for 1870. This would require global trade/global output ratio to have grown at an average yearly rate of growth of 3.49 percent. However, because data collected by Mitchell (2003) show that global trade expanded rapidly starting in the mid-1800s, then for the 1821 to 1845 period we assume that world trade/ world output ratio grew at half the rate of the 1846 to 1870 period. Therefore, during the 1821 to 1845 period, world trade/ world output is assumed to grow at 2.49 per year, while during the 1845 to 1869 period world trade/ world output ratio is assumed to grow at 4.49 per year.

Note 3: The 1951–2000 figure is based on Maddison (1995) and (2001) figures for 1950, 1973, 1995, and 1998 as reported by Estevadeordal, et al. (2002). Maddison's own data is found in Maddison (2003) and on the web at http://www.eco.rug.nl/~Maddison/. These numbers are used to estimate that the total world trade/ world output ratio grew at an average rate of 2.85 percent from 1950 to 1973, 1.33 percent from 1973 to 1992, and 3.92 percent from 1992 to 2000.

Note 4: War data from Gleditsch, K. "A Revised List of Wars between and within Independent States, 1816–2002." *International Interactions*. 30. 2004. Data provided by Gleditsch upon request. Author will make data available upon request.

(continued)

Box 6.1 *(concluded)*

Numerous empirical studies have supported the general observation in Table I that trade leads to peace.[2] Most of these studies focus on what are called **dyads.** A dyad is a pair of contiguous states (or pairs of states), one of which is a major power. Observing this relationship leads to this logical question: "Why does trade reduce the prevalence of international war?" Scholars have forwarded four main answers.[3]

1. Trade increases the costs of war. War can sever trade ties. Because trade is correlated with economic growth, then leaders who seek economic growth will not wish to lose exchange ties with trading partners or potential third parties.
2. Trade reduces the benefits of war. As a country develops economically, trade (not war) becomes a more efficient means of generating wealth. War simply eliminates wealth and can cause physical destruction of infrastructure
3. Trade promotes peace through communication and transnational ties that increase understanding among societies and that increase the potential for cooperation.
4. A domestic-political argument holds that as an economy develops, it creates a middle class who demands democracy. In turn, democratic leaders are less likely to go to war because the voting public will have to fight the war. Hence, no two democracies have ever gone to war with one another.[4]

Some scholars have added caveats to these arguments. Mueller (2004) maintains that the correlation between free trade and war is reversed. In Mueller's theory, free trade doesn't lead to less war. Instead, less war creates an environment in which free trade can prosper. Bearce and Fisher (2002) argue that the relationship between trade and war is contingent upon third factors such as the economic proximity of countries. They propose that because two countries have economic proximity, those countries can easily trade with one another and desire not to go to war with one another. Economic proximity can refer to geography, such as two countries that are adjacent to one another and in the same trading network. Proximity can also be seen in an interactive sense. This meaning of proximity pertains to linkages between two countries that are not adjacent but are highly linked through transportation (for instance, shipping lanes) and communication networks (such as language). For example, East and West Germany were geographically proximate, but the roads and highways connecting the two countries were blocked and even dismantled. This rendered the two countries interactively distant.

---

[1] McDonald (2004), p. 547 summarizes the first three of these arguments.
[2] See Oneal and Russett (1997), p. 268.
[3] Information for this section from Bandarage (1994), unless otherwise cited.
[4] Held (1999), page 113.

---

in developing economies. Those sections examine how economics often explains the cause and continuance of such conflicts. Section 4 considers case studies of two notable developing-country civil conflicts, so as to better illustrate the general statistics offered in Section 2. Section 5 ends the chapter by exploring the economics of peacekeeping—the developed world's common response to such conflicts.

6.2 ECONOMIC CONSEQUENCES OF CIVIL WARS

The Iron Law of War (that war can benefit an economy) is an economic idea only applicable to developed countries. As estimates from Paul Collier and Anke Hoeffler (2004) indicate, civil conflict is a major impediment to development in many less-developed countries.[3] In total, Collier and Hoeffler estimate that the average global economic cost of civil wars each year is $64 billion per war. This economic toll is the result of longer conflicts, reductions in real GDP and government services, forced migrations, and conflict spillover into neighboring countries.

Figure 6.2
Average Duration of Civil Wars, By Decade

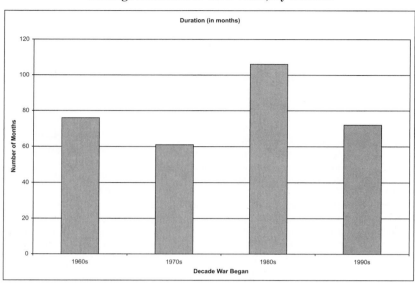

Source of data: Collier, Paul; Hoeffler, Anke; and Söderbom, Måns. "On the Duration of Civil War."
Center for the Study of African Economics. University of Oxford. October 2003. Appendix Table A.1 at
http://users.ox.ac.uk/~ball0144/warduration_oct03.pdf.

6.2.1   Conflict Duration

The typical conflict, on average, lasts seven years. Prior to the 1980s, the average duration
of a civil war was four years. Today, the average duration of a civil war is eight years. This
increase in the duration of civil wars is depicted in Figure 6.2. According to the data, the
duration of civil wars, measured in months, peaked in the 1980s but remained high into
the 1990s.

Full economic recovery can take, on average, a decade after a war's end. During the
recovery, total lost output is around 105 percent of the country's per-war annual GDP.
During the five years following a war that lasts one year, the growth rate is, on average, 2.1
percent lower than had the war not happened. By contrast, after a 15-year war, the postwar
growth rate increases by 5.9 percent annually. This difference in recovery rates is the result
of capital continuing to exit the country upon the conclusion of a short conflict, and capital
returning to the country after an extended conflict.[4]

6.2.2   Impact on GDP and Government Services

During the conflict, an economy's real GDP typically grows 2.2 percentage points a year
less than it would have in peacetime. According to Gupta et al. (2002), this downward
trend, in turn, negatively affects growth of per capita government revenue, which also leads
to lower growth of per capita government spending on education and health. This diversion
of government expenditures toward arms is estimated by Collier and Hoeffler (2004) to
reduce welfare by another 18 percent of GDP. In total, a typical civil war leaves a country
15 percent poorer than it would otherwise have been and with perhaps 30 percent more
people living in absolute poverty.[5]

Figure 6.3
Refugees and Malaria, 1962–1997

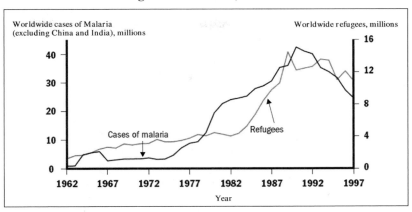

Source: Collier, P.; Elliot, V.L.; Hegre, H.; Hoeffler, A.; Reynal-Querol, M.; and Sambanis, N. *Breaking the Conflict Trap: Civil War and Development Policy.* Washington, D.C.: World Bank and Oxford University Press. May 2003. Figure 2.3, p. 37, available at www-wds.worldbank.org/ servlet/WDSContentServer/WDSP/IB/2003/06/30/000094946_0306190405396/Rendered/PDF/ multi0page.pdf. Reprinted here with permission.

Furthermore, the collapsing health care system, combined with the typical phenom-enon of forced migrations—which worsen disease—contribute to health costs of around $5 billion per conflict. As Figure 6.3 shows, worldwide cases of malaria (excluding cases in China and India) and the global refugee population, have a pronounced tendency to rise in tandem with conflicts.

6.2.3 Spillover Effects

The effects of civil wars are not isolated to the country in which the war originates. The effects typically spill over borders, even if the fighting does not. An average of 2.7 countries border each state mired in civil war. Economic losses to these neighboring countries—commonly from reduced trade and foreign investment—can often amount to 115 percent of their GDP, and these countries typically spend a total of 12 percent of one year's GDP on military spending—so as to guard against conflict spillover.

6.3 ECONOMIC CAUSES OF CIVIL WARS

One might be quick to dismiss conflict in less-developed countries as nothing more than irrational behavior spurred on by ethnic or religious rivalry. However, in reality, ethnic and religious divisions simply overlay economic conditions that are the true causes of conflict: poverty; resource exploitation; greed; extraction of resources from an ethnic minority; and inequality.

6.3.1 Poverty as a Cause

Studies have explored the probability of civil war onset conditional upon different income levels.[6] It has been found that a country with GDP per person of just $250 has a predicted probability of war beginning (at some point over the next five years) of 15 percent. The probability of war is cut in half when a country's GDP per person rises to $600. War's likelihood falls by half again—to below 4 percent—when a country's GDP per person is $1,250. Countries with an income per person of over $5,000 have a less than 1 percent chance of experiencing civil conflicts, all else being equal. Therefore, it should come as no surprise that the poorest one-sixth of the world endures four-fifths of the world's civil wars.[7]

Poverty and policing resources: Scholars argue that the primary reason conflict onset and poverty are related is because wealthier societies tend to have more effective policing and military capabilities that are able to reach into inaccessible regions.[8] Specifically, if the police are badly financed, they will not only lack resources, but they will also be susceptible to accepting bribes. This situation makes it possible for the insurgents to "buy off" the police. Also, if the government's police or military personnel are poorly informed about the "goings on" at the local level, they will be ill-prepared to counter any insurgent's attempts to use information as a recruiting tool. Furthermore, poorly equipped policing units will find it difficult to discern between insurgent and noninsurgent. Consequently, attempts to eliminate insurgents will tend to be highly disruptive to the lives of noninsurgents and, therefore, prove counterproductive as the attempts create additional antigovernment sentiment. In short, because wealth leads to better policing capabilities, wealthier societies are better able to protect assets. This protection lessens the attractiveness of violence for would-be rebels.

Poverty and opportunity costs: Opportunity costs (the next best activity that a person gives up in order to carry out an action) can also explain the correlation between poverty and conflict. As an example, consider the educational level of the male population in a country. The average years of schooling of the men is one measure of the opportunity costs for men to engage in risky behavior such as armed conflict. The higher the level of education among men, the less likely the men are to engage in armed conflict. Hence, even a slight increase in the level of male education can decrease the risk of conflict.[9]

Another opportunity cost that is related to education is employment opportunity. Whereas a government's army can build unity gradually, a rebel force must form quickly. Consequently, this need for rapid growth makes the rebel organization more sensitive to the current state of the labor market. If jobs are plentiful, a rebellion is unlikely since the rebel organization will be unable to amass sufficient personnel in a timely fashion.[10]

Additional links between poverty and conflict: Though persuasive, opportunity costs alone can not fully explain the positive relationship between poverty and conflict. For instance, Chapter 7 will discuss how suicide bombers are typically better off and more educated than the average populations from which they originate. Therefore, there are additional explanations for why poverty and conflict-onset are correlated.

Acute scarcity of resources in one area leads to migrations that result in conflicts between groups over resources in the other area. Finally, poverty and low or negative economic growth are often symptoms of a corrupt, incompetent government, which can provoke rebellion.[11] Of course, the causality between poverty and civil war could run in the opposite direction—rich countries tend to be rich because they have been fortunate enough to avoid conflict.

6.3.2   Resources as a Cause

Perhaps the single most powerful conflict risk factor is when a country has a substantial share of GDP coming from the export of **primary commodities** (natural resources such as minerals, jewels, or oil). Specifically, countries are most at risk when the level of primary-commodity dependence reaches 26 percent of GDP. This level of dependence raises the risk of conflict (for a typical less-developed country) from 14 percent to 23 percent. In contrast, if the country had no primary-commodity exports (but was otherwise the same), its risk of conflict falls to 0.5 percent.[12]

There are six main explanations for this relationship between conflict and natural resource exports.[13] First, natural resources can provide financing to rebel groups. The "conflict diamonds" in Sierra Leone are a classic example (see the Sierra Leone case study). Therefore, Collier and Hoeffler (2004) recommend taking international steps to ensure that commodities from countries engaged in civil wars receive a lower price on the global market. The result should be a shortening of the civil wars. Specifically, a 10 percent reduction in price for "conflict" commodities can produce a $5.9 billion peace dividend for the warring economy.[14]

Second, natural resources concentrated in a particular region of a country may lead a dissatisfied group to believe that a seceding state could be viable and prosperous. Examples of this type of thinking include southern Sudan (see the Sudan case study), as well as Biafra in Nigeria, Katanga in Congo, Cabinda in Angola, Casamance in Senegal, and Aceh in Indonesia.

Third, natural resources can create inequalities. This creation of inequalities can occur if the wealth the resources generate is unjustly distributed, or if the government forcibly moves an ethnic group who was living in the resource-rich area. Nigeria and Sierra Leone offer such examples. In fact, the claims of the Revolutionary United Front (RUF) rebel group in Sierra Leone, as expressed in the group's anthem, explicitly pertain to such grievances:

> "Where are our diamonds, Mr. President? / Where is our gold, NPRC? [....] Our people are suffering without means of survival. / All our minerals have gone to foreign lands."[15]

Fourth, governments that rely on natural resources rather than taxation for financing have little incentive to create strong institutions or respond to the demands of their citizens. The classic example is Zaire under Sesko Mobutu. Fifth, economies dependent on a few natural resources are more susceptible to terms of trade shocks (for example, international price fluctuations or changes in the weather conditions). Dissatisfaction within groups that suffer from such shocks can lead to conflict. Sixth, neighboring states may spur on a civil conflict in order to exploit the country's natural resources. The prime example of this type is the Democratic Republic of Congo; Zimbabwe and Rwanda justified their continued presence in the country on the need to guard raw materials.

6.3.3 Greed as a Cause

A rebel group's desire for profit may also provoke and perpetuate conflict.[16] To put it bluntly, though civil war is bad for the economy as a whole, *some* people actually benefit. If some people do well out of civil war, they may lack an incentive to restore peace.[17]

The rebellion may begin as a grievance (a desire to eliminate what the rebel group deems to be an unjust government), but its continuance could be the result of profiteering. Because civil wars can both provoke greed and be provoked by greed, it is sometimes difficult to determine if greed or grievance is the rebellion's driving force.[18]

Greed provokes civil war: Rebel groups may provoke and perpetuate a civil war so as to gain revenues through resource abundance. For example, when civil war resumed in Angola in 1993, the rebel National Union for the Total Independence of Angola (UNITA) earned, between 1993 and 2000, an estimated $4 billion from illegal diamond sales.[19]

Oil is another resource susceptible to profiteering by rebels.[20] Rebel groups rarely, if ever, pump the oil (it requires capital, skills, and technology; such assets are typically controlled instead by multinational firms who prefer to work with legitimate governments). Instead, rebels attempt to profit from oil by extorting money from these oil firms. In Colombia and Nigeria, rebel groups will either kidnap oil firm employees or threaten to blow up pipelines. In both cases a ransom or payment is demanded, which firms will usually provide. Hence, during the 1990s, European companies paid an estimated $1.2 billion to rebel groups. Now that ransom insurance is available, this has the potential of raising ransom demands, thereby increasing the profits to be made from violence.

Civil war provokes greed: On the flip side, civil wars also create incentives to become greedy.[21] Because life during a civil war can be less predictable, people will begin to think only in the short term. Whereas people may normally not engage in behavior harmful to their reputation, when the future is unclear (if not unlikely), individuals will have less incentive to maintain a reputation of trustworthiness. During the 1994 massacre of the Tutsi ethnic group in Rwanda, the killing was initially organized by the Hutu-dominated government. This government initiation gave the massacre the classification of **genocide** (government-sanctioned, systematic killing of a particular ethnic group). However, once the genocide began, numerous individuals joined the killing, not to rectify personal grievances against the Tutsi people, but as a form of personal economic gain:

> "[As the killing groups] went into action, they drew around them a cloud of even poorer people….For these people the genocide was the best thing that could ever happen to them….They could steal, they could kill with minimum justification, they could rape and they could get drunk for free. This was wonderful. The political aims pursued by the masters of this dark carnival were quite beyond their scope. They just went along."[22]

6.3.4   Ethnic Dominance as a Cause

Collier (2000) finds that in societies where the single largest ethnic group comprises 45 percent to 90 percent of the population, there is a 28 percent probability of conflict onset.[23] Relative ethnic homogeneity (a country in which the dominant group comprises less than 90 percent of the population) contributes to the probability of conflict because the dominant group may benefit from transferring resources from the minority group. However, near-perfect dominance (one ethnic group comprises 90 percent or more of the population) lessens the probability of conflict, because the minority group is so small that the benefit of exploiting the group may be swallowed up in the cost of actually carrying out the resource transfer.

Overall, in the 47 civil conflicts studied, Collier finds the risk of conflict in relatively ethnically homogenous countries near 23 percent, all things being equal; while the most ethnically diverse countries only had a probability of three percent. Widespread ethnic and religious diversity contributes to stability because in countries with diversity, it is difficult to recruit a force of sufficient scale to be viable. For example, in Africa the average group of ethnic and linguistic similarities has only around 250,000 people, of whom around 25,000 are young males. Thus, even before considering further divisions along, for example, religious lines, an organization of 5,000 fighters would need to recruit 20 percent of the young male age group. This percent will be difficult to achieve and so makes rebellion less likely.[24] Table 6.1 summarizes these figures, as well as other interesting findings from Collier's study.

Table 6.1

Collier's Findings Regarding Inequality and Probability of Conflict

Observation	Probability of Conflict
Sample average	14.00%
A country with 10% more youths in schools than average (55% instead of 45%)	10.00%
A country with a population growth rate 1% higher than	16.50%
A country with a growth rate of per capita income 1% less	15.00%
A country with a relatively dominant ethnic group (45 to 90% of the population)	28.00%
A country with an overwhelming dominant ethnic group	3.0%*

Source of data: Collier, Paul. "Economic Causes of Civil Conflict and their Implications for Policy." World Bank: The Economics of Civil War, Crime and Violence Project. June 15, 2000. Available at www.econ.worldbank.org/files/13198_EcCausesPolicy.pdf.

* maximum of sample

6.3.5 Inequality as a Cause

Related to ethnic group dominance is inequality. There are two forms of inequality: vertical inequality and horizontal inequality. **Vertical inequality** is income inequality between people. A common quantitative measure of vertical inequality is to measure the distribution of income in a society to determine how much is held by the wealthiest, relative to how much is held by the poorest. In a perfectly equitable society, 20 percent of the entire population would hold 20 percent of the wealth, 60 percent of the entire population would hold 60 percent of the wealth, and so on. In a vertically unequal society, 80 percent of the population may, for example, have only 5 percent of the wealth, while the other 20 percent of the population has 95 percent of the wealth. Though this may lead to animosity between rich and poor, studies using quantitative measures of income inequality find that vertical inequality does not lead to conflict. This is most likely because vertical inequality alone does not tell *who* is and is not wealthy.

In contrast, **horizontal inequality**—inequality between ethnic, religious, political or regional groups—may increase the risk of conflict-onset.[25] According to Stewart (2000), it is possible to have sharp vertical inequality without horizontal inequality.[26] An example of such an instance would be if the av erage income of all groups were the same and distribution within each group was highly unequal (i.e., there are both rich and poor people from the same ethnic group and all ethnic groups have about the same distribution of rich and poor people).

Horizontal inequality can lead to conflict when a group in power actively discriminates against another group. Consider a few examples. In Burundi, half of government investment went to the city of Bujumbura and its vicinity, from which the elite Tutsi ethnic group came. Additionally, there were deliberate attempts to limit the educational access of the Hutu ethnic group.[27]

Unfortunately, as compelling as the argument may be for horizontal inequality as a cause of civil war, it does suffer from some limitations. First, there are no quantitative measures of horizontal inequality that can be used for comparisons across countries. Without data analysis, it is difficult to make definitive arguments concerning horizontal inequality's role in provoking civil war. Second, horizontal inequality alone is not enough to provoke civil war. Civil war will result only if other risk elements are present.[28] These risk elements include greed, propaganda espoused by a charismatic leader, weak state institutions, and availability of resources with which to finance an insurgency—in short, the other factors highlighted in this section.

6.4   SMALL ARMS TRANSFERS TO THE DEVELOPING WORLD

Despite the numerous economic causes of civil wars, no war can be fought without weapons. Though numerous sophisticated weapons systems are sold to developing countries each year (see Box 6.2), most civil wars are fought with simple small arms. In fact, the most widely held weapon of insurgents in the developing world is the AK-47 assault rifle. Also known as the "Kalashnikov" (after the original Russian designer), these guns have been produced in a number between 70 million and 105 million since 1949.[29]

What makes the AK-47 such an attractive weapon? First, it is deadly, with the ability to shoot 650 rounds per minute.[30] Second, it is reliable (it is considered to very rarely fail to fire) and simple. Third, and perhaps most important, it is inexpensive. Its low price is primarily because the AK-47 (unlike major weapons systems) is produced in a competitive market.

6.4.1   The Supply of AK-47s

On the supply side, there is no monopoly producer of AK-47s. The Soviet Union began producing the rifles for its own army in 1949; but in the 1950s, the Soviets began exporting the rifles and manufacturing technology to states in its sphere of influence (particularly those in Eastern Europe). The Soviet Union entered into licensing agreements with 18 countries; but as the technology became more widely dispersed, eleven other countries began making AK-47 clones without the Soviet Union's approval. The Soviet Union, plus these additional 29 countries, comprised the initial primary market for AK-47s.

However, it is the **secondary arms market** that explains the virtual ubiquity of these weapons. It is in these markets that *used* AK-47s are sold. For example, Heckler & Koch, a British-owned, German-based maker of assault rifles, has licensed production agreements with Iran and Greece. In turn, Iran exports its rifles to Sudan, and Greece exports its rifles to Burundi and Libya.[31] These countries then export the rifles to Algeria, Egypt, Lebanon, and the West Bank. During the 1980s, the U.S. government bought AK-47s produced in China and Egypt and then supplied them to Islamic guerrillas fighting the Soviet Union in Afghanistan.

Other guns are smuggled through **black markets**—markets for goods that are illegal and, therefore, lack government regulation. For instance, Thailand has one of the world's largest and most efficient black markets. Guns are often brought here and then exported to Sri Lanka, the Philippines, Indonesia, and the Kashmir region separating India and Pakistan.[32]

Consequently, there is substantial evidence to suggest that as the supply of AK-47s rises in many developing countries, the price has fallen. For example, in northeastern Kenya, the barter rate for an AK-47 has dropped from 10 cows in 1986 to two cows in 2001.[33] In some areas of the world, an AK-47 can be bought for $15 or for a bag of grain.[34]

6.4.2 The Demand for AK-47s

The price of an AK-47 is also a function of demand.[35] Under stable conditions and in legal markets (such as the United States), a used AK-47 will sell for $200 to $400. Black market prices under $100 usually indicate a sudden arrival of peace after a period of intense conflict. Black market prices above $1,000 can serve as a warning of imminent or expanding conflict. High prices mean that people are desperate to own weapons and that normal supply chains cannot keep up with demand. For example, in Somalia in 1992, the cost of an AK-47 fell from $300 to $100 in a matter of days as U.S. Marines massed offshore; and to $50 shortly after they landed. However, the gun prices rose back to about $200 after the U.S. withdrawal.

6.4.3 Global Equilibrium and Implications

It is estimated that around 500 million small arms are circulating around the world, thereby making small arms more readily available than major weapons systems. What has been the consequence? It has been estimated that in Latin America alone the direct and indirect costs of small arms violence is between $140 and $170 billion per year; and worldwide, small arms are implicated in well over 1,000 deaths every day.[36]

BOX 6.2
Historical Perspective
Cold War Alliance-Forming[1]

During the Cold War, the United States and the Soviet Union fought numerous **proxy wars** (wars where, in place of direct confrontation, the two superpowers supported groups or governments in developing countries fighting one another). Both superpowers actively courted many developing country governments by offering favorable financing arrangements for weapons.

The result was a massive dumping of arms by superpowers into the developing world. Exports to developing countries rose from $1.1 billion in 1960 to $35 billion in 1987. The number of countries supplying arms to developing countries rose from 10 in 1970 to 25 in 1990.[2] Because the favorable financing offered by the superpowers contributed to the accumulation of third-world external debt, nearly 20 percent of the African and Latin American loans in the 1970s were geared toward the military.

As the end of the Cold War led the governments of the developed world to reduce their demand for light infantry weaponry (as they reduced the size of their armed forces), foreign arms sales to the developing world became an ever more important focus of arms dealers and producers.[3] From the years 1995 to 2002, the value of arms-transfer agreements with developing nations comprised 66.2 percent of all such agreements, worldwide. More recently, arms-transfer agreements with developing nations constituted 64.6 percent of all such agreements globally from 1999–2002, and 60.6 percent of these agreements in 2002. The $17.7 billion in arms-transfer agreements to developing countries in 2002 marked the second lowest year, with 1999 (approximately $29 billion) serving as the peak year.

China is the leading "developing" country that is buying weapons. From 1999 to 2002, China concluded $11.3 billion in arms-transfer agreements. China's lead was followed by the United Arab Emirates ($9 billion) and India ($8 billion). The United States has been the primary supplier of weapons to the developing world, accounting for $7 billion (constant 2002 dollars) in 2002. The United States was followed by the United Kingdom ($3.3 billion) and Russia ($2.9 billion). The majority of weapons sold to developing countries are land systems such as tanks, self-propelled guns, and armored vehicles. Some supersonic combat aircraft such as the MIG-29 (by Russia) are sold as well.

(continued)

Box 6.2 *(concluded)*

To summarize, Table I lists the leading developing country recipients of arms-transfer agreements and deliveries in 2002 and during the 1995–2002 period. Table II summarizes the weapons system types delivered (by supplier country).

Table I: Arms Trade to Developing Nations (Leading Recipients)
(in millions of current U.S. dollars)

Arms Transfer Agreements			Arms Deliveries		
COUNTRY	1995-2002	2002	COUNTRY	1995-2002	2002
China	17,800	3,600	Saudi Arabia	64,500	5,200
U.A.E.	16,300	N/A	Taiwan	20,200	1,100
India	14,100	1,400	Egypt	9,500	2,100
Egypt	12,900	1,200	China	9,300	1,200
Saudi Arabia	10,700	900	South Korea	8,800	600
Israel	10,000	700	U.A.E.	8,700	900
South Korea	8,700	1,900	Kuwait	7,300	1,300
South Africa	5,200	N/A	Israel	7,000	700
Malaysia	4,900	800	India	4,700	900
Pakistan	4,700	N/A	Pakistan	3,800	600

Source of data: Grimmett, Richard F. "Conventional Arms Transfers to Developing Nations, 1995–2002." *Congressional Research Service Report for Congress.* September 22, 2003. Table 1I, p. 49.

Table II: Number of Weapons Systems Delivered to Developing Nations by Major Suppliers and by Type
(1999–2002)

Weapons Category	US	Russia	China	Major West European*	All Other European	All Others	Total
Tanks and self-propelled guns	200	290	100	370	1,170	100	2,230
Artillery	263	190	380	20	680	580	2,113
APCs and armored cars	88	660	340	100	920	590	2,698
Major surface combatants	8	3	0	8	10	3	32
Minor surface combatants	2	4	19	27	75	52	179
Guided missile boats	0	0	1	8	0	0	9
Submarines	0	2	0	5	2	0	9
Supersonic combat aircraft	221	250	50	30	100	100	751
Subsonic combat aircraft	17	10	0	60	10	0	97
Other aircraft	48	40	70	110	110	80	458
Helicopters	145	350	10	60	120	80	765
Surface-to-air missiles	2,884	1,600	660	1,200	580	6,190	13,114
Surface-to-surface missiles	0	0	0	0	0	60	60
Anti-ship missiles	419	250	130	220	0	10	1,029
Total	**4,295**	**3,649**	**1,760**	**2,218**	**3,777**	**7,845**	**23,544**

Source of data: Grimmett, Richard F. "Conventional Arms Transfers to Developing Nations, 1995–2002." *Congressional Research Service Report for Congress.* September 22, 2003. Table 3, p. 65.

* France, U.K., Germany, and Italy combined.

[1] Information for this section from Bandarage (1994), unless otherwise cited.
[2] Held (1999), page 113.
[3] Data in this section from Grimmett (2003).

6.5 CASE STUDIES OF CONFLICT AND UNDERDEVELOPMENT IN AFRICA

So far, the economic impact of civil wars has been discussed in terms of overall statistics. To make the impact of civil wars more concrete, this section offers two case studies of prominent African civil wars: Sierra Leone and Sudan. Each case study begins with an overview of the conflict, delves into the causes of the conflict, and ends with a brief description of the conflict's impact on the economy.

6.5.1 Sierra Leone[37]

Overview of the conflict: Civil conflict began in Sierra Leone in 1991. The conflict in Sierra Leone exemplifies how civil wars in Africa are as much war against regional powers, as against internal insurgents. The Revolutionary United Front (RUF) pushed into Sierra Leone with support from neighboring Liberia and advanced through southern and eastern Sierra Leone in the first half of 1991. With the aid of Guinean and Nigerian troops, the forces of the Sierra Leone government pushed back the RUF rebels in the second half of 1991 and into 1992. From 1992 until 1996, the war remained a virtual stalemate until a tentative ceasefire was reached in 1996. Though cease fire agreements have been repeatedly broken and instituted since 1996, the period from 1991–1996 marks the heaviest fighting and will be the focus of this case study.

Causes of the conflict:[38] From the time of colonial rule, the Sierra Leone economy was based primarily on the extraction of largely unprocessed raw materials. This export dependence, combined with widespread corruption among the Sierra Leone politicians and traditional chiefs, served to create deep pools of resentment among those excluded from the economic system. For example, Sierra Leone President Siaka Stevens relied on food aid to pay off political clientele, despite the inability of Sierra Leone's rice production to keep pace with population increases.

In conjunction with this corruption was the government's inability to stop (and, at times, condone) diamond smuggling. This smuggling seriously reduced state revenues. For example, by the late 1980s, diamond smuggling reached nearly $300 million per year and, by 1985-86, domestic revenue collection had plummeted to just 18 percent of its 1977–78 levels. In particular, President Stevens built a fortune for himself and top political clientele by using government control of import/export licenses and the allocation of foreign exchange to acquire key roles in the private firms of the Sierra Leone diamond industry.

By the early 1980s, Stevens' nonbudgeted discretionary spending rose to more than 60 percent of the budget. In contrast, economic development spending fell to only 3 percent of the overall budget by 1984. The already inadequate education system of Sierra Leone was further hurt by public spending cuts. By the late 1980s, under the rule of Stevens' self-appointed successor, President Momoh, the economy's inequalities were ripe ground for civil discontent.

However, these inequalities did not lead directly to conflict. The war began when Charles Taylor, president of Liberia (Sierra Leone's southern neighbor) sought to deflect the attention of ECOMOG (Economic Community of West African States Monitoring Group) troops who would have been deployed against his own troops fighting a civil war in Liberia. To accomplish this distraction, Taylor sponsored an incursion into Sierra Leone of a small band of armed men (some from Sierra Leone, some armed mercenaries from Burkina Faso, others militants from Taylor's National Patriotic Front of Liberia group) called the RUF.

Economic inequalities came into play as the economically and educationally excluded portions of the Sierra Leone population began to support the chaos wrought by the RUF. These excluded populations used the chaos as a way to make money. These marginalized groups benefited from looting and participating in the illegal trading and production of diamonds (a trading network that had previously been tightly controlled by the government).

Economic consequences of the conflict:[39] Tactics on both sides involved indiscriminate violence against civilians, which caused major disruption and displacement in the labor force. By 1995, nearly 900,000 civilians had been displaced and 300,000 killed out of a total population of 4.3 million. Infant mortality rates rose to one-fifth of live births.

Figure 6.4
External Indebtedness (Sierra Leone)

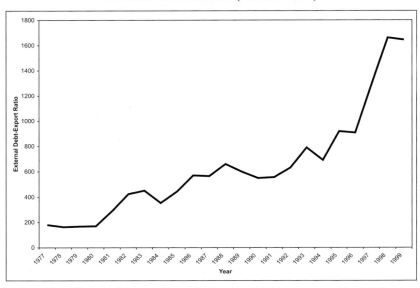

Source of data: Easterly, William and Sewadeh, Mirvat. Global Development Network Growth Database. Macro Time Series Dataset 2001. World Bank. Available at http://www.worldbank.org/research/growth/GDNdata.htm.

From 1985–1994, the combination of war and corruption led to an average per year decline in real GDP per capita of 1.9 percent. However, that most macroeconomic indicators declined sharply in the years prior to the war suggests that corruption played the primary role in Sierra Leone's economic travails.

Export earnings declined during the war years, and this decline contributed to a rise in the **external debt/export earnings ratio** (see Figure 6.4). This ratio, a measure of the sustainability of a country's external indebtedness (for example, how easily it can pay off its financial obligations to foreigners), had been in decline heading into the war period, but resumed its upward trend during the war.

6.5.2 Sudan

Overview of the conflict: Though much recent attention has been paid to human rights violations in the Darfur region of western Sudan, this case study will focus on the long-running conflict between the Arab Muslim Northerners of Sudan (the base of the Sudanese government), and the black Africans of the South. The Africans practice mainly Christian or animist beliefs and have been marginalized for centuries. Independence of Sudan was marked by an initial civil war (1955–1971). A peace agreement in 1972 ended the first civil war after independence, and Sudan made some movement towards federalism. However, tensions between the authorities in Khartoum and those in the Southern region, and divisions between different groups of southerners, led to further outbreaks of violence in the early 1980s, particularly between the government and the Sudan People's Liberation Army (SPLA). Since 1983, over 1.2 million people have been killed, and the civil war has devastated the Sudanese economy.[40]

Causes of the conflict: Sudan is a vast country populated by mainly Muslim Arab and Nubian peoples in the north; and in the South, mainly Animist or Christian Nilotic and Negro peoples. Because the Nile river basin runs down into the northern portions of Sudan, this fertile northern region has historically been an important farming and transportation locale; the Northerners of Sudan received privileged attention under both Turkish and then British rule. Consequently, Sudan developed a highly uneven resource-extractive and export-oriented form of economic development, where economic activity was concentrated in the northern, eastern, and central portions of the country, while the South was left economically underdeveloped.

Upon independence, the differences between Northerners and Southerners were evident. Southerners lacked land (which was being taken from Southerners as the Northerners used World Bank loans to clear southern land for mechanized farming). Southerners also lacked capital, and they had been discriminated against in educational opportunities. They also did not have the connections necessary to maximize the revenue of selling cattle in the lucrative northern livestock markets. In sum, the Southerners were not in control of their economic development and were dependent on the Northerners.

These conditions alone would not have sparked a second civil war. However, with the discovery of oil in southern Sudan in 1978, the government sought control over these reserves (see Figure 6.5). The government began to gradually transfer troops in the north to the southern regions, notably to the oil-rich Bentiu area in 1983. This troop mobilization, coupled with the Southerners' non-representation within the Sudanese government (so the Southerners could not stake an effective claim to these resources), led to the creation of the SPLA in 1983 and initiated a civil war.

Economic consequences of the conflict: Over 2 million people died during the 20 years of civil war, either directly from combat, or from the widespread government-sponsored famine in the South.[41] This death toll is a considerable number, given that Sudan had averaged a population of 25 million during the course of the conflict. The government not only extracted

Figure 6.5
Sudan's Oil Deposits

Source: *The Economist.* "Fleeing the Horsemen who Kill for Khartoum." May 13, 2004. Reprinted here with permission.

Figure 6.6
External Indebtedness (Sudan)

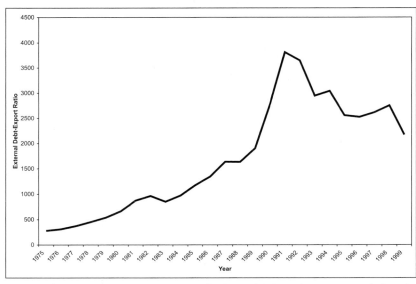

Source of data: Easterly, William and Sewadeh, Mirvat. Global Development Network Growth Database. Macro Time Series Dataset 2001. World Bank. Available at http://www.worldbank.org/research/growth/GDNdata.htm.

resources from the South, but Northern merchants also manipulated the grain prices in the northern markets, thereby rendering grain too expensive for Southerners to purchase.

Though usable internal data is not available for Sudan for many of the war years, it is still possible to use external economic data to illustrate the conflict's negative impact. Specifically, the conflict contributed to the diminishment of Sudan's export earnings; which, in turn, contributed to a drastic rise in Sudan's external debt. This increased the debt/export ratio from approximately 1,176 in 1983 (already an unsustainable level) to nearly 4,000 in the early 1990s (see Figure 6.6).

6.5.3 Lessons from the Case Studies

Table 6.2 provides a variety of data that summarize the economic toll of war on these two countries. The combination of declining population, increases in military expenditures, and resource displacement (as represented by the decline in food consumption) created large cumulative losses of GDP. Specifically, these countries are estimated to have lost the equivalent of between 147 percent and 172 percent of their 1995 GDP due to war (see the final column of Table 6.2).

Despite being a small sample of pertinent cases, these two conflicts do present four general lessons:

1) Ethnic and tribal differences (which are often blamed for civil wars in underdeveloped economies) have very little to do with the conflicts' origins. For example, the conflict in Sierrra Leone was a function of economic inequality, government abuse and corruption, and spillover of conflict into neighboring countries.

Table 6.2
Economic Performance of Case Study Countries: Summary Statistics

Country	Years Measured	Deaths	Deaths as Percent of Population	Miltary Expenditure in Start Year (Percent of GDP)	Military Expenditure in Peak Year (Percent of GDP)	Start Year Daily Calories per Person	End Year Daily Calories per Person	Estimated Cumulative GDP Loss (as a percent of 1995 GDP)
Sierra Leone	1991–95	30,000	0.7	0.8	2.6 (1993)	1,895	1,694	147
Sudan	1984–1995	611,000	4.8	2.9	3.2 (1989)	2,244	2,310	172

Source of data: Stewart, F.; Huang, C.; and Wang, M. "Internal Wars in Developing Countries: An Empirical Overview of Economic and Social Consequences," in *War and Underdevelopment,* vol. I. Stewart, Fitzgerald, and associates (eds). Oxford: Oxford University Press. 2001. Tables 4.5, 4.9, 4.11, and 4.16.

2) Though government corruption may be a fundamental cause of underdevelopment, conflict also plays a role in that it delays the development process or impedes a country from realizing its economic potential.

3) Sierra Leone illustrates that civil conflicts in Africa are intimately related to regional interstate conflicts.

4) Conflict appears to contribute to the external indebtedness of a less-developed country. However, conflict is neither the sole nor the primary cause of the external indebtedness of a less-developed country.

6.6   PEACE OPERATIONS: AN ECONOMICALLY INEFFICIENT RESPONSE?

Given the negative consequences of conflict, policy makers around the world have considered various options for stopping or preventing civil wars. Military intervention that is aimed at stopping these conflicts falls under the category of **Peacekeeping** or **Peacemaking.** Peacekeeping is the use of military personnel to observe and monitor whether or not a ceasefire is being obeyed. Soldiers in these operations are traditionally lightly armed and powerless to do much if either side in the conflict chooses to resume hostilities. This lack of force means that peacekeepers, in order to fulfill their assignment, require the consent of opposing sides.[42]

Peacemaking is taking actions to bring about a ceasefire. Such actions can entail the use of diplomacy, negotiations, and arbitration. The United Nations has been involved in numerous peacekeeping and peacemaking operations since its inception in 1950 (see Table 6.3). Such operations have also, more recently, been taken on by the North Atlantic Treaty Organization (NATO).

6.6.1   Expansion of Peacekeeping Operations

According to Sandler and Hartley (1999), U.N. peacekeeping operations have evolved through four distinct phases. From 1947–1956, the United Nations was involved in four missions (three were peacekeeping; one, UNEF I in the Sinai, was peacemaking). From 1957–1974, the United Nations became very active, engaging in nine new peacekeeping operations; while from 1975–1987, the United Nations engaged in only two new operations. From 1988–1997, U.N. peace operations expanded greatly, with thirty-three missions. Another ten missions have been added since 1998. In short, the first 40 years of

Table 6.3
UN Peacekeeping Operations

Current UN Peacekeeping Operations		Sierra Leone	July 1998–Oct. 1999
Region/Country	**Duration**	Central African Republic	April 1998–Feb. 2000
AFRICA		**MIDEAST**	
Western Sahara	April 1991–present	Middle East—1st UN Emergency Force	Nov. 1956–June 1967
Sierra Leone	Oct. 1999–present		
DRC	Nov.1999–present	Lebanon	June–Dec. 1958
Ethiopia and Eritrea	July 2000–present	Yemen	July 1963–Sept. 1964
Côte d'Ivoire	May 2003–present	Middle East—2nd UN Emergency Force	Oct. 1973–July 1979
Liberia	Oct. 2003–present		
ASIA		Iran/Iraq	Aug. 1988–Feb. 1991
India/Pakistan	Jan. 1949–present	**AMERICAS**	
East Timor	May 2002–present	Dominican Republic	May 1965–Oct. 1966
EUROPE		Central America Observer Group	Nov. 1989–Jan. 1992
Cyprus	March 1964–present		
Georgia	Aug. 1993–present	El Salvador	July 1991–April 1995
Kosovo	June 1999–present	Haiti	Sept. 1993–June 1996
MIDDLE EAST		Haiti	July 1996–July 1997
Middle East	May 1948–present	Guatemala	Jan.–May 1997
Golan Heights	June 1974–present	Haiti	Aug.–Nov. 1997
Lebanon	March 1978–present	Haiti	Dec. 1997–March 2000
Iraq/Kuwait	April 1991–present	**ASIA**	
		West New Guinea	Oct. 1962–April 1963
Completed UN Peacekeeping Operations		India/Pakistan	Sept. 1965–March 1966
Region/Country	**Duration**	Afghanistan/Pakistan	May 1988–March 1990
AFRICA		Cambodia	Oct. 1991–March 1992
Congo	July 1960–June 1964	Cambodia	March 1992–Sept. 1993
Angola	Dec. 1988–May 1991	Tajikistan	Dec. 1994–May 2000
Namibia	April 1989–March 1990	East Timor	Oct. 1999–May 2002
Angola	May 1991–Feb. 1995	**EUROPE**	
Somalia	April 1992–March 1993	Former Yugoslavia	Feb. 1992–March 1995
Mozambique	Dec. 1992–Dec. 1994	Croatia	March 1995–Jan. 1996
Somalia	March 1993–March 1995	Former Yugoslavia	March 1995–Feb. 1999
Rwanda/Uganda	June 1993–Sept. 1994	Rep. of Macedonia	
Liberia	Sept. 1993–Sept. 1997	Bosnia & Herzegovina	Dec. 1995–Dec. 2002
Rwanda	Oct. 1993–March 1996	Croatia	Jan. 1996–Jan. 1998
Chad/Libya	May–June 1994	Croatia	Jan. 1998–Oct. 1998
Angola	Feb. 1995–June 1997		
Angola	June 1997–Feb. 1999		

Source: United Nations Department of Peacekeeping Operations. Available at www.un.org/Depts/dpko/dpko/ops.htm.

U.N. peacekeeping operations witnessed only 15 missions; while in the next 18 years, the number of U.N. peace missions nearly tripled.

What explains the rise of U.N. peacekeeping missions? There are two reasons, both related to the end of the Cold War. First, the end of the Cold War made former Cold War rivals more likely to agree (rather than conflict) over involvement in such ventures. Second, after the Cold War, governments that were previously supported by the United States or the Soviet Union were overthrown. Examples of this second point include the flaring up of ethnic conflict in the Balkans, and power vacuums in the Middle East (leading to Iraq's invasion of Kuwait in 1990) and Africa. Peacekeeping operations were needed to stabilize these countries (the United Nations in the Middle East and Africa; NATO in the Balkans).

With the expansion of missions has come an expansion in costs. Prior to 1989, the United Nations spent about $200 million annually on peacekeeping. Since 1989, peacekeeping costs have risen, creeping to a little over $3 billion in the early 1990s.[43] Table 6.4 shows, overall, the estimated U.N. expenditures on peacekeeping operations from 1975 to 2003.

6.6.2 Peacekeeping as a Public Good

A **public good** is a good that is neither excludable nor rival. A good is *excludable* if people can be prevented from using the good. A good is *rival* if one person's use of a good diminishes another person's ability to enjoy a good. A country's national defense is held up as a typical example of a public good. If a country is secure from foreign aggressors, it is impossible to prevent a single member of the nation from enjoying that protection, even if that person did not pay taxes. Also, one person enjoying the benefit of national defense does not diminish the ability of another person to benefit from national defense. Are peacekeeping operations public goods, just like national defense?

Excludable: Peacekeeping provides peace, which benefits all nations, even those not contributing to the operation. [44] Because it is impossible to prevent a nation from benefiting from the peacekeeping operation, peacekeeping is a non-excludable good and is subject to the **free-riding problem** (where a person chooses to let other people pay for a good from which he or she also benefits). As a consequence of the free-riding problem, nations will rely on other nations to contribute the funds and troops for a peacekeeping mission.

Rival: Classifying a peacekeeping operation according to the operation's rival characteristics is slightly more complicated. For example, if NATO sends peacekeepers to Afghanistan, the fact that Pakistan (a neighbor to Afghanistan) benefits from peace in Afghanistan does

Table 6.4
U.N. Expenditures on Peacekeeping
(millions of current year U.S. $)

Year	Expenditure	Year	Expenditure	Year	Expenditure
1975	101.8	1986	183.7	1997	1,226.0
1976	134.6	1987	180.4	1998	907.0
1977	120.5	1988	205.5	1999	1,100.0
1978	213.9	1989	568.5	2000	1,800.0
1979	221.9	1990	388.9	2001	2,500.0
1980	190.0	1991	421.3	2002	2,284.0
1981	212.4	1992	1,676.0	2003	2,260.0
1982	248.9	1993	2,900.0		
1983	229.5	1994	3,500.0		
1984	212.4	1995	3,200.0		
1985	213.6	1996	1,350.0		

Source of data: 1975–1996 from Sandler, Todd and Hartley, Keith. *The Political Economy of NATO.* New York: Cambridge University Press, 1999, p. 90. 1997–2003 from Renner, Michael. "Peacekeeping Operations Expenditures: 1947–2003." *Global Policy Forum.* Available at www.globalpolicy.org/finance/tables/pko/expend.htm.

not diminish the ability of Iran (another neighbor of Afghanistan) to benefit from peace in Afghanistan. Alternatively, consider a country like Iraq. If NATO has committed extensive resources to Afghanistan, then Iraq—like all other countries—benefits from a stable Afghanistan. However, if Iraq also needs NATO peacekeeping forces, the NATO countries may lack the resources to supply the forces. Therefore, rivalry does exist with regard to the peacekeeping forces. This rivalry factor makes the forces used in a peacekeeping operation a **common resource,** rather than a public good (goods that are non-excludable, but *are* rival). Hence, the act of carrying out a peacekeeping operation is a public good. But the forces used to conduct the operation are a common resource.

Evidence: Sandler and Hartley (1999) argue that to determine whether peacekeeping operations do indeed fit the definition of a public good, one should look for evidence of disproportionate burden-sharing in terms of the percentage of income a country contributes to peacekeeping. Using data from 1980 through 1994, Sandler and Hartley rank the GDP and peacekeeping expenditures as a percent of GDP for 16 NATO members. In the 1980s, there is very little evidence that GDP and peacekeeping expenditures were related. For the 1990s, by contrast, it is found that the countries with the larger economies (as measured by GDP) spent a larger proportion of their money on peacekeeping operations. This difference between decades suggests that as peacekeeping missions became more prominent, major economic countries were required to carry more of the peacekeeping burden.[45]

The relationship between economic size and peacekeeping budget contributions is noticeable in the United Nations as well. In the 1990s, the bulk of peacekeeping was financed by the five permanent members of the Security Council (63 percent) and 22 other developed countries who were non-permanent members of the Security Council (35 percent). The primary contributors to U.N. peacekeeping funding since 1990 have been the United States, the United Kingdom, and France (see Table 6.5). Consequently, because peacekeeping operations are a public good, they are economically inefficient for countries to provide.[46]

6.6.3 Marginal Cost/Marginal Benefits of Peacekeeping

Evaluating the economic cost/benefits of deploying peacekeeping should be considered from two perspectives: that of the contributing country and that of the United Nations.

Table 6.5
U.N. Peacekeeping Funding 1991–1998
(constant 1998 U.S. $)

	1994	1995	1996	1997–98
US	1.08	0.43	0.29	0.3
France	0.15	0.27	0.09	0.07
UK	0.23	0.24	0.1	0.07

Source of data: Report on Allied Contributions to the Common Defense (1999) in Hentges, Harriet and Coicaud, Jean-Marc. "Dividends of Peace: The Economics of Peacekeeping." *Journal of International Affairs.* Spring 2002, p. 357.

Contributing country's perspective: Though the United States may be the largest contributor to the funding for U.N. peacekeeping, it does not contribute the most troops. This lack of troop contribution is because, from the U.S. perspective, it is economically inefficient for the United States to contribute troops. The United Nations reimburses countries contributing troops to peacekeeping operations at a flat rate of $1,000 per month for each soldier deployed. The cost of deploying one U.S. soldier can approach $4,500 per month. Consequently, for countries such as the United States, the **marginal benefit** (the additional benefit, measured in dollars, gained by an actor when it obtains—or in this case, contributes—one more of some item) of these operations is lower than the **marginal cost** (the additional cost, measured in dollars, incurred by an actor when it obtains or contributes one more of something). This is because such countries send well-trained troops. In contrast, countries sending poorly trained or less capital-intensive troops could spend as little as $300 per month deploying a troop.

Therefore, it should not come as a surprise that during 1994, for instance, the 10-largest troop contributors were, in descending order: Pakistan, France, India, Bangladesh, the United Kingdom, Jordan, Malaysia, Canada, Egypt, and Poland. In 1997, the top troop contributors, in descending order, were Pakistan, India, Russia, Bangladesh, Jordan, Poland, Canada, Brazil, Finland, and Austria. In 1998, the top troop contributors, in descending order, were Poland, Bangladesh, Austria, Ghana, Ireland, Norway, Argentina, Nepal, Fiji, and the United States. In short, for the United States and other developed countries, a marginal cost greater than a marginal monetary benefit is another example of peacekeeping proving to be an economically inefficient endeavor for such a country.[47]

The U.N.'s perspective: Though soldiers from developed countries are more expensive than soldiers from poorer nations, recall that higher-paid soldiers have a higher marginal productivity of labor (refer to the military labor market model in Chapter 4). Therefore, soldiers from developed countries should be much more capable than soldiers from poorer countries. For example, in 1999 the rebel forces and government of Sierra Leone signed the Lome peace accord. The United Nations sent a peacekeeping force into Sierra Leone at the beginning of 2000 in order to enforce the peace agreement. However, the U.N. forces, comprised mostly of troops from sub-Saharan Africa, the Middle East, and South Asia, had little experience either working together or carrying out peacekeeping missions. The peace deal soon broke down and the U.N. peacekeeping force was unable to stop the advance of rebel troops on the government. In fact, several of the peacekeeping-force members were taken hostage. The situation stabilized only when the United Kingdom sent British troops to support the peacekeepers and train the Sierra Leone army.[48]

In fact, from the perspective of the global economy, effective peacekeeping is an extremely economically efficient policy. Extrapolating from the British experience in Sierra Leone, it is estimated that military intervention in a dozen similar countries—once conflict has ended (so as to maintain the peace)—would cost $4.8 billion, but the intervention may generate economic gains of approximately $397 billion.[49]

Summary: It is now possible to understand why the United States is wary to engage in peacekeeping operations, even if the operation does not place soldiers in an overtly hostile location. Despite the fact that peacekeeping can generate economic benefits for the global economy, the free-rider problem and marginal cost greater than marginal benefit both mean peacekeeping is an economically inefficient use of U.S. military resources.

6.7 KEY POINTS

Key Macroeconomic Points:

- Civil wars have not only become more frequent, but have also grown longer.
- Civil wars not only leave the inflicted country poorer, but they also damage the economies of neighboring countries.
- Civil wars contribute to a country's external indebtedness

Key Microeconomic Points:

- Civil wars are primarily the result of economic factors such as poverty, horizontal inequality, and primary-product dependence.
- The small arms market is actually three markets: initial export market, secondary market, and black market.
- The forces of supply and demand mean that the price of an AK-47 can serve to indicate the degree of hostilities in a country.
- Peacekeeping operations are public goods (non-exclusive and non-rival). But peacekeeping forces are a common resource (non-exclusive, but rival).
- Peacekeeping operations are economically inefficient for the United States and other developed countries, because the marginal cost of military operations exceeds the marginal benefit.

Key Terms:

Vertical inequality	Peacekeeping
Horizontal inequality	Peacemaking
Primary commodities	Public good
Opportunity cost	Excludable
Genocide	Free-riding problem
Secondary arms market	Rival
Black market	Common resource
Proxy wars	Marginal benefit
External debt/export earnings ratio	Marginal cost

Key Questions:

1. Why does vertical-income inequality typically not start civil wars?
2. Why do civil wars commonly have a negative impact on neighboring countries?
3. In and of itself, can primary-commodity export dependence lead to civil war?
4. Why would people view the civil war in southern Sudan as a religiously driven conflict?
5. It has been shown that, with regard to the consideration of marginal benefit and marginal cost, the United States should not be involved in peacekeeping operations. However, are there any other economic arguments that can be made for the United States to involve itself in peacekeeping operations?

Endnotes

1. Churchill (1953), p. 430.
2. The Global Menace of Local Strife." Special report in *The Economist*. May 24, 2003, p. 23.
3. Collier and Hoeffler (2004), p. 8.
4. Collier (1999), p. 9.

5. "The Global Menace of Local Strife." Special report in *The Economist,* May 24, 2003, p. 25.
6. See Collier and Hoeffler (2002a) and Humphreys (2003).
7. "The Global Menace of Local Strife." Special report in *The Economist,* May 24, 2003, p. 24.
8. See Fearon and Laitin (2003), pp. 14–15.
9. De Soya (2000), p. 116 and Collier (2000), p. 94.
10. Collier and Hoeffler (2002b), p. 10.
11. "The Global Menace of Local Strife." Special Report in *The Economist,* May 24, 2003, p. 24.
12. Ibid., p. 6.
13. Found in Humphreys (2003), pp. 4–5.
14. Collier and Hoeffler (2004), p. 17.
15. From the RUF's key ideological document "Footpaths through the Forest" cited in Humphreys (2003), p. 5. Note: the NPRC (National Provisional Ruling Council) was the ruling authority in Sierra Leone during the early and middle 1990s.
16. Humphreys (2003), p. 4 warns of the pejorative consequences of using the term "greed."
17. Collier (2000), p. 104.
18. Mwanasali (2000), p. 145.
19. Duffield (2000), p. 82.
20. Information for this paragraph from "The Global Menace of Local Strife." Special report in *The Economist,* May 24, 2003, pp. 24–25.
21. See Collier (2000), pp 101–103.
22. Prunier, Gérard. *The Rwandan Crisis: History of a Genocide.* New York: Columbia University Press, 1995, pp. 231–232. Cited in Mueller (2004), pp. 98–99.
23. Collier (2000), p. 7.
24. Ibid., pp. 11- 14.
25. Humphreys (2003), p. 4.
26. Stewart (2000), pp. 252–253.
27. Ibid., p. 8.
28. Ibid., p. 8.
29. Chivers, C.J. "Who's a Pirate? Russia Points Back at the U.S." *The New York Times,* July 26, 2003, p. A1.
30. Oxfam. *Up in Arms: Controlling the International Trade in Small Arms.* Paper for the UN Conference on the Illicit Trade in Small Arms and Light Weapons in All Its Aspects. January 2001, p. 2, available at: www.oxfam.org.uk/what_we_do/issues/conflict_disasters/up_in_arms.htm.
31. Peck (2002)
32. Ibid.
33. Oxfam. *Up in Arms: Controlling the International Trade in Small Arms.* Paper for the UN Conference on the Illicit Trade in Small Arms and Light Weapons in All Its Aspects. January 2001. p. 2 available at: www.oxfam.org.uk/what_we_do/issues/conflict_disasters/up_in_arms.htm.
34. U.N. Secretary-General Kofi Annan. "Small Arms, Big Problems." *International Herald Tribune,* July 10, 2001. Peck (2002).
35. U.N. Secretary-General Kofi Annan. "Small Arms, Big Problems." *International Herald Tribune.* July 10, 2001. For instructors wishing to offer a more detailed account relating to the economics of the causes, consequences, and responses to the conflict in Sierra Leone, please refer to Davies (2000).
36. Adapted from Keen in Stewart and Fitzgerald. (2001), vol. 2, pp. 155–163.

37. Stewart and Fitzgerald (2001), vol. 2. p. 15.

38. For an excellent and easy-to-follow discussion of the conflict's background, see the BBC's World Analysis of Sudan. February 21, 1999. available at news.bbc.co.uk/1/hi/world/africa/84927.stm.

39. Lacy, Marc. "In Sudan, Militiamen on Horses Uproot a Million." *The New York Times,* May 4, 2004.

40. Sandler and Hartley (1999), p. 92.

41. Ibid., p. 90.

42. Ibid., p. 102.

43. Ibid., p. 108.

44. Hentges and Coicaud (2001), pp. 356–357.

45. Figures from Sandler and Hartley (1999), p. 101.

46. "Q&A: Sierra Leone's Troubles." *BBC NEWS,* June 1, 2000. Available at http://news.bbc.co.uk/1/hi/world/africa/737323.stm.

47. Collier and Hoeffler (2004), p. 21.

Chapter 7

Terrorism

7.1 INTRODUCTION

In the past, most American adults viewed the colors red, orange, and yellow as simply three of the seven primary colors taught to the average elementary school student. Today, the colors are known as the terrorist alert system. Specifically, they now signify the three highest threat levels on the U.S. Department of Homeland Security's color-coded system (representing, respectively, Severe, High, and Elevated). The threat level, reported each day on the news, is a constant reminder to all Americans that the possibility of a terrorist attack, though less likely than a serious car accident on the way to work, is ever-present.

Given that alterations in the country's threat level can influence people's travel plans, delay their movement through security checkpoints, and force cities to put more police on the streets, the economic implications of a terrorist threat are quite evident. For example, when the terror level was raised in New York and Washington in early August of 2004, Senator Charles Schumer of New York had to remind people that, "If every time they made a threat we stopped doing what we're doing, they'd win; and so we feel it's almost a moral imperative for everybody to go about their jobs." [1] Because terrorism is predicated not only on the destruction of an enemy, but also on influencing that enemy's behavior (particularly its ability to work), no text on the economics of war would be complete without this topic.

Sections 2 and 3 define terrorism and examine how frequently it occurs. Section 4 uses economic tools to understand why individuals join terrorist groups, why these groups resort to violence, and why some members of these groups attempt suicide bombing. Section 5 details the financial underpinnings of terrorist organizations. Finally, Section 6 offers an analysis of how terrorist incidents, such as the September 11, 2001 attacks on the United States, impact economies.

7.2 DEFINITION OF TERRORISM

Terrorism is a term heard widely, but few actually know what it means. For instance, how does one know whether a person should be classified as a "terrorist," a "rebel," a "patriot," or just a regular "soldier"? Terrorism will be defined as:

> "The premeditated, politically motivated violence perpetrated against non-combatant targets by sub-national groups or clandestine agents, to influence or intimidate a large audience beyond that of the immediate victims, and involving citizens or territory of more than one country." [2]

Let's take a moment to reflect on the phrases used in this definition.

Premeditated...

A terrorist attack is intentional, and planned in advance. It is not an extemporaneous, unplanned skirmish that breaks out in the midst of a heated argument, nor is it rioting by an angry mob.

...politically motivated...

If a robber or serial killer is seeking to do harm for monetary gain (or simply for the sake of inducing fear), then these individuals are not terrorists. The act must have some political objective (such as a grievance over the removal of land, or disenfranchisement).

...against noncombatants...

The U.S. government has interpreted noncombatants to include not just civilians, but also military personnel that are unarmed or not on duty. The term also covers military installations or armed military personnel when a state of military hostilities does not exist at the site of the terrorist attacks.

...sub-national groups or clandestine agents...

This phrase refers to groups not recognized as a country. Examples would be the Provisional Wing of the Irish Republican Army in Ireland, Hamas (Islamic Resistance Movement) in Palestine, Kahane Chai in Israel, or Al-Qaeda internationally. Therefore, a country cannot carry out a terrorist attack (but it can sponsor a terrorist group).

...influence or intimidate a large audience beyond that of the immediate victims...

Terrorist attacks are intended to send a message, not to the direct victims, but to the public or to policy makers. Terrorism is a powerful tool, not because of the direct damage it creates, but by the fear it promotes.

...involving citizens or territory of more than one country.

This final portion of the definition shows the focus of this text: international terrorism. Therefore, this text will examine those attacks where the perpetrator and the victim are of different nationalities, or where the perpetrators carry out an attack in a country other than their country of origin. Examples would include Colombian rebels kidnapping foreign aid workers, a Hamas suicide bomber destroying a bus in Jerusalem, or an Al-Qaeda bombing in Madrid, Spain. The highway shooter in Columbus, Ohio in 2003 and the Oklahoma City bombing in 1995 are not included.

7.3 INCIDENTS AND TRENDS IN INTERNATIONAL TERRORISM

How many incidents can be classified as international terrorism? Figure 7.1 depicts the trends in international terrorism incidents and the fatalities attributed to these incidents. It covers from 1968 (the first year in which the U.S. State Department considered an incident of international terrorism to have occurred) to 2003.

Three features of Figure 7.1 are notable. First, the incidents and fatalities are marked by short-term cycles. One year will produce a spike in incidents, followed by a dropoff in the subsequent year. This cycling effect results from the evolution between terrorist techniques and government responses to those techniques. For instance, terrorists will initially hijack airplanes. As the government improves the defense mechanisms in airports, this defense method will initially cause a reduction in terrorist incidents. However, the

Figure 7.1

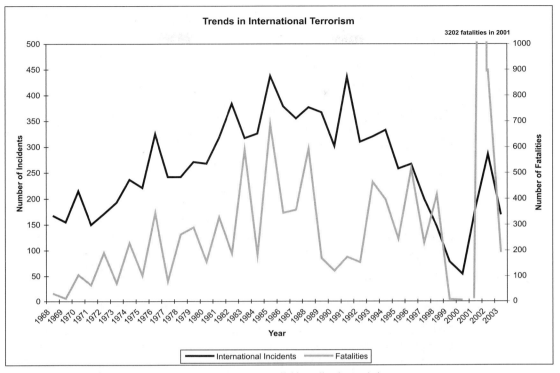

Source of data: RAND-MIPT Terrorism Incident Database. Available at db.mipt.org/mipt.

terrorists will eventually adopt new tactics, thereby creating a new spike in the number of incidents. This spike, in turn, provokes another government response.

Second, there is a noticeable, single long-term cycle in incidents over the past 30 years. There was a gradual rise of incidents in the early 1980s, which peaked in the late 1980s. Since then, there has been a gradual decline. This long-term cycle is attributable to the improved methods, techniques, and security measures that governments have employed against terrorists since the 1970s.

The third feature of Figure 7.1 is that since the mid-1990s, terrorist attacks have become more efficient. Specifically, the number of fatalities has grown to the point where the fatalities now consistently surpass the number of incidents each year. Social scientists pose two explanations for the increased efficiency of terrorist attacks, one economic and one political.

7.3.1 Substitution Effect

When selecting a target to attack, terrorists act rationally, according to Enders and Sandler (2000). In particular, when government policies raise the barriers to successful attack, terrorists will move to alternatives. For example, the tightening of security measures at embassies and government buildings provoked terrorists to turn to aircraft hijacking. As airports installed metal detectors, this provoked terrorists to select less-protected, civilian **soft targets** (targets such as malls, hotels, and public spaces). Because more civilians are present at soft targets, then one attack will result in more deaths.[3]

7.3.2 Rise of Religious Radicalism

Another important factor contributing to the increased efficiency of terrorist attacks relates to the changing motives of terrorists since the November 1979 takeover of the U.S. embassy in Tehran and the Soviet invasion of Afghanistan in the same period.[4] Specifically, U.S. forces taught groups fighting the Soviets in Afghanistan (including Al-Qaeda) many combat techniques. The extent that these groups acquired information, material, and skills, coupled with the chance to successfully practice against a real adversary, eventually enhanced their ability to carry out effective terrorist strikes. Furthermore, the eventual Soviet withdrawal, coupled with the overthrow of the U.S.-backed Shah of Iran, served as emboldening examples that radical groups could "defeat" a superpower.

7.4   IS TERRORISM RATIONAL?

Most people would not think of using terrorism to achieve some political end. For example, great civil rights leaders such as Dr. Martin Luther King, Jr., and Nelson Mandela denounced violence, instead choosing to employ methods of protest, boycott, non-cooperation, and civil disobedience. Most perplexing, why will people willingly become suicide bombers? As irrational as the behavior seems, it is thought reasonable by the terrorists.

7.4.1   Motivations to Join or Form a Terrorist Group

Public goods in failed states: [5] According to research by Eli Berman (2004), terrorist organizations, particularly those of a religious bent, often provide their members public goods that the state may not be able to supply. These goods include mutual insurance, education, and even law and order. Consider Hamas, which provided health care and schooling to Palestinians, or Hezbollah, which ran soup kitchens in Lebanon. Berman points to **failed states** (locations where public services are paltry or nonexistent, such as Somalia) as likely places where extremists will try to fill the gap in public services. In well-functioning countries, terrorists cannot maintain this role. Consider Gush Emunim, a movement of orthodox Jews that gave rise to the Jewish Underground and formed an Israeli militia that was active in the late 1970s and early 1980s. Like most extremist groups, it tightly regulated its members' lives, from their dress to their housing arrangements. However, this group failed to maintain its strength, most likely because it was composed of citizens of Israel, a country with a well-functioning government. Therefore, the extremist group was not the sole supplier of public goods to its members.

These groups finance their public goods by prohibiting work outside the group and expenses on activities deemed wasteful pleasures. These prohibitions are a kind of tax. Similar to how government taxes finance public services, the prohibitions keep both human and financial resources devoted to the group and its provision of services. A member's willingness to "pay" the prohibition "tax" also demonstrates commitment to the group (demonstration of devotion to the group can also include studying holy texts for years, or committing acts of destruction).

Of course, there are exceptions to this theory, such as Saudi Arabia. Despite a rich government that provides generous services, extremist activity persists. Another exception seems to be some of Al-Qaeda's terrorists, who have been neither poor nor deprived of public goods. Therefore, there must be additional explanations for the creation of terrorist groups.

Table 7.1

Comparison of Educational Distribution for Palestinian Suicide Bombers and Palestinian Population of Comparable Age

	Suicide Bombers	Palestinian Population
Poverty Rate	13%	33%
More than High School Education	57%	15%

Source of data: Krueger A. and Maleková, Jitka. "Education, Poverty and Terrorism: Is There a Causal Connection?" *Journal of Economic Perspectives,* Fall 2003, pp. 119–144, Figure 2 .

Lack of civil liberties: [6] Though poverty is surely a contributing factor to terrorism as a method, the stereotype that terrorists are driven to extremes by economic deprivation is flawed. Consider the Middle East. It has been found that only 13 percent of Palestinian suicide bombers are from impoverished families, while about a third of the Palestinian population lives in poverty. Fully 57 percent of suicide bombers have some education beyond high school, compared with just 15 percent of the Palestinian population of comparable age (see Table 7.1).

To further examine the claim that terrorists are drawn from society's elites, rather than the dispossessed, Krueger and Maleková (2003) analyzed State Department data on significant international terrorist incidents. In this data, the home countries of the perpetrators of each incident are identified. Looking at the nationality of the terrorists, there is a tendency for terrorists to come from poor countries, rather than rich ones. However, Kruger and Maleková find that more terrorists come from poor countries because those countries tend to lack civil liberties. They found that once a country's degree of civil liberties is taken into account (measured by Freedom House, a nonprofit organization, which looks at the extent to which citizens are free to develop views, institutions, and personal autonomy without interference from the state) income bears no relation to involvement in terrorism. Apart from the size of a country and the extent of its civil liberties, they found no other factor—including the literacy rate, infant mortality rate, terrain, ethnic divisions, and religious fractionalization—could predict whether people from that country were more or less likely to take part in international terrorism.

This finding suggests that the freedom to assemble and protest peacefully without interference from the government provides an alternative to terrorist actions; and that a country like Saudi Arabia, which is relatively economically well off, is more likely to spawn terrorists than a poor country with a tradition of protecting civil liberties. In short, terrorist attacks may increase in a repressive regime whenever the political situation is not heading in a direction the extremists prefer, regardless of the country's economic health.

7.4.2 Modeling the Choice of Terrorism

It is possible to use economic analysis (i.e., seeing how people behave when faced with certain incentives) to understand terrorism. Game theory, introduced in Chapter 3, can be used to explain the behavior of people faced with choices. Specifically, a **game tree** or **extended form game** will be used.[7] A game tree is a visual model that depicts not only the choices faced by an individual, but also the sequence in which those choices are made.

The game's setup: When setting up a game tree, it is important to make some assumptions. For this game tree, four assumptions will be made:

1. There is a group of wealth-maximizing individuals who wish to alter the status quo (perhaps they are unsatisfied with the level of public goods they presently receive).
2. An individual must be alive to change the status quo and, therefore, death is suboptimal for all legal or nonlegal actions. This assumption controls for suicide bombers, or the martyrdom benefits associated with government executions.
3. Any activity, legal or illegal, will generate media attention. This assumption simplifies the analysis by eliminating the possibility of the media failing to cover a government-sanctioned protest.
4. The degree of personal freedoms bestowed upon each individual of a populace is uniform. This assumption eliminates the possibility of government bias toward particular groups. Personal freedoms can be either high (groups are allowed to peacefully protest) or low (groups are not allowed to protest).

The model: Figure 7.2 shows the decisions of a group, called *I*, and the government, called *G*. Each point at which either the group or the government makes a decision is represented by a dot or **node.**

The group initially has three courses of action. They can do nothing to change the status quo. They can try to change the status quo through legal means, or they can try to change the status quo through illegal means. If the group chooses legal means, lobbying the government may go largely unnoticed by the government; while even a small protest can generate media attention. Therefore, protesting is considered less costly for the group than lobbying. Because achieving objectives through illegal means can negatively stigmatize the group in the eyes of the international community, the group will pursue legal means and (by accounting for costs) will protest.

However, if the government does not permit the exercise of legal means, then protesting becomes impossible. This government role will move the group directly to the "node" offering the choice of illegal means or no action. If group *I* perceives the status quo as

Figure 7.2
Why Individuals Join Terrorist Groups

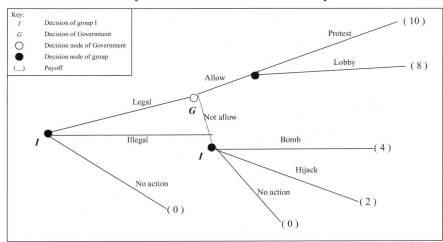

intolerable, then it will choose to take action through illegal means. Having chosen to take illegal action, the group now has two methods through which it can have its message heard—bombing or hijacking.

If government defense expenditures are adequate, hijacking is the most costly method, a factor that also makes hijacking the least attractive method. For instance, metal detectors, bolted doors, and armed pilots raise the per-incident cost of skyjacking above other hostage-taking methods. Also, the logistical complexity of securing, monitoring, and/or transporting hostages gives all hostage incidents a higher per-incident cost than bombing. Therefore, in order to minimize costs, the group will choose to engage in a bombing rather than hijacking.

It is now possible to construct **payoffs** for the scenarios considered. Payoffs are number categories that indicate how much the group values the result of its decisions. Higher numbers suggest a more valuable payoff. Assuming the status quo has the lowest payoff, if a group **discounts the future** (i.e., takes the future consequences of actions into consideration) and seeks to minimize costs, the payoffs for each scenario would be ordered as follows:

$$Status\ quo < hijacking < bombing < lobbying < protesting,$$

meaning hijacking is favored over the status quo, bombing is favored over hijacking, and so on. Assigning numerical payoffs to each scenario generates:

$$0 < 2 < 4 < 8 < 10$$

The core lessons of this model should be clear—a group that cares about its public image will pursue legal recourse, unless a lack of civil liberties eliminates this option. At that point, it will resort to bombing, as it is the lowest-cost option.

There are exceptions to this model. First, consider Iran, a country with limited civil liberties, particularly towards women. Shirin Ebadi, the 2003 winner of the Nobel Peace Prize, continues to protest the Iranian government's policies towards women through literature and legalism, rather than violence. Second, Timothy McVeigh chose to bomb the Oklahoma Federal Building as a statement of his dissatisfaction with the U.S. government, even though he was free to organize a rally, write an editorial, or file a petition. Such exceptions aside, the model nevertheless illustrates the general choices and behavior of individuals faced with a lack of civil liberties.

7.4.3   Is Suicide Bombing Rational?[8]

Committing suicide is irrational to most. However, even rational people may consider it. As such, the rationality of suicide may consist not in the "content" of the action, but in the reason for conducting the action.

Autonomy and solidarity: Assume that an individual has a certain set of beliefs; and, corresponding to this set of beliefs, a certain identity. This identity is the individual's **autonomy.** An organization can give an individual a sense of belonging to a community. An organization promotes "belonging" by holding events where the individual can get to know others in the organization. The group provides a framework of beliefs that the individual can adopt and identify with. When a person joins an organization, part of the "price" of admission to that organization is that he or she must adopt and demonstrate adherence to the beliefs sanctioned by the group. These cohesive actions represent the person's **solidarity** with the group.

From the organization's point of view, the more united the membership is in its beliefs, the greater the willingness of the members to sacrifice their time, energy, and resources in support of the goals of the organization. Consequently, *individuals face a tradeoff between autonomy and solidarity.*

Autonomy and solidarity as essential goods: Think of *autonomy* and *solidarity* as being two **essential goods.** An essential good is a good that is indispensable (as needed as water and air). With an essential good, there is no price that is too high for the person to pay for the good. Figure 7.3 depicts an individual's preference for solidarity on the horizontal axis and preference for autonomy on the vertical axis, when both are perceived as essential goods. The downward sloping line, *AB,* represents a **budget constraint line.** The budget constraint line shows, all things being equal, the possible bundles of *autonomy* and *solidarity* that an individual can possibly achieve, given his or her personal resources (personal experiences and self-esteem). "Personal resources" seems like a vague concept, but simply realize that point *B* depicts the maximum autonomy that this particular individual can attain and point *A* depicts the maximum solidarity that this individual can obtain. Any combination of solidarity and autonomy below (or on) the budget constraint line is an **attainable bundle** (a combination of the two goods that a person has the ability to obtain). The indifference curve, IC_1, is a standard concave indifference curve (meaning it bends inward), like that curve presented in the arms race section of Chapter 3. However, instead of depicting a country's preferences for bundles of perceived security and butter, it now depicts an individual's preferences for bundles of *autonomy* and *solidarity.* Notice that IC_1 touches neither the vertical nor the horizontal axis. This nonintersection means that IC_1 represents *autonomy* and *solidarity* as being essential goods.

Point *C* shows the location at which the indifference curve is tangent to the budget constraint line. This point shows the bundle of autonomy and solidarity that the individual thinks is best. Recall from the arms race discussion in Chapter 3 that the space created by the solidarity and autonomy axes is full of indifference curves. For now, IC_1 is the only important indifference curve. We ignore the indifference curves below IC_1 because they represent bundles of solidarity and autonomy that are not as good as those offered by IC_1.

Figure 7.3
The Solidarity and Autonomy Tradeoff

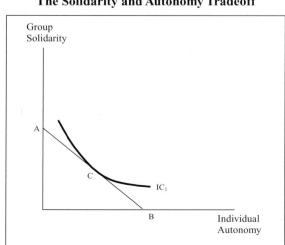

We ignore the indifference curves above IC_1 because they represent bundles of solidarity and autonomy that, given the budget constraint line, are unobtainable. Therefore, a rational individual would want to be on the highest indifference curve possible, while still touching the budget constraint line.

Autonomy as an inessential good: Refer to Figure 7.4, which illustrates a person's wish for complete solidarity. An individual must be willing to trade some autonomy for solidarity, if he or she wishes to join the organization. The group would ideally wish for the individual to be in complete solidarity with the group. Thus the organization would like the individual to view solidarity as an essential good and view autonomy as an **inessential good** (a good for which none will be bought, if the price for it becomes high enough). If autonomy is viewed as an inessential good, then this means there is a price for autonomy that is high enough to provoke the individual not to want it. Hence, he or she would no longer strive for autonomy. This situation is depicted in Figure 7.4. In this figure, the indifference curve IC_2 intersects the vertical axis. This graph shows that it is possible for the individual to consume no autonomy (represented by point A). This scenario is called a **corner solution.** A corner solution is when an individual will consume a positive quantity of one good and zero quantity of the other good.

But how can autonomy ever be viewed as an inessential good? The ability of the organization to convert new members is a function of the charisma of the leader, as well as the group's rituals, reputation, prestige, and resources. Resources are particularly important, if the group's main attraction is its ability to supply public goods. Let's say that the individual chooses more group solidarity over autonomy. Then (because he or she has given up some autonomy), he or she has also given up some ability and capacity to choose. As the individual loses some of the desire to have his or her own interests, he or she begins to think more and more along the lines of the group's interest. Because solidarity is in the

Figure 7.4
The Solidarity Corner Solution

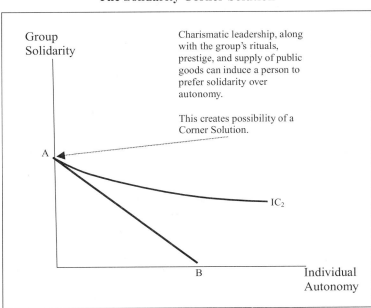

best interest of the group, the person begins to prefer even more solidarity. As the person begins to prefer more and more solidarity, the process becomes self-reinforcing. In other words, there is now a point (point A) at which the person would prefer no autonomy and all solidarity. Hence, to this person, autonomy has become an inessential good.

Therefore, once a person views autonomy as an inessential good, that person's interests may become completely those of the group (zero autonomy attained). Once this total transition occurs, a person will carry out an action that maximizes the group's well-being. If the group must resort to bombing (given Figure 7.2), then, from the group's perspective, suicide bombing is one of the most economical forms of attack. **Cost-benefit analysis** (comparing the cost and benefits of an action, in order to find the optimal action) can illustrate why bombing by suicide is economically effective.

Cost-benefits of suicide bombing:[9] Suicide bombing first emerged in Lebanon in 1983, but it has become an increasingly common occurrence in Israel, particularly since the start of the 2000 Palestinian *intifada* (uprising). Palestinian suicide bombers have taken nuts, bolts, screws, ball bearings, and metal shards or bits of broken machinery and packed them together with homemade explosives. This bomb package (usually in the form of a belt) is then strapped onto the body of a willing group member who is then dispatched to any place where people gather—bus stops, train stations, restaurants, cafés, supermarkets, shopping malls, or street corners. The attacker does not need an escape plan—often the most difficult aspect of a terrorist operation—and the attacks are accurate and deadly.

According to data from the Rand Corporation, suicide attacks on average kill four times as many people as other terrorist acts. Once more, a typical suicide bus bombing in Israel costs no more than perhaps $150 to carry out. Hence, it has been frequently considered the "poor man's smart bomb."

Therefore, if a group member's interests are completely aligned with that of the group's, then he or she will be willing to carry out a suicide bombing because it is an action that maximizes the group's well-being. Additionally, once a person reaches a state where his or her own self-interests are irrelevant, the individual is theoretically indifferent to life or death. At this point, the person, in theory, could be swayed to live or die with even the smallest of financial incentives. Therefore, financial incentives of $10,000 to $25,000 to the families of suicide bombers, offered by extremist Islamic charities and even from the Iraq regime under Saddam Hussein, have been enough to sway a person to commit a suicide attack.[10]

7.5 TERRORIST FINANCING

Much like the conflicts of states, the militant actions of terrorist organizations require financing. Table 7.2 shows the estimated annual financial flows of a selection of Arab Islamic terrorist organizations. Though these sums pale in comparison to the financial resources available to states, given the low cost of terrorist operations, the amounts are still significant.

Disrupting this financing is the key to neutralizing terrorist organizations. However, the small sum of money necessary for individual terrorist attacks is only the first of several problems facing the financial institutions and the international organizations (like the International Monetary Fund, IMF, and the Financial Action Task Force division, FATF) who attempt to stop terrorist financing.

The second problem is that terrorist financing is different from **money laundering** (the process criminal organizations use to disguise the origin of illegally obtained money).[11]

Table 7.2
Overview of Annual Financial Flows of Select Arab Islamic Terror Organizations

Name	Estimated Financial Flows (2001–2002) millions of U.S. $
Al-Qaeda	20–50
Front Islamique du Salut	5
Hamas	10
Hizbullah	50
PKK (Turkey)	10

Source of data: Schneider, F. "Money Supply for Terrorism—The Hidden Financial Flows of Islamic Terrorism Organisations." Berlin, Germany: German Institute for Economic Research (DIW). *The Economic Consequences of Global Terrorism Workshop,* June 14–15, 2002, p. 29.

Overall, the IMF calculates that the total sum of laundered money per year is between U.S. $500 billion and $1.5 trillion. This sum is nearly 5 percent of total world production. Therefore, financial flows of Islamic terrorist organizations only comprise approximately 1 to 5.8 percent of the total sum of laundered money.[12] Problems for regulators arise because whereas money laundering takes illegal money and places it in legal activities, terrorist financing will often take legally obtained money and place it towards illegal activities. Often, because the illegal activity of a terrorist attack has not yet taken place, it is difficult for authorities to know if money is financing terrorists.

The third problem relates to **layers and redundancies**—when money is raised from a variety of sources and moved in a variety of ways so as to obscure the quantity, origin, and destination of the money.[13] Because organizations such as the Irish Republican Army, Hezbollah, and Hamas use financing tactics similar to Al-Qaeda, this section will use Al-Qaeda to describe what is known about the usage of "layering" by terrorist organizations.[14]

7.5.1 Multiple Sources [15]

Table 7.3 lists many of the various sources of terrorist financing and provides an estimate of what fraction of total funding is comprised by each source. Looking at this table, it is clear that terrorists obtain funds from both legitimate (donations) and illegal (drug money) sources.

Legitimate sources: Al-Qaeda's message of radical Islam and disenchantment with the Saudi Arabian monarchy resonates with some legitimate groups. Therefore, these groups become a source of income. Al-Qaeda's finances have been tracked to corporations in Sudan and honey traders in Yemen. Al-Barakaat, a financial intermediary that enabled Somali nationals to send money back to relatives in Somalia (called **remittances**), allowed a portion of the millions of dollars moved through it to be diverted to Al-Qaeda.

Additionally, many devout Muslims give a religious duty of 2.5 percent of their income to humanitarian causes (a responsibility called the *zakat*). In many communities, the *zakat* is often provided in cash to prominent, trusted community leaders or institutions. These community figures then combine and disperse the funds to charities and persons they determine to be worthy. Sadly, though most of the funds are directed to legitimate ends, the unregulated, seldom audited, and undocumented makeup of this system has enabled some of its funds to be obtained by terrorist groups.

Table 7.3
The Sources of Finance for Al-Qaeda and Other Terror Organizations

Source	Percentage of Total Finances (%)
Drug business (mainly transport)	30-35
Donations/tribute payments of governments or wealthy individuals or religious groups	25-30
Classic crime activities (blackmail, kidnapping, ransom)	10-15
Illegal diamond trading	10-15
Additional unknown financial means (legal and illegal)	25-50

Source of data: Schneider, F. "Money Supply for Terrorism—The Hidden Financial Flows of Islamic Terrorism Organisations." Berlin, Germany: German Institute for Economic Research (DIW). *The Economic Consequences of Global Terrorism Workshop,* June 14–15, 2002, p. 28.

Finally, some charities knowingly donate funds to Al-Qaeda. These charities include the Afghan Support Committee in Afghanistan, the Al Rashid Trust in Pakistan, the Revival of Islamic Heritage Society in Kuwait, the Al-Haramain organization in Saudi Arabia, and the Holy Land Foundation for Relief and Development in the United States.

Criminal sources: Smuggling, fraud, and theft have been employed by local terrorist cells to garner funds. In particular, the drug trade has been associated with the financing of many terrorist organizations. For example, the Kurdistan Worker's Party (PKK) in Turkey will tax ethnic Kurdish drug traffickers in order to finance operations.[16] Additionally, some states that provide material and financial support to terrorist organizations obtain a fair portion of revenue from taxing the local drug trade. For instance, the Taliban in Afghanistan imposed a 10 percent tax rate on the cultivation of opium poppy in Afghanistan.[17] It is estimated that in 1999, the drug trade brought at least $40 million to the Taliban government. This sum enabled the Taliban government to survive **international sanctions** (restraints placed by other countries on goods, services, and financial flows entering and leaving a country with the intent of changing the behavior of the inflicted country) imposed on it for offering sanctuary to Al-Qaeda.

Other sources: Other sources of financing to terrorists are unintended on the part of the donor. For example, charities, nongovernmental organizations, mosques, fundraisers, and financial intermediaries (particularly those located in Saudi Arabia) gave money to the **mujahideen** (holy warriors) fighting the Soviets in Afghanistan in the 1980s. These mujahideens then became the Al-Qaeda organization.

Other times, people donate money to the "political wing" of an organization (such as Sinn Fein in Northern Ireland, and Hamas in Palestine), believing the money will not go to the militant wing (the Irish Republican Army or the radical militant groups of Hamas).

Still, there are some who knowingly give funds to a terrorist organization. Some radical members of the Saudi royal family (there are 30,000 members overall), such as the son of King Fahd, Abdul Aziz, give money directly to Al-Qaeda. However, because Aziz also supports many local mosques, his family has been reluctant to stop his actions.[18]

7.5.2   Multiple Transfer Methods

Other than simply transporting the funds by land (which can be used if all other methods fail), terrorist organizations will store and transfer money by exploiting financial districts with limited or no regulation. Districts with limited banking supervision, no anti-laundering laws, ineffective law enforcement, or a no-questions-asked secrecy culture are particularly attractive to terrorist groups. Regionally, examples include financial districts in Kuwait, Bahrain, and the Dubai emirate of the United Arab Emirates. Also, **offshore** financial districts (meaning districts not subject to the laws of a major country) operating in Liechtenstein and the Bahamas have been shown to have transferred funds that eventually financed a terrorist operation.

Additionally, terrorist groups will create their own businesses to transfer the funds. These ventures are known as **front companies.** In front companies, the real, illegal business is covered by an apparently legitimate business located in the "front" of the shop. For example, Al-Qaeda had an agricultural company, a construction business, a transportation business, and two investment companies located in Sudan in 1991. Asma Limited in Kenya and Tanzanite King Jeweler in Tanzania were other Al-Qaeda front companies.[19]

Finally, money is transferred through the loosely regulated, Islamic banking system called *Hawala.*

7.5.3   Case Study: the *Hawala* Network [20]

What it is: The *hawala* system is an ancient, trust-based method of sending money legally across borders. *Hawala* dealers have none of the features commonly associated with banks such as big buildings and uniform paperwork. Their methods date back to first millennium China. There, a system known as *fei qian,* or flying money, allowed people in the southern provinces to pay money to the emperor in the north without the risk of traveling and being robbed.

How it works: In the *hawala* system, there is no physical movement of money. Instead, money is transferred by means of a telephone call or fax between *hawala* dealers in different locations. No legal contracts are involved, and recipients are given only a code number, a verse from the Koran, or a simple token to prove that money is due (see **Example of how it works** below). Over time, transactions in opposite directions cancel each other out, so physical movement is minimized. If an imbalance forms (where one *Hawala* dealer owes a substantial sum to another), cash or jewelry is carried across borders or conventional banks are used. *Hawala* dealers do not charge traditional forms of interest (the Koran's ban on charging prohibitively high interest rates is known as the **riba**) and usually charge a commission of only 1 to 2 percent for a transfer (whereas Western Union charges nearly 15 percent commission). Dealers also can arrange for money to be delivered to people's homes, even in small villages.[21] In short, because the whole system is based on trust, *hawala* can be an inexpensive and efficient worldwide money-transmission service.

Example of how it works:[22] Figure 7.5 provides a visual schematic of how a *hawala* transaction takes place. A client who wishes to transfer a certain sum of money meets with

Figure 7.5
Operation of a *Hawala* Transaction

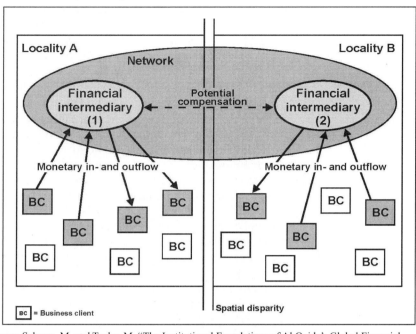

Source: Schram, M. and Taube, M. "The Institutional Foundations of Al Qaida's Global Financial System." Berlin, Germany: German Institute for Economic Research (DIW). *The Economic Consequences of Global Terrorism Workshop*, June 14–15, 2002, p. 5. Reprinted here with permission.

the local *hawala* intermediary in his village, city, or country and tells him the amount of the payment and where and when the payment is to take place. The *hawala* intermediary takes the sum and a small commission and gives the client a code: a simple word, a short combination of numbers, or a particular verse from the Koran. Then the intermediary contacts his partner in the relevant target area and tells him the code and the amount to be paid out. In passing on this information, the *hawala* intermediary in the transaction's place of origin has completed his part. If it had been necessary for him to keep any written record of the transaction up to this time, such records can now be destroyed.

Next, the client tells the code to the recipient of the money, who then goes to the *hawala* intermediary in the target area (whose identity is usually indicated in the code), passes on the code, and accepts payment. Once the payment has been issued, the intermediary in the target area destroys any notes or other indications of the transfer. Such transactions are concluded within 24 hours, leaving no bookkeeping notes or other evidence of the movement of money.

How it prevents opportunism:[23] The system maintains its credibility because, by being simultaneously community and internationally based, information can spread rapidly through the network as to who is trustworthy and who is not. Not only does this method prevent an untrustworthy individual from continuing to use the low-transaction cost system of the *hawala,* it can also cause that person to be ostracized in the local Muslim community. In short, both the client and the *hawala* intermediary, if they wish to continue using the system, have incentives to maintain their reputation.

Impact of system:[24] The largest proportion of people using *hawala* networks are overseas workers sending earnings to their families. Besides the low fees, *hawala* networks are attractive because many foreign workers do not trust official institutions. In 2001, Pakistan's finance minister, Shaukat Aziz, a former Citibank executive, complained that only $1.2 billion of the $6 billion sent annually to Pakistan from overseas arrives through the official banking system. In some countries, such as Somalia, *hawala* systems form the only efficient payments system. Globally, it is estimated that every year approximately $200 billion moves through *hawala* networks without ever becoming subject to any kind of official regulation.

Criminals also have a history of using this system. Historically, *hawala* networks have played a vital role in the smuggling of gold from Europe to India, through Dubai. The National Criminal Intelligence Service of Britain estimated in 2001 that the use of London-based *hawala* dealers by criminals has been on the rise in recent years. In the United States, al-Barakat, the financial group based in Dubai and mentioned previously, had *hawala* operations exploited by Al-Qaeda.

Government regulation:[25] Governments concerned with terrorist use of *hawala* networks are seeking to more tightly regulate the systems. Starting in 2002, the United States, United Kingdom, Pakistan, and United Arab Emirates all began pressing *hawala* dealers to register with the government.

Will these regulations work? *Hawala* transactions can be carried out anywhere (a home, a mosque, even at a coffee house table), with small sums of money and require only a phone and a couple trustworthy individuals (which, unfortunately, aren't always easy to find). Given the large global demand for such services, it is feared that if regulations are too strict, the networks will simply move more underground. In fact, *hawala* dealers thrive in environments with high-import tariffs and currency controls (which both limit and tax the movement of funds into a country). For example, when the Philippines abolished exchange controls in 1992, official remittances from abroad quadrupled. Therefore, a balance must be struck between too much regulation and too little.

7.6 ECONOMIC IMPACT OF TERRORISM

7.6.1 Macroeconomic Level

At the macroeconomic level, a singular terrorism event typically has little impact. If the event does negatively impact the economy, it is only in the short-run with little effect on the economy's medium- to long-term performance. To illustrate this point, consider the largest terrorist attack in history—the September 11, 2001 attacks on the United States.

Short-run impact: Some economists have estimated that these attacks were perhaps the most costly one-day event in the history of the United States. If one totals the loss of human capital (3,000 individuals, most of whom were highly skilled), physical capital (the two flattened World Trade Center towers and surrounding buildings, four destroyed airplanes, and the damage to the Pentagon), and clean-up costs, then the attack generated an estimated direct cost of between $30 billion and $50 billion dollars.[26]

However, there are additional indirect economic effects.[27] Shopping centers and restaurants across the country were closed for at least 24 hours. High-risk office buildings (such as the Sears Tower in Chicago) were evacuated. Planes were grounded and the stock market ceased trading for four consecutive days. As a result, the economy stalled for most of what remained of September. Retail sales fell by $6 billion (2.1 percent). New orders of **durable goods** (goods that will last for longer than three years) fell $11.6 billion (6.8 percent). Durable goods shipments fell by $9.2 billion due to tighter security. Industrial production fell 1 percent in September and when stocks finally opened for trading on September 17, the S&P 500 fell 7 percent while the NASDAQ fell 9.9 percent (before bottoming on September 21). Major airlines immediately cut scheduled flights by 30 percent and many of the remaining flights were not full. Hotels experienced a surge in vacancies. Through December 29, 2001, the Bureau of Labor Statistics attributed 408 major layoff events (defined as those shedding 50 or more jobs) as a direct or indirect result of the attacks, with 70 percent of those layoffs in the air transportation and travel industries. As a consequence, new claims for unemployment insurance surged by 50,000 in September, the biggest monthly jump since August of 1982.

Furthermore, the possibility of a short-term stall or even all-out collapse in the financial markets was of such a concern to officials in the Federal Reserve that the Fed issued the following public release to all banking institutions on the morning of September 11: "The Federal Reserve System is open and operating. The discount window is available to meet liquidity needs." This statement was to encourage banks to view the discount window as a source of financial funds.[28] The **discount window** allows banks to obtain funds directly from the Fed. The Fed prefers that banks borrow additional funds from other banks through the federal funds market and leave the discount window as a last resort. The Fed can change the quantity of funds available in the federal funds market through the purchase and sale of bonds to financial institutions. These purchases are called **Open Market Operations.** On a typical day the Fed issues approximately $20 billion worth of funds, with only about $1 billion through the discount window (the rest is through OMOs injecting liquidity into the federal funds market). Because the attacks on September 11 occurred just before the markets opened, the interbank lending market was not able to properly distribute funds.

In addition to making the discount window statement, the Fed injected nearly $45 billion of funds into the banking system on that day alone. A large portion of this injection was through the use of overnight **repurchasing agreements** (RP). An RP is an agreement between two parties where one party, a bank, sells a security (such as a bond) to another party, the Fed, at a specified price with a commitment to buy that security back at a later date for another specified price. The Fed can use overnight repurchasing agreements as a means of temporarily increasing the liquidity in the financial system. The Fed followed the $45 billion on September 11 with an injection of $110 billion on September 12, $120 billion on September 13, $110 billion on September 14, and $45 billion on September 17. By September 18, the Fed began returning funding balances to more normal levels (see Figure 7.6).[29]

Long-run impact: Within days, consumer and business activity began returning to normal.[30] Car sales soared as automobile manufacturers instituted zero percent financing. Auto sales only fell from an annual rate of 16.4 million units in August 2001 (meaning that 16.4 million units would be sold that year if consumers continued purchasing at that pace for the rest of the year) to a rate of 15.9 million units in September. This continuity of business is attributable to the late-month initiation of the incentives. The declines in September were offset by gains in October. Specifically, October auto sales rose to an annual rate of 21.3 million units, an all-time record high.

Because other retailers also cut prices, retail sales, excluding automobiles, rose 1.2 percent in October after falling by 1.2 percent in September. Following a similar pattern, new orders for durable goods fell 6.8 percent in September, only to rebound 9.2 percent in October. New home sales also rose to a record level in 2001, while electronic and appliance store sales rose by an annual rate of 23.3 percent during the last three months of the year. Most interesting, a surge in demand for U.S. flags after September 11 also contributed to

Figure 7.6

Outstanding Term and Overnight RPs around September 11
billions of dollars

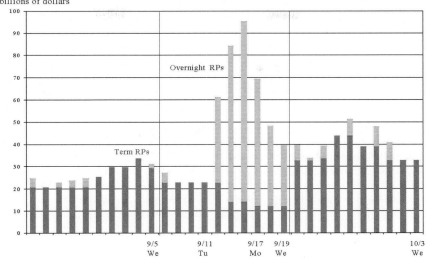

Source: Federal Reserve Bank of New York. "Domestic Open Market Operations During 2001." February 2002, p. 23, chart 15. Available at www.ny.frb.org/markets/omo/omo2001.pdf.

lifting the global economy, as domestic manufacturers turned to Chinese factories to help supply more than half of the record $51.7 million of flag imports in 2001.

Overall the quick rebound in business activity returned the economy to its pre-September 11 growth rate almost without delay. Despite the devastation from the terrorist attacks, real GDP grew at an annual rate of 2.7 percent in the fourth quarter of 2001. In short, consumer behavior may have changed, but the overall pace of spending was barely affected by the September 11 attacks.

The long-term economic impact of the September 11 attacks was minor for two final reasons. First, the Federal Reserve moved quickly to cut interest rates three more times in late 2001, pushing the federal funds rate down to 1.75 percent by the end of 2001. This made loans in the U.S. economy more widely available. Secondly, there were no additional attacks. This lull allowed consumers and businesses to return to their normal behavior.

7.6.2 Microeconomic Level

The most profound ongoing economic impacts of terrorist attacks are felt at the micro level. In particular, terrorist attacks force businesses to incur several types of **transaction costs** (the cost that businesses incur in the process of agreeing and following through on a sale or bargain).[31] First, a terrorist attack can raise insurance premiums. For insurers, the cost of the September 11 attacks surpassed that of Hurricane Andrew in 1992 ($15.5 billion), Hurricane Hugo in 1989 ($4.2 billion), and even the Northridge, California, earthquake of 1994 ($12.5 billion).[32] Consequently, some insurance premiums rose 300 percent (or more) from their pre-September 11 levels.[33] To place a rise of insurance premiums into perspective, it is estimated that a 20 percent rise in commercial insurance can cost U.S. businesses $30 billion more per year.

Second, because businesses have to install tighter security measures so as to prevent a terrorist attack, this security can disrupt the flow of goods and force companies to engage

---

Box 7.1
Historical Perspective
The Economic Impact of another Day in September

Much has been made of the $1.5 billion Athens spent on security for the 2004 Summer Olympics. This figure is easily the largest expenditure ever for Olympic security, eclipsing the $310 million, $210 million, and $300 million spent on security for, respectively, the Salt Lake City, Sydney, and Atlanta Games.[1]

The reasons for the high expenditures are numerous: hostilities towards American and British athletes after the 2003 invasion of Iraq; the heightened sensitivity towards catastrophic terrorist incidents after the terrorist attacks of September 11, 2001; and the ongoing presence of leftist terrorist groups (such as *November 17* and the Revolutionary People's Struggle) in Greece.

However, this is not the first or most dramatic rise in security expenditures in Olympic history. Between the Summer Games in Munich of 1972 and the Summer Games in Montreal in 1976, security expenditures rose from $2 million (Munich) to $100 million (Montreal).[2] This cost increase contributed to the massive cost overruns of the Montreal games, which nearly bankrupted the city. Yet, whereas the rise in security expenditures for the Athens games was driven by events outside the games themselves, the cost increase incurred by Montreal was in direct response to the tragic hostage incident at the 1972 Munich games.

In the morning of September 5, 1972 the Palestinian terrorist group *Black September* snuck into the sparsely guarded Olympic village and took hostage ten Israeli athletes and officials and killed one Israeli coach.[3] For the next two days the ten hostages were held captive while the terrorists and German officials negotiated the terms for their release. *Black September* demanded the release of over 200 political prisoners held by the Israeli government. Additionally, they sought safe passage for themselves and their hostages to an airport of their choice in the Middle East. With the Israeli government unwilling to accede to any of the terrorists' demands, the West Germans decided to implement a plan to free the hostages on German soil. They allowed the terrorists and hostages to leave the Olympic Village and proceed to a nearby airfield, where an attempt was made to free the hostages. When the terrorists realized that they had been ambushed, they threw hand grenades into the helicopters containing the hostages, killing the hostages and themselves.

---
[1] Chang, Andrew. "Major Competition: Athens on High Alert as the 2004 Olympics Summer Games Approach." *ABC News,* June 26, 2004.
[2] Montreal figure taken from CBC. "Montreal 1976." *Athens 2004: The Olympic Games Official Site.* Available at www.cbc.ca/olympics/history/1976.html (8/2/04)..
[3] Account of the Munich terrorist incident taken from Toohey and Veal (2000), pp. 92–93.

---

in the highly inefficient activity of holding additional inventory. Estimates indicate that if companies in the United States have to carry 10 percent more inventory, this inventory will cost businesses $7.5 billion per year.

Third, tourism is hurt immensely by terrorism. After the bombings in Bali, Indonesia in 2002, tourist arrivals to Indonesia fell by 2.2 percent. If a country is small and tourism-dependent, like Indonesia, then this loss of tourists can translate into a macroeconomic impact. Because tourism accounts for 3.4 percent of Indonesia's GDP (one of the highest ratios in the world), market analysts placed the financial loss to the Indonesian economy at approximately 1 percent of GDP. Israel, Turkey, and Greece are other economies where a terrorist-induced decline in tourism can negatively impact the economy as a whole. Studies have found that a terrorist incident in either of these countries decreases their global tourism market share by 1 percent for Greece, 0.78 percent for Turkey, and 0.44 percent for Israel. These percentages are significant, because a 1 percent decline can represent the loss of hundreds of thousands of tourists and hundreds of millions of dollars.[34] However, it should be stressed that tourism is most affected when a country experiences a series of attacks. For example, tourism to Spain, the second most popular tourist destination in the world (after France), was barely impacted by the March 11, 2004 bombings in Madrid that killed over 190 people, primarily because it was a single attack.

7.6.3   International Trade

Several studies indicate that perhaps the biggest impact from a terrorist attack is on **economic globalization**—the process of integrating and interconnecting economies world-wide.

First, acts of terrorism can reduce international trade between economies as countries seek to tighten security measures. Sending products abroad is delayed as ports take additional time to inspect cargo. Foreign buyers, wishing to enter the country and inspect a prospective product, can face higher barriers to obtaining a visa. Nitsch and Schumacher (2000) studied over 200 countries from 1968 to 1979 and found that a doubling of the number of terrorist incidents decreased bilateral trade between targeted economies by about 6 percent.

Second, terrorism can raise the **risk premium** of investing in a country (the additional interest a borrower must pay, relative to the most preferred borrower). A raised risk premium will increase the cost of obtaining **Foreign Direct Investment** (FDI). FDI is investment by foreigners to build fixed assets such as factories, warehouses, and office buildings. When it costs more to obtain FDI, inflows of FDI are reduced. Specifically, Enders and Sandler (1996) found that from 1975 to 1991, heightened terrorism reduced average annual net FDI inflows to Spain by 13.5 percent and to Greece by 11.9 percent.

Third, currencies of those economies seen as carrying a higher risk premium may experience exchange-rate volatility and sudden declines in currency value when a terrorist event occurs. Because the exchange rate determines the international price of a country's goods, exchange rate volatility can reduce a country's trade flows as buyers look to purchase from countries with more stable exchange rates.

7.7   KEY POINTS

Key Macroeconomic Points:

- Terrorist financing is difficult to trace because it uses small quantities of money and relies on a variety of methods to raise and transfer funds. Unlike money laundering, terrorist financing often directs legal money toward a future illegal activity.
- A single terrorist attack, even one on the scale of the September 11, 2001 attacks, will have a negative short-term economic impact, but almost no perceptible effect in the long-term.
- The Federal Reserve used a combination of open market operations and discount window liquidity to assist the U.S. economy through the immediate aftermath of the September 11 attacks.
- Tourism and economic globalization are the primary victims of repeated terrorist attacks.

Key Microeconomic Points:

- The substitution effect explains why terrorist attacks became more efficient. Specifically, as security became tighter on government installations and aircraft, terrorists substituted with soft targets.
- The desire of people to have public goods, and the government's inability to supply such goods, helps to explain why people join terrorist groups.
- An extended form game can explain why groups will choose illegal forms of expression if governments do not permit civil liberties. The game illustrates why groups will choose bombing over other illegal forms of expression.

- When an individual reaches a corner solution—meaning his or her indifference curve intersects one axis—then it can be rational for him or her to become a suicide bomber.
- Cost-benefit analysis explains why a terrorist group prefers suicide bombing over other forms of bombing.
- Terrorist incidents can raise the transaction cost of doing business.

Key Terms:

Soft targets	Zakat
Failed states	Economic sanctions
Game tree/extended form game	Mujahideen
Node	Off-shore
Payoffs	Front companies
Discount the future	Hawala
Essential good	Riba
Budget constraint line	Transaction costs
Attainable bundle	Durable goods
Inessential good	Discount window
Corner solution	Open Market Operations
Cost-benefit analysis	Repurchasing agreements
Intifada	Economic globalization
Money laundering	Risk premium
Layers and redundancies	Foreign Direct Investment
Remittances	

Key Review Questions:

1. Do suicide bombings against U.S. soldiers in Iraq fall under the definition of international terrorism?
2. Use economic tools to explain why suicide bombing is rational.
3. Perform a cost-benefit analysis to determine if you should use a regular bank or a *hawala* system to store and transfer money.
4. Did the September 11 attacks cause the U.S. economy to enter a recession?

Endnotes

1. Neilan, Terence. "Americans Urged to Stick to Routines Despite Terror Alert." *The New York Times,* August 2, 2004.
2. Definition applied by U.S. Department of State. Also used by scholars of terrorism such as Enders and Sandler (2004).
3. Enders and Sandler (2000), p. 330.
4. Enders and Sandler (2004).
5. Berman (2004). Also see "Rational Extremist." *The Economist,* January 15, 2004
6. Krueger, Alan B. "Poverty Doesn't Create Terrorists" *The New York Times,* May 29, 2003 and Krueger and Maleková (2003).
7. This model is based in part on that offered by Lapan and Sandler (1988). In their model, they try to account for the probability of success, the likelihood that bombings or protests will fail logistically (thereby generating no attention), and the likelihood that the government will capitulate to the group's demands (whether made legally or illegally) or retaliate to illegal actions. These factors have been left out of the model so as to make the core lesson clear.

8. Adopted from Wintrobe (2002), pp. 9–15. Modifications based on the discussion of indifference curves found in Eaton and Eaton (1995), Chapters 2 and 3.

9. Information for this section from Hoffman, Bruce. "The Logic of Suicide Terrorism." *The Atlantic Monthly,* June 2003, unless otherwise cited.

10. Krueger, Alan B. "Poverty Doesn't Create Terrorists." *New York Times,* May 29, 2003. p. C2.

11. "Basic Facts about Money Laundering." OECD. Financial Action Task Force on Money Laundering. Available at http://www1.oecd.org/fatf/MLaundering_en.htm.

12. Schneider (2002), p. 10.

13. Weschler and Wolosky (2002), p. 1.

14. Ibid, p. 6.

15. Ibid, pp. 5–12.

16. NARCO Terrorism (Global and regional overview). Southeast European Cooperative Initiative (SECI) Center Anti-Terrorism Task Force. March 8, 2004. Available at www.osce.org/documents.

17. Perl (2001), p. 3.

18. Baer (2003), p. 57.

19. United States v. Usama bin Laden et al., United States District Court. Southern District of New York. Counts One Through Six: Conspiracies to Murder, Bomb and Maim Count One: Conspiracy to Kill United States Nationals." 1998. Available through Federation of American Scientists website at www.fas.org/irp/news/1998/11/98110602_nlt.html.

20. Information from "Cheap and Trusted." *The Economist,* Nov. 22, 2001 unless otherwise cited.

21. According to Professor Timur Kuran, University of Southern California, "In practice interest is often waived [in the Hawala system] when the duration is short. Over longer terms, interest is charged routinely, though usually disguised as a commission, or fee, or service charge. The same was true historically. In medieval times the Middle East had a sophisticated financial system by the standards of the day; many transactions were based on what we would call interest." E-mail correspondence between author and Timur Kuran, August 12, 2003.

22. Schramm (2003), pp. 2–8.

23. Ibid.

24. Ibid.

25. "Fears over U.S. hawala crackdown." *BBC News,* UK Edition, February 6, 2004.

26. Miller, Benjamin, and North (2003), pp. 23–25.

27. See Wesbury (2002).

28. Markets Group of the Federal Reserve Bank of New York, 2002. "Domestic open market operations during 2001." Federal Reserve Bank of New York. Available at www.ny.frb.org/markets/omo/omo2001.pdf.

29. Martin (2004), pp. 6–11.

30. Information from this section from Wesbury (2002).

31. Information for this section from Raby (2003) unless otherwise cited.

32. In 2003 U.S. dollars. Insurance Information Institute. "The Ten Most Costly World Insurance Losses, 1970–2004." available at www.iii.org/media/facts/statsbyissue/catastrophes/. Note, since the September 11, 2001 attacks, Hurricane Charley (August 2004) surpassed the damage total of Hurricane Hugo.

33. From Wesbury (2002).

34. Drakos and Kutan (2001), pp. 17–19.

Chapter 8

Weapons of Mass Destruction Proliferation

8.1 INTRODUCTION

In January 2004, Mohammed El Baradei, the head of International Atomic Energy Agency (the United Nation's watchdog agency on atomic weapons), commented on how Libya's now-relinquished nuclear program was the result of "the Wal-Mart of private sector proliferation."[1] El Baradei was referring to the global dispersal of nuclear, chemical, and biological weapons. Because these weapons can inflict enormous destruction and casualties, they are commonly referred to as **Weapons of Mass Destruction** (WMD). The dispersal of WMD is called "proliferation," and this is arguably the biggest security threat facing nations in the twenty-first century. The fear of proliferation stems not solely from the thought of states using these weapons against one another, but also from the possibility that these weapons could be obtained and used by sub-state actors such as terrorist organizations. This fear is especially acute, given the presence of the international black market in weapons technology referred to by El Baradei.

This chapter will explore the economic motivations for obtaining and proliferating weapons capable of inflicting massive casualties. Section 2 provides an overview of three types of WMDs and concludes with an explanation for why only nuclear weapons will be the focus of the remaining sections. Section 3 provides a very brief introduction into the science of nuclear weapons. Sections 4 and 5 explore the reasons why states demand and supply these weapons. Section 6 concludes with a discussion of international treaties, one of the primary means by which states try to counter WMD proliferation.

8.2 OVERVIEW OF CHEMICAL, BIOLOGICAL, AND NUCLEAR WEAPONS

8.2.1 Types of WMD[2]

Chemical: Chemical weapons are man-made toxic chemicals that cause fatal or incapacitating injuries. Once injected into the air, a chemical agent (such as sarin gas, VX gas, or mustard gas) can enter the body through inhalation or absorption through the skin. Once in the body, these agents can have a variety of effects, including damaging the lungs, blistering the skin, or disrupting the nervous system.

These weapons are not as difficult to store as biological agents (see **biological** section below), but because chemical agents must be dispersed in large volumes to be effective against more than a few individuals, they must be produced on a large scale. This large-scale production process can create other problems, because the agents must be stored carefully and kept away from corrosion. Also, they must be handled with extreme care as even the smallest release of the chemical can kill those people surrounding the container if unprotected. Currently, twenty-eight countries are known to have existing or former chemical weapons programs (Table 8.1).

Chemical weapons were used widely in World War I, but have since been used only on a very limited scale. The most widely documented recent usage of chemical weapons was by Iraq against Iran (and possibly Iran against Iraq) during the 1980–1988 Iran-Iraq war.

Table 8.1
Chemical Weapons Programs (by Country)

Country	Program Status
Algeria	Possibly
Canada	Formerly
China	Likely
Cuba	Possibly
Egypt	Likely
Ethiopia	Likely
France	Formerly
Germany	Formerly
India	Formerly
Iran	Known
Iraq	Formerly
Israel	Likely
Italy	Formerly
Japan	Formerly
Libya	Known
Burma	Likely
N. Korea	Known
Pakistan	Likely
Russia	Known
USSR	Likely
S. Africa	Formerly
S. Korea	Formerly
Sudan	Possibly
Syria	Known
Taiwan	Likely
U.K.	Formerly
U.S.A.	Formerly
Vietnam	Possibly
TOTAL	28

Key:
Possibly: where states have been widely identified as possibly having a program, by sources other than government officials.
Likely: where states have been publicly named by government or military officials as likely possessing a program.
Formerly: where states have acknowledged having a program or stockpile in the past.
Known: where states have either declared their programs or there is clear evidence of possession.

Source: Monterey Institute of International Studies. "Chemical and Biological Weapons." Monterey, California: Center for Nonproliferation Studies (CNS). April 9, 2002. Available at http://cns.miis.edu/research/cbw/possess.htm.

Biological: Biological weapons are bacteria or viruses that, when inhaled, can cause fatal or incapacitating injuries. Two well-known examples of biological weapons are anthrax and small pox.

Though relatively inexpensive (see **cost comparison** section below), biological weapons are difficult to produce for two reasons. First, many biological agents are sensitive to their environments and require special handling. Therefore, it can be extremely difficult to ensure that the pathogens will survive storage and deployment. Second, it is difficult to produce pathogens in particles small enough to be inhaled and retained in the victims' lungs. Additionally, infectious agents are difficult to contain and so are less useful. Therefore, it is not surprising to see that fewer countries have (or attempt to have) a biological weapons program, compared to chemical weapons programs (Table 8.2).

Table 8.2
Biological Weapons Programs (by Country)

Country	Program Status
Algeria	Research
Canada	Formerly
China	Likely
Cuba	Likely
Egypt	Likely
France	Formerly
Germany	Formerly
India	Research
Iran	Likely
Iraq	Formerly
Israel	Possibly
Japan	Formerly
Libya	Possibly
N. Korea	Possibly
Pakistan	Possibly
Russia	Likely
USSR	Formerly
S. Africa	Formerly
Sudan	Possibly
Syria	Possibly
Taiwan	Possibly
U.K.	Formerly
U.S.A.	Formerly
TOTAL	21 (+2 research)

Key:
Possibly: where states have been widely identified as possibly having a program, by sources other than government officials.
Likely: where states have been publicly named by government or military officials as likely possessing a program.
Formerly: where states have acknowledged having a program or stockpile in the past.
Known: where states have either declared their programs or there is clear evidence of possession.
Research: agents studied, but no evidence of weaponization.

Source: Monterey Institute of International Studies. "Chemical and Biological Weapons." Monterey, California: Center for Nonproliferation Studies (CNS). April 9, 2002. Available at http://cns.miis.edu/research/cbw/possess.htm.

The only widespread contemporary use of biological weapons was by the Japanese on the Chinese during the 1930s and World War II. Since then, there have been several instances of limited usage, including the anthrax mail scare in the United States during late 2001 and early 2002.

Nuclear: Nuclear weapons detonate by creating energy through the splitting of a heavy atom (a process called **fission**), often combined with the merging of very light atoms (a process called **fusion**). Upon explosion, a shock wave spreads out, creating flying debris and pressurizing the air, tearing objects apart or blowing them over. A fireball is also produced that ignites flammable materials at great distances. The end result is massive destruction.[3] Currently, nine countries possess or are believed to possess nuclear weapons (Table 8.3).

The size of nuclear explosions is measured in **tons.**[4] One (metric) ton equals the energy release of 1,000 kg (2,205 lbs) of TNT or 40,000 sticks of dynamite.[5] A kilo-ton (kT) is 1,000 tons or 1 million kg (2.2 million lbs) of TNT. A mega-ton (MT) is 1 million

Table 8.3

Nuclear Weapons Programs (by Country)

Country	Program Status	Weapons
China	Known	400
France	Known	350
India	Known	30 to 50
Israel	Likely	75 to 200
N. Korea	Likely	5 to 7
Pakistan	Known	24 to 48
Russia	Known	20,000
U.K.	Known	200
U.S.A.	Known	10,600
TOTAL	9	32,000

Key:

Likely: where states have been publicly named by government or military officials as likely possessing a program.
Known: where states have either declared their programs or there is clear evidence of possession.

Source: Nuclear Threat Initiative. "Country Profiles." Prepared by the Center for Nonproliferation Studies. Monterey, California: Monterey Institute of International Studies, 2003. Available at www.nti.org/e_research/profiles/index.html.

Table 8.4

Radius of Damage of Nuclear Weapon by Weapon Size

Damage	Weapon size		
	20 KT	500 KT	10 MT
Reinforced Buildings Collapse	0.5 miles	1.5 miles	2.5 miles
Wood-Frame Homes Collapse	2 miles	6 miles	17 miles
Windows Shatter	5 miles	15 miles	32 miles
Most Materials Ignite/ Massive 3rd Degree Burns	1 mile	4 miles	12 miles
2nd Degree Burns/ Paper and Dry Leaves Ignite	2 miles	7 miles	19 miles

Source of data: Burbach, David. "Nuclear Weapons Primer." November 1997.
Available at http://classes.lls.edu/spring2003/natsec-manheim/Nuclear_Primer.pdf.

tons or 1 billion kg (2.2 billion lbs) of TNT. The atomic bomb dropped over Hiroshima released energy equal to about 15 kT. The typical U.S. nuclear bomb in 1997 was 200–500 kT (compared to 5 MT in 1965), while the largest nuclear weapon ever tested was a 53 MT bomb by the Soviet Union in 1960.

Table 8.4 provides a summary of the damage that the blast and fireball of different sizes of nuclear weapons can create.

Table 8.5
Cost Efficiency of WMDs

Weapon type	Q50 cost (in 1969 US $)
Conventional	$2,000
Nuclear	$800
Chemical	$600
Biological	$1

Source of data: North Atlantic Treaty Organization (NATO). *The NATO Handbook on the Medical Aspects of NBC Defense Operations.* Part II Biological Weapons; Chapter 1; Section 3. Brussels, Belgium: NATO, 1996. Available at www.fas.org/nuke/guide/usa/doctrine/dod/fm8-9/2toc.htm.

Cost comparison: Perhaps the best measure for comparing the cost and efficiency of various weapons is the **Q-50.** Q-50 refers to the cost of operations against civilian populations needed to produce 50 percent casualties per square kilometer. As Table 8.5 shows, despite the deployment difficulties of biological weapons, at a cost of only $1 per Q-50, biological agents are superior with regard to cost efficiency.

The fact that biological weapons are so cost-effective may go a long way toward illustrating how difficult they are to use. Consider that even though chemical weapons are 600 percent more costly to use than biological weapons, as Tables 8.1 and 8.2 show, 25 percent *fewer* countries have pursued biological rather than chemical weapons programs.

8.2.2   Why Focus on Nuclear Weapons?

While biological and chemical weapons are of great concern, nuclear weapons will be the focus of this chapter's analysis. This emphasis is for two reasons.

First, several scholars question the inclusion of chemical and biological weapons in the WMD category. Former Assistant Secretary of Defense Ashton Carter highlights how chemical weapons are not much more lethal than conventional explosives and are unable to destroy infrastructure. Similarly, weapons proliferation expert Graham Allison of Harvard University points out that biological weapons cannot destroy infrastructure, and that deaths resulting from them can be contained by effective medical countermeasures.[6]

Second, Perkovich (2003) highlights how nuclear weapons raise more intriguing issues than biological or chemical weapons. Specifically, because chemical and biological weapons are legally prohibited by treaty, the challenge they pose is simply one of enforcement. In contrast, nuclear weapons are legal in five countries, not illegal in three others, and forbidden everywhere else. Therefore, this complex and inconsistent arrangement presents a unique dilemma that is worth exploring (see section 8.6).[7]

8.3   BASICS OF PRODUCING NUCLEAR WEAPONS MATERIAL

Although this is not a science text, to fully appreciate the economic issues surrounding nuclear weapons proliferation, it is important to understand the basic elements of producing the material needed for a nuclear weapon. In fact, in order to understand this section, it is useful to quickly review a few basic science terms (see Box 8.1).

In order to build a nuclear weapon, a country or organization must possess fissile material that can be split so as to create a nuclear reaction. The two most common forms of fissile material for nuclear weapons include highly enriched uranium and plutonium.

Box 8.1
Important Science Terms[1]

Element: any of more than 100 known substances (most of which are naturally occurring) that cannot be separated into simpler substances and that, either by itself or in combination, constitute all matter. Examples of elements include hydrogen, helium, and uranium.

Atom: the smallest possible particle of an element that can still have the properties of that element.

Nucleus: the center of an atom containing protons, neutrons, and most of the atom's mass.

Protons: positively charged particles.

Neutrons: particles with no charge.

Isotope: a variation of an element. Specifically, isotopes of an element have the same number of protons, but a different number of neutrons.

Fission: the process of splitting the nucleus of an atom of a heavy element (such as uranium) into two roughly equal parts. This splitting is then accompanied by the release of relatively large amounts of energy.

Fissile material: any material capable of undergoing fission.

---

[1] A good online source for chemistry definitions is the Argonne National Laboratory—West at www.anlw.anl.gov/anlw_history/glossary.html.

8.3.1 Highly Enriched Uranium

Highly Enriched Uranium (HEU) is a form of uranium that can be used for a nuclear bomb. What does it mean for uranium to be highly enriched?

More than 99 percent of uranium found in nature is of the isotope called U-238 (meaning it has 92 protons and 146 neutrons).[8] Because it is difficult to split the atoms contained in U-238, this isotope is not useful either as fuel for a nuclear power reactor or for a bomb. Another 0.7 percent of natural uranium is of the isotope called U-235 (meaning it has 92 protons, but only 143 neutrons). U-235 is much easier to split than U-238 when bombarded by neutrons. U-235 also produces additional neutrons when splitting, enabling chain reactions to take place. Hence, U-235 is useful for creating and sustaining nuclear reactions.

However, most nuclear power reactors cannot run on natural uranium, and so enrichment is required if a country wishes to build nuclear weapons or have its own supply of fuel for its nuclear reactors. These reactors require low-enriched uranium fuel (meaning the uranium must contain 3 to 5 percent of the U-235 isotope); and so the fraction of U-235 in natural uranium must be increased, or enriched.

This enriching process uses a centrifuge.[9] Here's how a centrifuge works. First, the natural uranium is converted into a gas. The gas is then injected into the centrifuge, which is a cylinder that spins the gas at faster than the speed of sound. As the centrifuge spins, it subjects the uranium gas to a force thousands of times greater than gravity. A higher fraction of the lighter U-235 isotope gathers at the center of the cylinder, while the heavier U-238 isotopes are pushed to the outside of the cylinder. This "enriched" uranium can be put through the process again and again, each time further enriching the uranium.

Highly Enriched Uranium (HEU) is uranium over 20 percent comprised of the U-235 isotope. It is only at 20 percent enrichment that uranium is able to create a self-sustaining chain reaction in which the two nuclei created by the original fission are split into two more and so on. Such a chain reaction is required to create a nuclear explosion. Nuclear bombs require HEU enriched to at least 90 percent, a level well above what is needed for a nuclear energy reactor.[10]

How long does it take centrifuge enrichment to produce uranium fuel usable in a nuclear bomb? If the cylinders are stacked onto one another (with bellows between each cylinder), then this stacking can create a taller centrifuge capable of separating U-235 at a faster rate. It can take one year for 1,500 of these stacks to create enough HEU for one bomb (typically 35 pounds of U-235).[11]

8.3.2 Plutonium

An alternative source of fissile material is plutonium.[12] Plutonium (Pu), unlike uranium, is not a natural substance, but results from U-238 capturing a neutron to create U-239, which then decays to Pu-239. When a nuclear reactor is operated, U-235 splits into lighter elements and releases additional neutrons, some of which turn U-238 into Pu-239. Some of the U-235 in the fuel is not consumed, because once the fraction of U-235 drops below a certain percentage, it can no longer be used in that reactor. Because the uranium and plutonium remaining in the fuel are capable of sustaining another nuclear reaction once separated and reenriched, they can be reused as nuclear fuel. However, it is currently much cheaper to mine and enrich uranium ore than it is to reprocess spent nuclear fuel and remove the plutonium and uranium to be reused.

Reprocessing is the procedure for recovering the uranium and plutonium so that it can be used again as new fuel. It requires a chemical processing facility where the used nuclear fuel is pulverized, dissolved into nitric acid, and converted into usable uranium and plutonium. It typically requires at least 4 kilograms (8.4 pounds) of plutonium to have an amount sufficient for producing a bomb. With only a single reactor and reprocessing plant, it takes over a year to create this amount of plutonium.

8.4 DEMAND FOR NUCLEAR WEAPONS

Having now obtained a brief understanding of how the materials needed to build a nuclear weapon are created, one can better understand the supply and demand of nuclear weapons proliferation. When looking at the process of nuclear weapons supply and demand, one should keep in mind not only which countries currently have weapons, but also what prompted these countries to acquire these weapons, and why other countries attempt to acquire nuclear weapons. This information is summarized in Box 8.2.

There are two primary reasons why countries demand nuclear weapons: the security dilemma hypothesis and a substitution effect called "More Bang for the Buck."

8.4.1 Security Dilemma Hypothesis

The **security dilemma** was originally presented in Chapter 3. When two countries perceive each other as a threat, both countries will buy and construct weapons in an attempt to have more than the other; each action causing an opposing reaction.

As the explanations in Box 8.2 illustrate, the security dilemma hypothesis provides an excellent explanation for why Israel, Pakistan, and India acquired nuclear weapons. Each of these countries saw an opponent's massive conventional forces or possession of nuclear weapons as a threat that it perceived as diminishing its security. Each of these countries felt the only way to restore its perceived security was to acquire nuclear weapons.

Box 8.2
Historical Perspective
The Early Proliferation of Nuclear Weapons[1]

Proliferation among the five post-WW II powers: By the end of the 1940s, both the United States and Soviet Union possessed and had tested nuclear bombs. Britain, with U.S. assistance, became the next nuclear power by testing a weapon in 1952. France had pursued nuclear energy production in the late 1940s; but because it did not receive as much American assistance as the British, it did not successfully test a nuclear weapon until 1960.

Throughout the 1950s and early 1960s, the United States followed a policy of nuclear energy promotion, embodied in President Eisenhower's Atoms for Peace program initiated in 1953. Though the program authorized the United States to assist only in the construction of civilian nuclear reactors for energy production, the Eisenhower administration recognized that sovereign nations had the right to pursue weapons on their own. The Kennedy/Johnson administration was more aware of the ever-growing desire of technologically advanced and politically determined countries to acquire nuclear weapons. Due to the nuclear scare brought on by the Cuban missile crisis, that administration was aware of weapon proliferation's deadly implications.

China was helped by the Soviets through the 1957 Soviet-Sino New Defense Technical Accord. When in 1964 China became the last of the five permanent members of the United Nations Security Council to test a nuclear weapon, the United States switched from a policy of energy promotion to nonproliferation. This policy switch eventually culminated in the signing in 1969 of the Nuclear Nonproliferation Treaty (NPT).

Proliferation to Israel: Israel's desire to possess a nuclear weapon grew from two sources. First, the Israeli government held a conviction that the Holocaust justified any measures Israel would take to ensure its survival. Second, the conflagrations between Israel and its Arab neighbors upon the country's creation in 1948 and again in 1956 illustrated the need for an effective military deterrent. The Suez crisis of 1956 enabled Israel to provoke France's President Charles De Gaulle to begin assisting Israel with its program (a program the United States only became aware of with U2 surveillance flights in 1962). To this day, Israel's status as a nuclear power is intentionally ambiguous. It neither confirms nor denies possessing nuclear weapons, though it is almost certain that it possesses a stockpile of a few hundred warheads.

Proliferation to India and Pakistan: Whereas the proliferation of nuclear weapons among the United States, Soviet Union, United Kingdom, France, and China may be a matter of the five permanent members of the UN Security Council wishing to establish great power status, proliferation among many secondary powers fits well with the security dilemma hypothesis explanation. After India's defeat by the larger Chinese conventional forces in the 1962 Sino-Indian War, India was motivated to obtain a nuclear weapon so as to restore the region's military balance. India would eventually develop such a bomb (with Soviet help) by 1974, when it conducted a "Peaceful Nuclear Explosive" test. This test, combined with its own defeat to superior Indian conventional forces in the 1970–71 Bangladesh War, motivated Pakistan to obtain the bomb.

Pakistan's efforts to develop a bomb received a large boost in 1979 when the Soviet Union invaded Afghanistan. This invasion prompted the United States to give military aid to Pakistan, which in turn enabled Pakistan to dedicate its own resources toward nuclear research. Pakistan eventually tested a nuclear weapon in 1998.

Temporary nuclear states: After the collapse of the Soviet Union in 1989, Ukraine, Belarus, and Kazakhstan were all left with nuclear weapons. However, in order to bring themselves into the western fold, these countries agreed to return the weapons to Russia.

Though other nations attempted to develop nuclear weapons (including Argentina, Brazil, Algeria, and Libya), South Africa is the only nation to have successfully developed nuclear weapons and then voluntarily relinquish them. South Africa originally developed the weapons as a response to Cold War superpower (particularly Soviet) intervention on the African continent and the alienated status of South Africa due to its discriminatory apartheid policies. Yet, once the Cold War ended, the South African government saw an opportunity to reenter the community of nations by abandoning not only its apartheid polices, but also its weapons program.

---

[1] Information for this section from *The Nuclear Weapons Archive* website at http://nuclearweaponarchive.org and Cohen (1998), pages 2–5. Also see the Federation of American Scientists' (FAS) *Nuclear Forces Guide* at http://fas.org/nuke/guide/index.html; Washington, D.C.: FAS.

8.4.2 "More Bang for the Buck" Substitution Effect

Though the security dilemma is a useful strategic explanation for the procurement of nuclear weapons, it is not the sole explanation. Another justification for the acquisition of nuclear weapons is the **substitution effect.** The substitution effect is the process of using a less expensive item that can perform the same task as a more expensive item. In the context of security, there is a belief that nuclear weapons can provide a relatively inexpensive means of deterring a potential enemy. Once constructed, a handful of nuclear bombs mounted on long-range missiles could prevent a potential adversary from invading. Hence, a country could substitute the cost of maintaining a massive army for just a few nuclear weapons.

Despite this belief, the development of nuclear weapons is not an inexpensive venture, with estimates of costs varying significantly. According to an Office of Technology Assessment 1993 report, a state can expect to invest a minimum of $200 million in order to create just one small bomb.[13] The same report acknowledged that a secretive program could more realistically place the cost between $2 billion and $10 billion because of the obvious difficulties in acquiring widespread foreign assistance. Yet, South Africa constructed a secretive nuclear program (which it gave up in the early 1990s) at an estimated cost of $800 million.[14] Nuclear weapons proliferation expert Graham Allison places the cost of developing fissile material alone at $1 billion.[15]

Regardless of the estimate used, it is evident that constructing a nuclear program is costly. The major contributor to this high cost is its scientific complexity. Even if a country or organization is able to obtain fissile material, constructing a bomb requires high-level expertise in a broad range of subjects including the physical, chemical, and metallurgical properties of the materials; engineering; nuclear physics; the nuclear and biological effects of radiation; high explosives technology; hydrodynamics; and precision electrical circuitry.[16]

Nevertheless, once these high fixed costs have been incurred and the country has finely calibrated its production capabilities, it is then possible to build additional bombs for a marginal cost of between $2 and $4 million each (measured in 2003 dollars).[17] Additionally, from 1940 to 1996 the U.S. government spent nearly $5.9 trillion on its nuclear program.[18] This figure sounds like a large sum of money, until one considers two points: 1) it was less than half what the United States spent on conventional forces during the same time period, and 2) it gave the United States a far greater destructive capability than the more expensive conventional forces (see Box 8.3).

Therefore, nuclear weapons could have a substitution effect because the cost per destructive capability is far less than conventional weapons. Overall, a handful of nuclear weapons (perhaps even one nuclear weapon) may have the same deterrent impact as thousands of troops. Therefore, if the marginal price of producing additional nuclear weapons is lower than that of maintaining conventional forces, the demand for troops will fall. Likewise, if the price for troops rises, then the demand for nuclear weapons will rise. For a country like North Korea, which currently spends over 30 percent of GDP on its military, nuclear weapons could profoundly lower total military expenditures, thereby freeing resources to be spent elsewhere.

8.5 SUPPLY OF NUCLEAR WEAPONS

However, the security dilemma hypothesis and "more bang for the buck" substitution effect fail to explain the prevalence of nuclear weapons. This fact is because the security dilemma hypothesis would deem it irrational for countries to share nuclear technology. Remember that the security dilemma hypothesis maintains that countries will seek nuclear

Box 8.3
Historical Perspective
U.S. Nuclear Weapons Program: More Bang for the Buck?[1]

The massive U.S. nuclear weapons arsenal (at one point reaching nearly 15,000 warheads in the mid-1980s) did not come at a low cost. According to data collected by Steven Schwartz of the Brookings Institute, from 1940 to 1996 the U.S. nuclear weapons program cost a grand total of nearly $6 trillion. This figure, over 50 percent of the current U.S. GDP, was derived from adding the cost to the U.S. government of not just bomb construction, but also maintenance, security, and other miscellaneous tasks associated with maintaining a nuclear arsenal. Table I breaks down the costs considered by Schwartz.

Table I: Estimated Minimum Incurred Costs of U.S. Nuclear Weapons Programs, 1940–1996*

Total: $5,821.0 billion (figures in billions of constant 1996 dollars)

- Nuclear secrecy programs, $3.1
- Congressional oversight, $0.9
- Victim compensation, $2.1
- Building $409.0
- Nuclear waste management and environmental regulation $365.0
- Nuclear dismantling $31.0
- Defending against enemy nuclear weapons $937.0
- Targeting and controlling $831.0
- Deploying $3,241.0

Source of data: Schwartz, S. Atomic Audit: The Costs and Consequences of Nuclear Weapons Since the 1940s. Washington, D.C.: Brookings Institute, 1998.

*Includes average projected future-year costs for nuclear weapons dismantlement, fissile materials disposition, environmental remediation, and waste management. Total actual and estimated expenditures through 1996 were $5,481.1 billion.

This enormous cost initially calls into question the notion of nuclear weapons providing security on the cheap. However, if this cost is compared to the cost incurred by the United States over the same time frame for maintaining its conventional weapons arsenal, this cost appears more reasonable. Specifically, U.S. conventional forces over the 1940–1996 period cost the United States nearly $13 trillion. Therefore, the deterrent effect of the American nuclear forces (which carried the ability to destroy the planet several times), cost less than half of U.S. conventional forces (which possessed not nearly the destructive capacity). This seems to support the idea of nuclear weapons, despite their large overall expense, being a more cost-effective defensive tool than large conventional forces.

---

[1] All data for this section comes from Schwartz, S. *Atomic Audit: Cost and Consequences of Nuclear Weapons Since the 1940s.* Washington, D.C.: Brookings Institute, 1998.

weapons because other countries have nuclear weapons. Therefore, according to the security dilemma hypothesis, the last thing a country would want to do is make it easier for another country (that may become a threat) to obtain nuclear weapons.

However, such sharing of nuclear technology is quite prevalent. Sharing among allies may be logical (as it would have been during the Cold War), but many countries have willingly shared information on either nuclear power technology (as is the case with Russia) or nuclear weapons construction (Pakistan and North Korea) with countries whose allegiance is questionable. Additionally, the security dilemma fails to explain the involvement of companies (such as the British-owned Gulf Technical Industries, or the Malaysian company Scope) in the illegal proliferation of nuclear components.

Instead, nuclear proliferation by second-tier military powers, like Pakistan and North Korea, and private actors can be best explained with two economic motivations: the ability of such technology to facilitate a bartering exchange and the ability of nuclear material to generate large revenues.

8.5.1 Nuclear Bartering

Bartering is the direct exchange of goods and services for other goods and services. Nuclear bartering is best illustrated by the relationship between Pakistan and North Korea.[19] The armaments trade relationship between these two countries began during the 1970–1971 Bangladesh War. Pakistan approached North Korea (a heavily militarized state, thanks to military aid from the Soviet Union and China) to obtain artillery, multiple rocket launchers, and a variety of spare parts. Pakistani ballistic missile engineers developed working relationships with North Korean engineers in the mid-1980s when both assisted Iran during the 1980–1988 Iran-Iraq war. In fact, the close resemblance of Iran's *Shahab* missile and the Pakistani *Ghauri 1* has led many to conclude that probably around 1993 the development of the missiles was coordinated between the three countries.

In the early 1990s, Pakistan was seeking ballistic missile technology so as to have strike capability against targets in India. In 1992, Pakistani officials visited North Korea to view a *No Dong* medium-range missile prototype, and again in 1993 for a *No Dong* flight test. North Korea is believed to have subsequently sent five to 12 *No Dong* missile assembly sets to Pakistan between 1994 and 1997. Between 1997 and 1998, flights between North Korea and Pakistan became more regular, about nine flights per month. Overall, it is believed that Pakistan accepted between 12 and 25 complete *No Dong* missiles in the late 1990s.

At the same time, Pakistan is believed to have provided North Korea with technical assistance in developing solid propellant technology. This technology would allow North Korea's *Taepo Dong* missile to have a third stage, thereby potentially enabling it to cross the Pacific Ocean. Simultaneous to these events, Pakistan began nuclear cooperation with North Korea. It is a matter of debate whether this cooperation was begun with the blessing of the Pakistani government, or solely at the behest of Dr. A.Q. Khan (a German-educated metallurgist who headed the Khan Research Laboratory, which conducted the research that developed Pakistan's nuclear bomb). While information exists that point in either direction, there are some known facts.

First, starting in the 1980s and 1990s, Khan developed a secret network that wound through Dubai, United Arab Emirates, and Switzerland. This network transferred nuclear technological know-how to Iran, Libya, and, in particular, to North Korea. Second, Khan profited from these technology transfers, as he obtained several properties in Pakistan, Dubai, and elsewhere. Third, according to former officials in the Pakistani Inter-Services

Intelligence (ISI), Pakistan's military intelligence service, the Pakistani government had begun investigating Khan's activities back in the late 1980s and 1990s, yet did nothing to stop his transactions.[20]

Fourth, in 1996 Pakistan was experiencing a foreign currency reserves crisis. This problem meant that Pakistan did not have enough foreign currency to purchase imports from other countries. Its reserves stood at $773 million, the equivalent of about three weeks of imports. Because this problem infers that Pakistan lacked an ability to use money to pay for the missiles from North Korea, it presents the likelihood that Pakistan used nuclear technology as a barter payment for the missiles. Pakistan, in exchange for assisting North Korea with expertise on nuclear plant and weapons construction, received the *No Dong* missiles.

8.5.2 Bartering and Gains from Trade

Economically, it could be said that Pakistan had a comparative advantage producing nuclear weapons technology, while North Korea had a comparative advantage producing missiles. **Comparative advantage** is the ability of a person or country to perform an activity or produce a good or service at a lower opportunity cost than someone else. **Opportunity cost** is the next best thing someone must give up in order gain something else. Consider Figure 8.1. The two **production possibility frontiers (PPF)** illustrate the ability of each country (North Korea and Pakistan) to produce two goods (missiles and kg of HEU), given the resources available to each country. To simplify the example, notice that these production possibility frontiers have a constant slope (recall from Chapter 3 that a production possibility frontier is typically outward bowing, so as to illustrate increasing opportunity costs).

PPF $_{NK}$ in Figure 8.1 shows that if North Korea dedicates all of its resources towards missile production, then it can produce 50 missiles; while dedicating all of its resources to HEU production, it can only produce 1 kilogram of HEU. Conversely, *PPF $_{PAK}$* shows that

Figure 8.1
North Korea and Pakistan HEU and Missiles Production Possibilities Frontiers

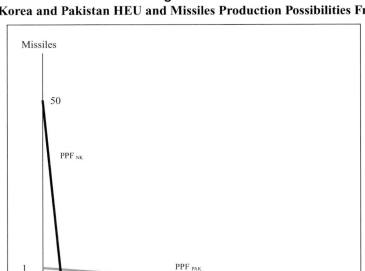

if Pakistan dedicates all of its resources towards missile production, it can only produce one missile; while dedicating all of its resources to HEU production allows it to produce 40 kilograms of HEU.

Calculating each country's opportunity cost is a matter of determining what each country must give up to produce certain items. This can be done by determining the HEU/ missile ratio for each country. This ratio measures the amount of HEU a country must give up to construct missiles (the opportunity cost of missile production).

Suppose North Korea starts by dedicating all of its resources towards HEU production. This effort gives it 1 kg of HEU. Suppose it then switches all of its resources to missile production. This switch gives it 50 missiles. Therefore, in order to switch all of its resources to producing 50 missiles, it had to give up 1 kg of HEU. This means that North Korea's HEU/missile ratio is 1/50 (quantity of HEU produced with all resources/ quantity of missiles produced with all resources). Alternatively, one can say that North Korea's *opportunity cost* for missile production is 1/50.

If Pakistan dedicates all of its resources to HEU production, it can produce 40 kg of HEU. If it then switches all of its resources to missile production, it can produce only 1 missile. Therefore, in order to switch all of its resources to producing 1 missile, it had to give up 40 kg of HEU. This means that Pakistan's HEU/missile ratio is 40/1. Alternatively, this ratio means Pakistan's *opportunity cost* for missile production is 40. *It should now be clear that North Korea has the lower opportunity cost with regard to missile production. Therefore, North Korea should focus on missile production.*

What about Pakistan? Does it have a comparative advantage? As it turns out, its comparative advantage is in HEU production. How is this determined? It is determined by looking at the missile/HEU ratio (the number of missiles a country must give up in order to produce HEU). Notice that the missile/HEU ratio is simply the inverse of the HEU/missile ratio. Because the HEU/missile ratios for North Korea and Pakistan were 1/50 and 40, respectively, the missile/HEU ratio for North Korea is 50 and the missile/HEU ratio for Pakistan is 1/40. *Therefore, Pakistan has an opportunity cost in HEU production that is lower than North Korea's. This lower ratio means that Pakistan has a comparative advantage in HEU production and should therefore focus on HEU production.*

What is the benefit of both countries deciding to focus on production of goods for which each has a comparative advantage? By specializing in the production of the goods for which each has a comparative advantage, total production of both HEU and missiles is higher. Before specializing, if Pakistan wanted both missiles and HEU, it had to dedicate half of its resources to each. This strategy allows Pakistan to possess 20 kg of HEU, but only 0.5 a missile. Similarly, North Korea, by dedicating half of its resources to each good, would possess 25 missiles, but only 0.5 a kg of HEU. Total production between the two countries would be 20.5 kg of HEU and 25.5 missiles.

However, once the two countries specialize, the total production of missiles rises to 50 and the total production of HEU rises to 40 kg. Therefore, Pakistan could, for example, give 10 kg of HEU to North Korea, while North Korea could give Pakistan 10 missiles. This trade would enable Pakistan to possess 30 kg of HEU and 10 missiles, and North Korea to possess 40 missiles and 10 kg of HEU. *Both countries gained by specializing and trading with one another.* This result is illustrated in Figure 8.2.

8.5.3 Acquiring Revenue

North Korea, an extremely impoverished country of 23 million people, has a well-documented tendency to sell its weapons technology in order to acquire revenues to finance its communist state. Experts estimate that North Korea sells about $500 million annually (2.5 percent

Figure 8.2
Gains from Black-Market Weapons Trade between North Korea and Pakistan

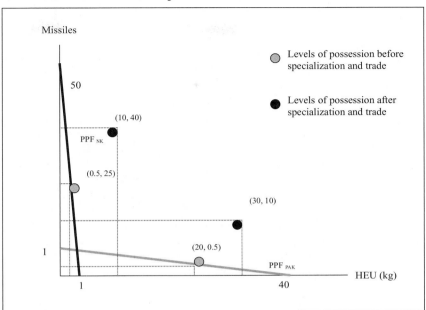

of its GDP) in weapons to other nations, mostly missiles and missile parts.[21] Consequently, many experts are concerned that North Korea will also try to sell nuclear materials and weapons.

But what kind of price could the North Koreans receive for either a black-market nuclear weapon sale or, more likely, the sale of weapons-grade radioactive materials (probably plutonium)? Figure 8.3 provides a count of the number of known nuclear material black-market transactions during the 1990s.

Pricing of nuclear weapons material on the international black market: How much revenue would these transactions generate? Needless to say, black market pricing is not common knowledge. However, Table 8.6 offers several reported prices from various black-market transactions.

Looking at Table 8.6, notice the variance in price. This price difference is due to variances in the material's quality, the patience of the seller, the location of the sale, the type of buyer, the number of suppliers, and the availability of substitutes. Let's examine these six factors.

1) Quality: Uranium usually has a lower price if it is less than 90 percent enriched with U-235 isotopes, because such uranium is less suitable for bomb construction. Plutonium with a higher fraction of Pu-239 is also more desirable. In the North Korean case, the plutonium would be high quality, thereby increasing the price.

2) Patience of the seller: In many past instances, if the individual is eager to be rid of the fissile material, then this eagerness would likely lower the price. It can be assumed that North Korea can afford to be deliberate in its sale of weapons, thereby increasing the price.

187

Figure 8.3
Incidents of Illicit Nuclear Material Trafficking (1993–2003)

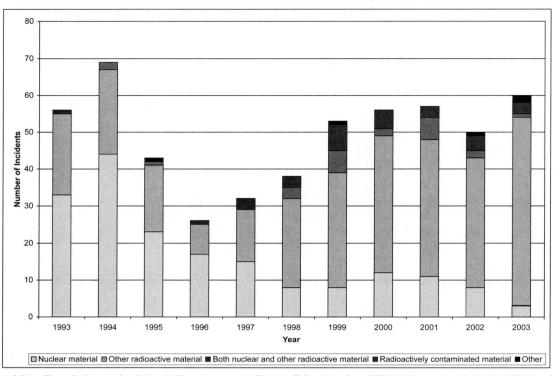

Source of data: From the International Atomic Energy Agency's *Illicit Trafficking Database* (ITDB). Vienna, Austria: IAEA. ITDB statistics, 1993–2003. Available at www.iaea.org/NewsCenter/Features/RadSources/Fact_Figures.html.

Notes: "Nuclear material" includes plutonium and enriched and non-enriched uranium. "Other radioactive material" includes non-fissionable radioactive material (used in industrial, medical, and research applications).

3) Location: In Western Europe or North America (due to more stringent regulations and adept law enforcement) the price is higher than in Central, East, or South Asia or the Middle East. North Korea would most likely be selling in these lower price regions, thereby placing downward pressure on the price.

4) Buyer: Commonly, governments will have the resources and willingness to pay more, while sub-state terrorist groups will not. Given the disparaging nature of North Korea's finances, North Korea is probably willing to supply to either group.

5) Number of suppliers: When the Soviet Union collapsed in the late 1980s, its vast nuclear weapons stockpile was strewn throughout the former empire. Though countries such as Ukraine and Belarus gave these weapons back to Russia, there was concern that years of neglect had left many nuclear material storage facilities in Russia without adequate security measures. Therefore, with the help of the United States, the U.S.-Russia "megaton-for-megawatt" exchange program initiated by U.S. Senators Richard Lugar and Sam Nunn in the early 1990s helped Russia to begin consolidating and securing thousands of metric tons of fissile material. Through this program, the United States has spent nearly $1 billion a year trying to secure the former Soviet Union's (FSU) nuclear stockpile. However, this

Table 8.6
Black Market Pricing of Nuclear Materials, Selected Incidents[1]

1. 2 to 3 times the prevailing official price[2]
2. $112 million for 1.3 kg of HEU[3]
3. $12.2 million for 190 g of HEU, though would have sold for only $60,000 to $100,000 in the commercial market (where it is not intended to become a bomb)[4]
4. $1 million for 12 lbs of uranium[5]
5. $4 million for 6 lbs of HEU[6]
6. $700,000 for 1 kg of uranium[7]
7. $800,000 for l kg of uranium[8]
8. $250–$265 million for 4 kg of weapons-grade plutonium[9]
9. $150 million for a cylinder of "uranium"[10]
10. $3 million for used centrifuge parts (note that it takes a few thousand centrifuges to efficiently produce enough uranium to make a nuclear weapon)[11]
11. $10 million for technical support to upgrade ballistic missiles for WMD delivery (paid by Iraq to North Korean government)[12]
12. $60 million for nuclear fuel (uranium hexafluoride), centrifuges, and one or more warhead designs—nuclear deterrent starter kit (paid by North Korea to A.Q. Khan of Pakistan; similar package sold to Libya for $100 million)[13]
13. $1.5 million purchase of 2-foot long cylinder of uranium from South Africa in 1993 (eventually found to be fake)[14]

Sources:

[1] Suggested reading: Lee, Rensselar W. *Smuggling Armageddon.* New York: St. Martin's Press. 1998. This work contains details on many instances of smuggling, as well as prices for various other attempted sales.

[2] "How Much is a Bomb These Days?" *Russian Press Digest.* September 30, 1995, pp. 1, 3.

[3] Goldstein, Steve. "Nukes on the Loose." *Philadelphia Inquirer.* January 11, 1999 Available through the Russian American Nuclear Security Advisory Council in Washington, D.C., 2003. Read the article at http://www.ransac.org/new-web-site/primary/secure/mpca/loosenukes.01.10.99.html.

[4] Ibid.

[5] Ibid.

[6] Ibid.

[7] Cernick, A. "The Nuclear Black Market." *International Review.* Spring, 1994. Available at http://www.geocities.com/Paris/Rue/4637/terr6a.html.

[8] "'Soviet' Nuclear Materials Sold in Black Market Scams." Toronto Star Newspaper, Ltd. April 4, 1992.

[9] Lee, Rensselar W. *Smuggling Armageddon.* 1998. p. 95; and "Russia Nuclear Means Must be Curtailed." Knoxville, Tennessee: *The Daily Beacon,* University of Tennessee, August 26, 1994.

[10] Grier, Peter. "Loose Nukes." *Christian Science Monitor,* December 5, 2001. Available at http://www.csmonitor.com/2001/1205/p1s3-wogi.html.

[11] Paid by Iran to Dr. Abdul Qadeer Khan of Pakistan in 1994–1995. Ravilious, Emmeline. "Pakistan's Khan Sold Nuclear Parts to Iran and Libya." *Financial Times,* February 20, 2004.

[12] Risen, James. "Russian Engineers Reportedly Gave Missile Aid to Iraq." *The New York Times,* March 5, 2004.

[13] Sanger, David. "U.S. Widens View of Pakistan Link to North Korean Arms." *The New York Times,* March 14, 2004.

[14] *United States v. Usama bin Laden et al.*, United States District Court, Southern District of New York. 2001. Trial Transcript. P. 360. Available at news.findlaw.com/cnn/docs/binladen20701tt.pdf.

amount of money is widely considered inadequate, because even though the program has been in effect for over a decade, the lax manner by which some of the material is stored continues to be a concern.

As Figure 8.4 shows, as of 2003, 63 percent (378 metric tons out of a total of 600 metric tons) of the non-warhead weapons-usable nuclear material had not been given even minor upgrades to its security, even though the U.S. Department of Energy, under its

Figure 8.4
Status of Security Upgrades on Russian Weapons-Usable Nuclear Material (2003)

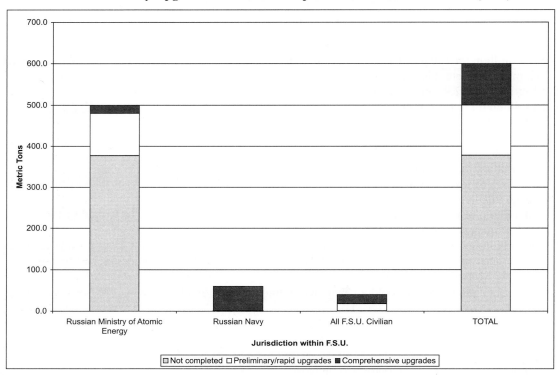

Source of data: Bunn, M., Wier, A., and Holdren, J.P. "Controlling Nuclear Warheads and Materials: A Report Card and Action Plan." *Nuclear Threat Initiative and the Project on Managing the Atom.* Boston, Mass.: Harvard University, 2003. Figure 5.2, p. 67.

Material Protection, Control, and Accounting program (MPC&A) has the goal of securing and accounting for every kilogram of nuclear material in the FSU.[22]

On a brighter note, if one considers the sites within the FSU containing this material, rather than the quantity of the material itself, then one sees that 62 percent (33 of 53) of the sites have been secured (Figure 8.5).

6) Availability of substitutes: Non-fissile radioactive material must be secured, and here's why. If a government (or organization) is unable to obtain fissile material, it may substitute a nuclear weapon for a nonnuclear **dirty bomb** (also called a radiological dispersal device). A dirty bomb is a conventional bomb surrounded by radioactive material that, when detonated, will scatter the radioactive material. A dirty bomb does not cause a nuclear explosion.

Such bombs can be rather crude. For example, they may simply consist of cesium-137 (one of the most common radioactive materials used in heavy industry), packed into a bundle of dynamite. When detonated, the radioactive material is pulverized and spreads outward. Such a device may not cause a large degree of physical damage (depending on the amount of dynamite used), but the radioactive material can contaminate the environment surrounding the explosion, potentially rendering it uninhabitable.

Figure 8.5
Status of Security Upgrades for Sites with Weapons-Usable Material within the F.S.U.

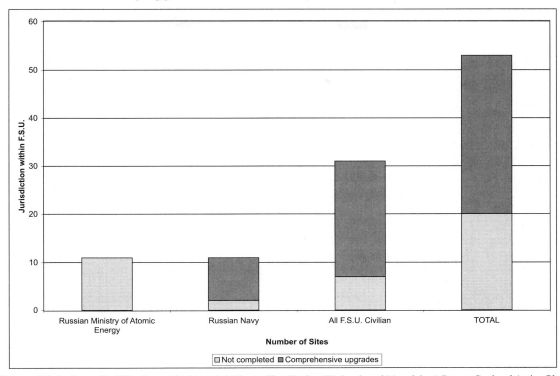

Source of data: Bunn, M., Wier, A., and Holdren, J.P. "Controlling Nuclear Warheads and Materials: A Report Card and Action Plan." *Nuclear Threat Initiative and the Project on Managing the Atom.* Boston, Mass.: Harvard University, 2003. Figure 5.3. page 68.

Because such weapons do not require incurring the research costs of achieving a nuclear reaction, they are likely to be attractive to sub-state actors. However, despite the scientific simplicity of such weapons, constructing and deploying them entails another set of costs. Specifically, making an effective bomb requires a lot of radioactive material. Consequently, an individual constructing the bomb must either make a shield to protect him or her from radiation (which can make the bomb extremely heavy) or not make a shield, but succumb to instant death from radiation poisoning.[23]

Therefore, if fissile or radioactive material is not available (or the person cannot find a suitable way to handle the radioactive material), then the individual will probably turn to chemical or biological weapons. This option will probably be available at a price lower than fissile and radioactive material. In the case of chemical weapons, they are more easily produced. In the case of biological weapons, they more difficult to deploy. For example, a few thousand to a few hundred thousand dollars could be used to purchase a chemical agent like Sarin. Perhaps a few hundred dollars could purchase a small quantity of biological agent, such as anthrax, bubonic plague, or ricin (a nerve agent).[24]

Benefits to North Korea of a nuclear sale: The prices listed in Table 8.6 provide a useful illustrative benchmark. In particular, price 8 is of the most relevance when looking at North Korea. First, this price is one of the highest and the majority of the six determinants

Figure 8.6
Impact of North Korea on Black Market for Fissile Material

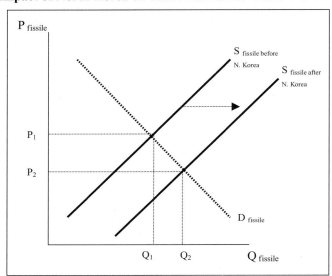

of a black-market price indicate that North Korea could expect a higher price. Second, the product sold in the price 8 transaction was plutonium, and the product was deemed by authorities to be weapons grade. This product is similar to the type of material North Korea would sell. Also, notice that the transaction is for 4 kg of plutonium, which is enough to construct a viable nuclear bomb.

North Korea could have up to 30 kg of plutonium. If North Korea sells all 30 kg at $250 million for 4 kg, it will generate nearly $2 billion of revenue for the country. This figure is about 10 percent of North Korea's 19.4 billion GDP. More importantly, this amount could finance 40 to 70 percent of North Korea's military (depending on whether you accept the official numbers for North Korea's military expenditures as a percentage of GDP—15 percent—or the U.S. numbers—25 to 30 percent of GDP). In short, a price of $250 million for 4 kg could make the sale of weapons-grade fissile material financially lucrative for North Korea.

However, because the addition of North Korea as a fissile material supplier will increase the supply of fissile material on the black market, Figure 8.6 shows that this addition would cause the price of fissile material to fall.

Though a reduction in the price of fissile material will obviously benefit terrorist organizations with limited disposable income, a price reduction is not in the interest of North Korea. The fall in price lowers the revenues gained by North Korea. Therefore, North Korea may be more interested, from the perspective of gaining revenue, in creating a new market by engaging in an unprecedented black-market sale of a full nuclear weapon. Because North Korea would have a monoploy on this market, it would have the ability to obtain a higher price. If North Korea were to sell a full nuclear weapon, then estimates are that the bidding price would start around $1 billion and could quickly rise.[25] Of course, revenue is only one consideration. North Korea may decide to not sell a nuclear weapon for diplomatic reasons. Nevertheless, given North Korea's history of weapons sales, one should seriously consider the incentives it has to engage in a nuclear weapons sale.

8.6 TREATIES: AN EFFECTIVE RESPONSE?

Stopping the spread of nuclear weapons and inhibiting the flow of terrorist financing (covered in Chapter 7) requires cooperation among countries. For example, to stop the flow of terrorist financing, an individual government can try to more stringently regulate its financial markets by requiring more transparency in disclosing account ownership, background checks into persons opening an account or withdrawing a large deposit, and sufficient record keeping. However, the efficacy of such efforts is compromised by the transnational nature of terrorist financing. Hence, it is not sufficient for one country to regulate its financial markets. Similarly, if only one country with nuclear technology decides to stop proliferating nuclear technology, this decision does not obligate other nuclear powers to follow suit.

8.6.1 Treaties in Theory

Economic theory predicts that cooperative efforts towards non-proliferation are unlikely to be successful.

The costs of treaty compliance: Whenever a country signs a treaty, it benefits from the treaty's provisions. However, this benefit is not without cost. These costs are typically associated with monitoring its own compliance, being subject to outside monitoring, giving up the item that is prohibited, and assisting in the monitoring of other countries.

Free-rider problem: Keeping in mind the cost associated with treaty compliance, Figure 8.7 illustrates, in game theoretic form, the costs/benefits associated with joining a treaty. Assume that country A is looking to propose a treaty. There are four other countries. The benefit gained to country A for each country that joins and abides by the treaty, including itself, is a payoff of 5. The cost incurred by country A for joining the treaty is one negative payoff of 10 (remember that these numbers merely provide an illustration). Therefore, if country A and two other countries sign and abide by the treaty, then the payoff to country A is 5 (plus 5 for each country that joined, minus 10 for the cost to country A of joining).

One can see that the more countries that join and abide by the treaty, the bigger the payoff for country A. However, in each instance (be it none, one, two, or more countries signing on to the treaty), country A receives a larger payoff if it does not join the treaty. Consequently, country A has an incentive to not join the treaty, even though it would like for everyone else to comply with the treaty. This consequence is known as the **free-rider problem**—the absence of an incentive for people to pay for what they consume. The free-rider problem is commonly

Figure 8.7
Game Theoretic Depiction of Why Treaties Fail

		No other countries abide	1 other country abides	2 other countries abide	3 other countries abide
COUNTRY A	ABIDE	-5	0	5	10
	NOT ABIDE	0	5	10	15

associated with **public goods.** Public goods are goods and services that can be consumed simultaneously by everyone, and from which no one can be excluded. For example, if countries *X, Y,* and *Z* all agree to stop terrorist financing in their own countries, country *A* benefits from their actions regardless of whether country *A* takes any action itself. Country *A* could add to the overall benefit by signing and complying with the treaty, but then it would have to incur a cost. Its best option would be to wait until every other country has signed the treaty before it even considers joining.

What is the result? Because every country has the same incentives as country *A,* then no country would rationally sign and abide by the treaty. Hence the treaty will never come into effect! How can the free-rider problem be overcome? Consider the economy of a single nation. Public goods in a national economy include roads and national defense. The government of the country must provide these public goods because it is virtually impossible to prevent citizens of the country from using or benefiting from them, regardless of whether the citizen pays taxes or not.

Role of a hegemonic state: Internationally, there is no overall government that can provide public goods. Instead, **Hegemonic Stability Theory** holds that the international system must rely on a hegemonic state to provide such goods. A **hegemonic state** is a country that far surpasses the wealth and military power of any other country. Because it is so much wealthier than the other countries, it is the only one that can incur the cost of proposing and enforcing a treaty. In the nineteenth century, the United Kingdom was a hegemonic state. As we learned in chapter 2, it provided the financing to maintain a military alliance against Napoleon. It also used the Royal Navy to enforce a ban on slavery (imposed in 1807) and to rid the seas of pirates. After World War II, the United States became the world's hegemonic state. It provided such international public goods as the International Monetary Fund, World Bank, and General Agreement on Trade and Tariffs. In short, international treaties are more likely to succeed if a hegemonic state proposes, signs, and abides by the treaty.

8.6.2   Treaties in Reality: The Nuclear Nonproliferation Treaty

Is the theory true that cooperative efforts are likely to fail? Perhaps the best illustration of such cooperative breakdown in the security realm is the effort to regulate and prevent the spread of nuclear weapons. The primary international treaty to prevent nuclear proliferation is the 1970 Nuclear Nonproliferation Treaty (NPT).

Treaty provisions: When the NPT was agreed upon in 1969 (it was ratified by all signatory nations in 1970), it contained two primary provisions. Under Article VI, the existing five nuclear states (U.S., U.S.S.R., U.K., France, and China), agreed to work towards the eventual elimination of their nuclear stockpiles. In exchange, the non-nuclear countries agreed not to pursue nuclear weapons programs (Article II) and would instead receive assistance from the nuclear states with developing civilian programs (Article IV). The treaty created the International Atomic Energy Agency (IAEA) to oversee compliance.

Treaty flaws: However, as theory would predict, this treaty has been prone to defection and free-riding. With regard to free-riding, India, Pakistan, Israel, and Cuba are not members of the NPT. Three of these four countries (India, Pakistan, and Israel) became nuclear states after the creation of the NPT. With regard to defection, though North Korea is the only country to withdraw from the NPT (which it did in 2003, so as to pursue a nuclear weapons program) many other countries have violated the spirit of the treaty. Defection and free-riding are due to weaknesses within the NPT.

Why the NPT allows defection: Under the NPT provisions, a country that signs the NPT as a nonnuclear-weapon state agrees not to acquire nuclear weapons. However, because the NPT does allow states to create nuclear reactors for civilian energy purposes, the NPT does not prevent states from acquiring nuclear materials and components. Because many of the components needed to construct a nuclear weapon are also used for civilian energy purposes, the NPT requires states that are pursuing a civilian program to allow inspectors from the IAEA to oversee their nuclear program's development. However, there are few incentives for countries to be completely open about their activities with IAEA officials. Therefore, some countries (such as Iraq throughout the 1990s and Iran more recently) will refuse to allow inspectors into certain nonnuclear locations even if the inspectors suspect that important nuclear components are in those locations.

North Korea went a step further (as did Iraq in 1998) by kicking out IAEA inspectors and openly admitting its desire to obtain nuclear weapons. Iran is still a member of the NPT and claims its nuclear program is solely for civilian use. However, the United States and European Union question Iran's motivation on several grounds. First, Iran has failed to disclose work on centrifuges to enrich uranium (a step unnecessary in civilian nuclear power production).[26] Second, Iran is the fifth-largest net exporter of petroleum in the world, with the world's fifth-largest oil reserves supply.[27] Therefore, many states question why Iran would need nuclear power when it sits on top of such vast oil reserves.

Even the United States, which in 2002 agreed with Russia to dismantle deployable nuclear missiles, is potentially violating the spirit of the NPT by pursuing the development of "mini-nukes" (nuclear weapons of less than 5 kT). These mini-nukes could be used to destroy underground bunkers, but as the head of the IAEA Mohammad El-Baradei stated in 2003, "The U.S. government demands other states not to own nuclear weapons. On the other hand it is perfecting its own arsenal....I don't believe it [the development of the mini-nukes] complies with the treaty which it [the United States] signed."[28]

8.7   KEY POINTS

Key Macroeconomic Points:

- Building nuclear weapons, though more cost-effective than conventional weapons, is still an expensive enterprise that can absorb a large portion of a government's defense budget.
- Selling nuclear weapons on the international black market could generate government funds that can be used to finance the military or create social programs.

Key Microeconomic Points:

- Chemical, biological, and nuclear weapons are more efficient (in terms of their ability to inflict casualties at a low cost) than conventional weapons.
- Countries base the decision to acquire and distribute nuclear weapons on considerations of supply (bartering and acquisition of revenue) and demand (security dilemma and substitution effect).
- Just like any other market, prices in the international black market are susceptible to changes in the number of suppliers, the availability of substitutes, and the quality of the product.
- North Korea and Pakistan specialized in the production of the goods for which each had a comparative advantage, meaning they had the lower opportunity cost in producing that good. This enabled both countries to obtain gains from trade in the international weapons black market.

- Treaties are international public goods that are susceptible to free-riding. Hence, hegemonic stability theory holds that only a hegemonic state (like the government within a country) can provide treaties and/or ensure their enforcement.

Key Terms:

Weapons of mass destruction
Fission
Tons
Q-50
Highly enriched uranium
Reprocessing
Security dilemma
Substitution effect
Bartering

Comparative advantage
Opportunity cost
Production possibility frontier
Dirty bomb
Free-rider problem
Public goods
Hegemonic Stability Theory
Hegemonic state

Key Questions:

1. Is there evidence that nuclear weapons provide "more bang for the buck"? Which of the weapons commonly referred to as "Weapons of Mass Destruction" is most economically efficient with regard to generating fatalities?

2. Why have more countries attempted chemical weapons programs, even though biological weapons programs are more economically efficient?

3. Why do the prices for uranium vary so widely on the international black market?

4. Use the supply and demand model to explain why North Korea, from an economic perspective, would be more likely to sell a nuclear weapon (rather than fissile material) on the international black market.

5. The Ottawa Convention, created in 1997, is an international treaty banning the use of land mines. As of 2005, over 150 countries have signed the treaty; but the United States, China, and Russia have not. Can economic theory explain why these three countries have decided not to sign this treaty? Given that these three countries have not joined the treaty, what does Hegemonic Stability Theory predict will be the likely outcome of the treaty?

Endnotes

1. Landler, Mark. "UN Official Warns of a 'Wal-Mart' in Nuclear Trafficking." *The New York Times,* January 23, 2004.

2. Information from the Nuclear Threat Initiative's "WMD 411: A Primer on WMD," authored by the Monterey Institute's Center for Nonproliferation Studies, 2004. Available at www.nti.org/f_wmd411/f1a.html.

3. For an excellent and easy-to-understand summary of the effects of a nuclear weapons and their operation, please refer to the "Nuclear Weapons" entry in the *Microsoft Encarta* encyclopedia on-line. Available at www.encarta.msn.com. One can also refer to the FAQ section of the nuclear weapons archive website at nuclearweaponarchive.org.

4. Information from Burbach, David. "Nuclear Weapons Primer." November 1997. Available at http://classes.lls.edu/spring2003/natsec-manheim/Nuclear_Primer.pdf, unless otherwise cited.

5. Allison (2004), p. 47.

6. See Carter (2004), p. 73, and Allison (2004), p. 219.

7. Perkovich (2003), p. 2.

8. Argonne National Laboratory—West. Available at www.anlw.anl.gov/anlw_history/glossary.html.

9. There are other enrichment methods such as gaseous diffusion and electromagnetic isotope separation.

10. "Nuclear Weapons," in *Special Weapons Primer.* Federation of American Scientists (1998). Available at www.fas.org/nuke/intro/nuke/.

11. Sanger, David and Broad, William. "From Rogue Nuclear Programs, Web of Trails Leads to Pakistan." *The New York Times,* January 4, 2004. p. A1.

12. Information for this paragraph comes from the Nuclear Energy Institute's web-page, "Plutonium and Uranium Reprocessing," Washington, D.C., January 2003. Available at www.nei.org/doc.asp?docid=663.

13. U.S. Congress, Office of Technology Assessment. *Proliferation of Weapons of Mass Destruction: Assessing the Risks.* OTA-ISC-559. Washington, D.C.: U.S. Government Printing Office, August 1993. Available at www.wws.princeton.edu/~ota/disk1/1993/9341_n.html Table 1-1, p. 11 I.

14. "Rising Cost of High-Tech Weapons Fuels Developing World's Nuclear Ambitions." Washington, D.C.: *Jewish Institute for National Security Affairs,* March 1, 1995. Available at www.jinsa.org/articles/articles.html/function/view/categoryid/148/documentid/391/history/3,2360,652,148,391.

15. Allison (2004), p. 212.

16. Information from the Nuclear Threat Initiative's "WMD 411: A Primer on WMD," authored by the Monterey Institute's Center for Nonproliferation Studies, 2004. Available at www.nti.org/f_wmd411/f1a.html.

17. Perkovich (1999), p. 67.

18. See Schwartz, S. *Atomic Audit: Cost and Consequences of Nuclear Weapons Since the 1940s.* Washington, D.C.: Brookings Institution. 1998. Available at http://www.brook.edu/fp/projects/nucwcost/weapons.htm.

19. Account from Squassoni (2004) unless otherwise cited.

20. Fidler and Burnett. "What did Pakistan know about Khan's deals?" *Financial Times,* April 5, 2004.

21. Dunham, Will. "U.S. Worries North Korea Will Sell Nuclear Bombs." Reuters. January 19, 2003. Available through globalsecurity.org web site at www.globalsecurity.org/org/news/2003/030119-dprk01.htm and Hiscock, Geoff. "North's Economy Still in decline." *CNN.com*, August 25, 2003. Available at http://edition.cnn.com/2003/BUSINESS/08/24/nkorea.economy.biz/.

22. Bunn, et al (2003), p. 65.

23. "The Mechanisms of A Dirty Bomb." *CBSNEWS.com* from a news report by Jim Stewart. April 23, 2002. Available at www.cbsnews.com/stories/2002/04/23/attack/main507031.shtml.

24. Cameron (1999), p. 141.

25. Dunham, Will. "U.S. Worries North Korea Will Sell Nuclear Bombs." Reuters, January 19, 2003. Available through globalsecurity.org web site at www.globalsecurity.org/org/news/2003/030119-dprk01.htm.

26. See the April 27, 2004 statement of John Bolton (U.S. Under Secretary for Arms Control and International Security), "The NPT: A Crisis of Non-Compliance," presented at the Third Session of the Preparatory Committee for the 2005 Review Conference of the Treaty on the Non-Proliferation of Nuclear Weapons, New York City. Available at the U.S. Department of State, www.state.gov/t/us/rm/31848.htm.

27. Energy Information Administration (EIA). "Top Petroleum Net Exporters, 2003." U.S. Department of Energy, August 18, 2004. Available at www.eia.doe.gov/emeu/security/topexp.html.

28. "El Baradei Accuses U.S. of Violating NPT." Berlin, Germany: Islamic Republic News Agency (IRNA). 8/26/2003. Available at http://globalsecurity.org/ and www.globalsecurity.org/wmd/library/news/usa/2003/usa-030826-irna01.htm.

References:

Books:

Allison, Graham. *Nuclear Terrorism: The Ultimate Preventable Catastrophe.* New York: Henry Holt. 2004.

Bade, Robin and Parkin, Michael. *Foundations of Microeconomics.* Second Edition. Boston, MA: Addison-Wesley. 2004.

Cameron, Gavin. *Nuclear Terrorism.* New York, NY: St Martin's Press. 1999.

Churchill, Winston. *The Second World War, Volume 6: Triumph and Tragedy.* Cambridge, MA.: Houghton-Mifflin. 1953.

Davies, Glyn. *A History of Money: From Ancient Times to the Present Day.* Cardiff, Wales: Wales Press. 2002.

Dickenson, H.T. (ed.) *Britain and the French Revolution, 1789–1815.* New York: St. Martin's Press. 1989.

Duncan-Jones, Richard. *Money and Government in the Roman Empire.* New York, NY: Cambridge University Press. 1994.

Ehrenberg, R.G. and Smith, R.S. *Modern Labor Economics: Theory and Public Policy.* Boston, MA.: Addison-Wesley. 2003.

Feinstein, Charles H.; Temin, Peter; and Toniolo, Gianni. *The European Economy Between the Wars.* Oxford, U.K.: Oxford University Press. 1997.

Garraty, John and Gay, Peter. *The Columbia History of the World.* New York, NY: Harper and Row. 1981.

Gordon, Robert. *Macroeconomics.* 7th Edition. New York: Addison-Wesley. 1998.

Harrison, Mark (ed.). *The Economics of World War II.* New York, NY: Cambridge University Press. 1998.

Hartley, Keith and Sandler, Todd (eds.). *Handbook of Defense Economics: Volume 1.* New York, NY: Elsevier Science. 1995.

Held, David and McGrew, Anthony; Goldblatt, David and Perraton, Jonathan. *Global Transformations.* Stanford, CA: Stanford University Press. 1999.

Higgs, Robert (ed.). *Arms, Politics, and the Economy.* New York: Holmes & Meier Publishers. 1990.

International Institute for Strategic Studies, "Military Balance." 2002–2003. London, UK: International Institute for Strategic Studies. 2002–2003.

Josselin, Daphné and Wallace, William (eds.). *Non-state Actors in World Politics.* Houndmills, U.K.: Palgrave. 2001.

Kapstein, Ethan. *The Political Economy of National Security: A Global Perspective.* Columbia, SC: South Carolina Press. 1992.

Kagan, Donald. *On the Origins of War and the Preservation of Peace.* New York: Doubleday. 1995.

Keller, William W. *Arm in Arm: The Political Economy of the Global Arms Trade.* New York: Basic Books. 1995.

Kennedy, Paul. *The Rise and Fall of the Great Powers.* Boston, MA.: Unwin Hyman. 1988.

Lee, Rensselar W. *Smuggling Armageddon: The Nuclear Black Market in the Former Soviet Union and Europe.* New York: St. Martin's Press.1998.

Maddison, Angus. *The World Economy: Historical Statistics.* Paris, France: Development Centre of the Organization for Economic Cooperation and Development. 2003.

Mankiw, N. Gregory. *Principles of Microeconomics.* Second Edition. Fort Worth, TX: Harcourt College. 2001.

McCormick, Thomas J. *America's Half-Century: United States Foreign Policy in the Cold War and After.* 2nd Edition. Baltimore, MA: John Hopkins University Press. 1995.

Meltzer, Allan. H. *A History of the Federal Reserve: Volume 1.* Chicago: University of Chicago Press. 2003.

Miller, Roger; Benjamin, Daniel and North, Douglass. *The Economics of Public Issues.* 13th Edition. Boston, MA.: Addison-Wesley. 2003.

Mishkin, Fredric. *The Economics of Money, Banking, and Financial Markets.* 7th Edition. Boston, Mass.: Addison-Wesley. 2004.

Mitchell, Brian R. *International Historical Statistics: The Americas, 1750–2000.* New York: Palgrave Macmillan. 2003.

Mosley, Hugh. *The Arms Race: Economic and Social Consequences.* Lexington, MA.: Lexington Books. 1985.

Mueller, John. *Retreat from Doomsday: The Obsolescence of Major War.* New York: Basic Books. 1989.

Mueller, John. *Remnants of War.* Ithaca, NY: Cornell University. 2004.

Neal, Larry (ed.). *War Finance: Volume I: War from Antiquity to Artillery.* Cheltenham, U.K.: Edward Elgar Publishing. 1994.

Parkin, Michael. *Macroeconomics.* Seventh Edition. Boston, MA: Addison-Wesley. 2005.

Perkovich, George. *India's Nuclear Bomb: the impact of global proliferation.* Berkeley, CA: University of California Press. 1999.

Rosen, Harvey. *Public Finance.* 5th Edition. New York: Irwin McGraw-Hill. 1999.

Rothgeb, John M. *Defining Power: Influence and Force in the Contemporary International System.* New York: St. Martin's Press. 1993.

Sandler, Todd and Hartley, Keith. *The Economics of Defense.* New York: Cambridge University Press. 1995.

Sandler, Todd and Hartley, Keith. *The Political Economy of NATO.* New York, NY: Cambridge University Press. 1999.

Sandler, Todd and Hartley, Keith (eds.). *The Economics of Defense: Volume I.* Cheltenham, U.K.: Edward Elgar Publishing. 2001.

Sargent, Thomas J. *The Conquest of American Inflation.* Princeton, NJ: Princeton University Press. 1999.

Sislin, John and Pearson, Frederic S. *Arms and Ethnic Conflict.* Lanham, MD: Rowan and Littlefield. 2001.

Starr, Chester. *The Roman Empire 27 B.C.–A.D. 476.* New York, NY: Oxford University Press. 1982.

Stewart, Frances and Fitzgerald, Valpy (eds.). *War and Underdevelopment: Volumes 1 and 2.* Oxford, U.K.: Oxford University Press. 2001.

Thucydides. *The Peloponnesian War.* Translated by Steven Lattimore. Indianapolis, IN: Hackett. 1998.

Toohey, K. and Veal, A.J. *The Olympic Games: A Social Science Perspective.* Wallingford, U.K.: CABI Publishing. 2000.

Von Clausewitz, Carl. *On War.* Indexed Edition. Princeton, NJ: Princeton University Press. 1984.

Williams, Cindy (ed.). *Filling the Ranks: Transforming the U.S. Military Personnel System.* Cambridge, MA.: MIT Press. 2004.

Zachary, G. Pascal. *Endless Frontier: Vannevar Bush, Engineer of the American Century.* New York: The Free Press. 1997.

Separate Articles:

Aizenman, Joshua and Glick, Reuven. "Military Expenditure, Threats, and Growth." *NBER Working Paper No. W9618.* April 2003.

Alexander, Kern. "Extraterritorial U.S. Banking Regulation and International Terrorism: The Patriot Act and the International Response." *Journal of International Banking Regulation.* Vol. 3, No. 4, 2002, pp. 307–326.

Allen, Douglas. "The British Navy Rules: Monitoring and Incompatible Incentives in the Age of Fighting Sail." *Explorations in Economic History,* 39, 2002, 204–231.

Allison, Graham and Kokoshin, Andrei. "The New Containment." *The National Interest.* Fall 2002, pp. 35–43.

Anderson, J.L. "A Measure of the Effect of British Public Finance, 1793–1815." *Economic History Review,* 17, 1974, pp. 610–619.

Anderton, Charles. "Teaching Arms Race Concepts in Intermediate Microeconomics." *Journal of Economic Education.* Vol. 21, 1990, pp. 148–166.

Angrist, Joshua D. "The Draft Lottery and Voluntary Enlistment in the Vietnam Era." *Journal of the American Statistical Association.* September 1991, pp. 584–595.

Aninat, Eduardo; Hardy, Daniel; and Johnston, R. Barry. "Combating Money Laundering and the Financing of Terrorism." *Finance and Development.* September 2002, pp. 44–47.

Baack, Ben, and Ray, Edward. "The Political Economy of the Origins of the Military-Industrial Complex in the United States." *The Journal of Economic History.* June 1985, pp. 369–375.

Baer, Robert. "The Fall of the House of Saud." *The Atlantic Monthly.* June 2003, pp. 53–62.

Banadarage, Asoka. "Global Peace and Security in the Post-Cold War Era: A 'Third World' Perspective," in *Peace and World Security Studies.* 6th Edition. Michael Klare (ed.). Boulder, CO: Lynne Rienner Publishers. 1994.

Barnett, Arnold; Stanley, Timothy; and Shore, Michael. "America's Vietnam Casualties: Victims of a Class War?" *Operations Research.* September–October 1992, pp. 856–866.

Bish, Robert and O'Donoghue, Patrick. "A Neglected Issue in Public-Goods Theory: The Monopsony Problem." *Journal of Political Economy.* November-December 1970, pp.1367–1371.

Bordo, M.D. and White, E.N. "A Tale of Two Currencies: British and French Finance during the Napoleonic Wars." *Journal of Economic History,* 51, June 1991, pp. 303–316.

Brauer, Jurgen. "On the Economics of Terrorism," in *Phi Kappa Phi Forum.* Spring 2002, pp. 38–41.

Brayton, Steve. "Outsourcing War: Mercenaries and the Privatization of Peacekeeping." *Journal of International Affairs.* Spring 2002, pp. 303–329.

Bridbury, A. R. "The Hundred Year's War: Costs and Profits," in *Trade, Government and Economy in Pre-Industrial England.* Colman, D.C. and John, A.H. (eds.). London, U.K.: Weidenfeld and Nicolson. 1976.

Bunn, M., Wier, A., and Holdren, J.P. *Controlling Nuclear Warheads and Materials: A Report Card and Action Plan.* Nuclear Threat Initiative and the Project on Managing the Atom. Boston, MA.: Harvard University. 2003.

Carter, Ashton. "How to Counter WMD." *Foreign Affairs.* September/October 2004, pp. 72–85.

Cohen, Avner. "Israel and the Evolution of U.S. Nonproliferation Policy: The Critical Decade (1958–1968)." *The Nonproliferation Review.* Winter (1998), pp. 2–5.

Collier, Paul. "Doing Well out of War: An Economic Perspective," in *Greed and Grievance: Economic Agendas in Civil Wars.* Berdal, Mats and Malone, David (eds.). International Peace Academy. Boulder, CO: Lynne Rienner Publishers. 2000. pp. 91–112.

Collier, Paul. "The Market for Civil War." *Foreign Policy.* May/June 2003. pp. 38–45.

Collier, Paul and Hoeffler, Anke. "On the Incidence of Civil War in Africa." *Journal of Conflict Resolution.* 2002. pp. 13–28.

Cooper, Richard. "William Pitt, Taxation, and the Needs of War." *Journal of British Studies.* 22 Autumn (1982). pp. 94–103.

Davies, Victor. "Sierra Leone: Ironic Tragedy." *Journal of African Economies.* Vol. 9, No. 3, 2000, pp. 349–369.

De Soya, Indra. "The Resource Curve: Are Civil Wars Driven by Rapacity or Paucity?" in *Greed and Grievance: Economic Agendas in Civil Wars.* Berdal, Mats and Malone, David (eds.). International Peace Academy. Boulder, CO: Lynne Rienner Publishers. 2000. pp. 113–136.

Duffield, Mark. "Globalization, Transborder Trade, and War Economies," in *Greed and Grievance: Economic Agendas in Civil Wars.* Berdal, Mats and Malone, David (eds.). International Peace Academy. Boulder, CO: Lynne Rienner Publishers. 2000. pp. 69–90.

Enders, Walter and Sandler, Todd. "After 9/11: Is It All Different Now?" *Mershon Center presentation.* Columbus: Ohio State University. Spring 2004.

Enders, Walter and Sandler, Todd. "Is Transnational Terrorism Becoming More Threatening?" *Journal of Conflict Resolution.* June 2000, pp. 307–322.

Enders, Walter and Sandler, Todd. "Terrorism and Foreign Direct Investment in Spain and Greece." *Kyklos.* Vol. 49, 1996, pp. 331–352.

Falconer, Bruce. "U.S. Military Logistics." *The Atlantic Monthly.* May 2003, pp. 50–51.

Fallows, James. "Uncle Sam Buys An Airplane." *The Atlantic Monthly.* June 2002, pp. 62–74.

Fearon, James D. and Laitin, David D. "Ethnicity, Insurgency, and Civil War." *American Political Science Review.* February 2003. pp. 75–90.

Fisher, Kenneth and Statman, Meir. "Consumer Confidence and Stock Returns." *Journal of Portfolio Management.* Fall 2003. pp. 115–127.

Gleditsch, Kristian. "A Revised List of Wars between and within Independent States, 1816–2002." *International Interactions.* 30. 2004.

Goff, Brian and Tollison, Robert. "The Allocation of Death in the Vietnam War." *Southern Economic Journal.* October 1987. pp. 316–321.

Graham, Thomas W. "Weapons of Mass Destruction: Does Globalization Mean Proliferation?" *Brookings Review.* Fall 2001, pp. 38–40.

Hamilton, James D. and Herrera, Ana Maria. "Oil Shocks and Aggregate Macroeconomic Behavior: The Role of Monetary Policy." *Journal of Money, Credit, and Banking.* April 2004, pp. 265–286.

Hengre, Håvard. "Size Asymmetry, Trade, and Militarized Conflict." *Journal of Conflict Resolution.* June 2004, pp. 403–429.

Hentges, Harriet and Coicaud, Jean-Marc. "Dividends of Peace: The Economics of Peacekeeping." *Journal of International Affairs.* Spring 2002, pp. 351–367.

Higgs, Robert. "The Cold War Economy: Opportunity Costs, Ideology, and the Politics of Crisis." *Explorations in Economic History.* July 1994, pp. 283–312.

Hoffman, Bruce. "The Logic of Suicide Terrorism." *The Atlantic Monthly.* June 2003.

Jansen, Jos and Nahuis, Niek. "The Stock Market and Consumer Confidence: European Evidence." *Economics Letters.* April 2003, pp. 89–98.

Jehn, C. and Selden, Z. "The End of Conscription in Europe?" *Contemporary Economic Policy.* Vol. 20, Issue 2, April 2002.

Korb, Lawrence. "Fixing the Mix: How to Update the Army's Reserves." *Foreign Affairs.* March/April 2004, pp. 2–7.

Krueger A. and Maleková, Jitka. "Education, Poverty and Terrorism: Is there a Causal Connection?" *Journal of Economic Perspectives.* Fall 2003, pp. 119–144.

Lapan, H. and Sandler, T. "To Bargain or Not to Bargain: That is the Question." *The American Economic Review.* May 1988, pp. 16–21.

Lee, Dwight. R. "Free Riding and Paid Riding in the Fight Against Terrorism." *The American Economic Review.* 1988, pp. 22–26.

Martin, Antonie. "Reconciling Bagehot with the Fed's response to September 11." *Ohio State University Macroeconomic Workshop.* Columbus: Ohio State University. March 2004.

McDonald, Patrick. "Peace through Trade or Free Trade?" *Journal of Conflict Resolution.* August 2004, pp. 547–572.

Morris, Ian. "The Athenian Empire (478–404)." First-draft manuscript.

Mwanasali, Musifiky. "The View from Below," in *Greed and Grievance: Economic Agendas in Civil Wars.* Berdal, Mats and Malone, David (eds.). International Peace Academy. Boulder, CO: Lynne Rienner Publishers. 2000. pp. 137–153.

Newhouse, John. "The Threats America Faces." *World Policy Journal.* Summer 2002, pp. 21–37.

Nikiforuk, Andrew. "The Business of Bioterror." *Canadian Business.* Nov. 26, 2002. Vol. 74, Issue 22, pp. 22.

Nordhaus, William and Tobin, James. "Is Growth Obsolete?" *The Measurement of Economic and Social Performance, Studies In Income and Wealth.* Vol. 38. National Bureau of Economic Research 1973.

Oneal, John and Russett, Bruce. "The Classical Liberals Were Right: Democracy, Interdependence, and Conflict, 1950–1985." *International Studies Quarterly.* Vol. 41, 1997, pp. 267–294.

Oneal, John and Russett, Bruce. "The Kantian Peace: The Pacific Benefits of Democracy, Interdependence, and International Organizations, 1885–1992." *World Politics.* Vol. 52, Issue 1, 1999a, pp. 1–37.

Oneal, John and Russett, Bruce. "Assessing the Liberal Peace with Alternative Specifications: Trade Still Reduces Conflict." *Journal of Peace Research.* July 1999b, pp. 423–442.

Peck, Don. "The Gun Trade." *The Atlantic Monthly.* December 2002, pp. 46–47.

Postan, M.M. "The Costs of the Hundred Year's War." *Past and Present.* April 1964, pp. 34–53.

Perkovich, George. "Bush's Nuclear Revolution." *Foreign Affairs.* March/April. 2003.

Reppy, Judith. "The Economics of Peace and Security," in *Peace and World Security Studies.* 6th Edition. Michael Klare (ed.). Boulder, CO: Lynne Rienner Publishers. 1994.

Sagan, Scott D. "Why Do States Build Nuclear Weapons?" *International Security.* Vol. 21, No. 3, Winter 1996/97, pp. 54–86.

Sandler, Todd. "Collective Action and Transnational Terrorism." *The World Economy.* Vol. 26 Issue 6. June 2003, pp. 779–802.

Sandler, T. and Enders, W. "An Economic Perspective on Transnational Terrorism." *European Journal of Political Economy.* June 2004, pp. 301–316.

Sandler, T.; Tschirhart, J. T.; and Cauley, Jon. "A Theoretical Analysis of Transnational Terrorism." *The American Political Science Review.* March 1983, pp. 36–54.

Sanderson, John. "The Changing Face of Peace Operations: A View from the Field." *Journal of International Affairs*. Vol. 55, No. 2, Spring 2002, pp. 277–288.

Singer, P.W. "War, Profits, and the Vacuum of Law: Privatized Military Firms and International Law." *Columbia Journal of Transnational Law*. Spring 2004, pp. 521–550.

Singer, P.W. "Corporate Warriors. The Rise and Ramifications of the Privatized Military Industry." *International Security*. December 2001, pp. 186–220.

Stewart, Francis. "Crisis Prevention: Tackling Horizontal Inequalities." *Oxford Development Studies*. Vol. 28, No. 3, Oct 2000, pp. 245–262.

Taylor, John B. "The Great Inflation, the Great Disinflation, and Policies for Future Price Stability," in Blundell-Wignall (ed.). *Inflation, Disinflation, and Monetary Policy*. Sydney: Ambassador Press. 1992, pp. 9–34.

Warner, John T. and Asch, Beth J. "The Record and Prospects of the All-Volunteer Military in the United States." *Journal of Economic Perspectives*. Spring 2001, pp. 169–192.

Zhou, Xianming. "A Graphical Approach to the Standard Principal-Agent Model." *Journal of Economic Education*. Summer 2002, pp. 265–276.

Papers and Sources Available Online:

Alesina, Alberto. "More Military Spending in Europe is Needed." May 2002. Available at http://post.economics.havard.edu/faculty/alesina/columns.html.

Bandow, Doug. "Fixing What Ain't Broke: The Renewed Call for Conscription." Cato Institute Policy Analysis. August 31, 1999, p. 10. Available at www.cato.org/pubs/pas/pa351.pdf.

Bearce, David, and Fisher, Eric. "Economic Geography, Trade, and War." *Journal of Conflict Resolution*. June 2002, pp. 365–393. Available at http://economics.sbs.ohio-state.edu/efisher/egtw/docs/BearFish.pdf.

Berman. E."Hamas, Taliban, and the Jewish Underground: An Economist's View of Radical Religious Militias." NBER Working Papers. Available at http://dsl.nber.org/papers/w10004.pdf.

Buddin, Richard and Do, Phuong. *Assessing the Personal Financial Problems of Junior Enlisted Personnel*. Santa Monica, CA: RAND Corporation. 2002. Available at www.rand.org/publications/MR/MR1444/.

Bunn, M., Wier, A., and Holdren, J.P. "Controlling Nuclear Warheads and Materials: A Report Card and Action Plan." *Nuclear Threat Initiative and the Project on Managing the Atom*. Boston, Mass.: Harvard University. 2003. Available at www.nti.org/e_research/cnwm/overview/cnwm_home.asp.

Bush, Vannevar. "Science: The Endless Frontier." A report to the President by Vannevar Bush, Director of the Office of Scientific Research and Development, National Science Foundation. July 1945. Available at http://www.nsf.gov/od/lpa/nsf50/vbush1945.htm#transmittal.

Chamberlin, Jeffrey. "Comparisons of U.S. and Foreign Military Spending: Data from Selected Public Sources." Congressional Research Service Report for Congress. January 28, 2004. Available at http://fas.org/man/crs/RL32209.pdf.

Collier, Paul. "On the Economic Consequences of Civil War." *Oxford Economic Papers*. Vol. 51, 1999. Available at econ.worldbank.org/files/13201_CollierEcConsequences.pdf.

Collier, Paul. "Economic Causes of Civil Conflict and their Implications for Policy." World Bank: The Economics of Civil War, Crime and Violence Project. June 15, 2000. Available at www.econ.worldbank.org/files/13198_EcCausesPolicy.pdf.

Collier, Paul. "Military Expenditure: Threats, Aid and Arms Races." World Bank: The Economics of Civil War, Crime and Violence Project. June 11, 2002. Available at www.econ.worldbank.org/files/15711_CollierHoefflerMilitarySpillovers.pdf

Collier, Paul and Hoeffler, Anke. "Greed and Grievance in Civil War." *Center for the Study of African Economies.* Working Paper Series/ 2002-01. March 2002b. Available at www.csae.ox.ac.uk/workingpapers/pdfs/2002-01text.pdf.

Collier, P.; Elliot, V.L.; Hegre, H.; Hoeffler, A.; Reynal-Querol, M.; and Sambanis, N. *Breaking the Conflict Trap: Civil War and Development Policy.* Washington, D.C.: World Bank and Oxford University Press, May 2003. Available at www-wds.worldbank.org/servlet/WDSContentServer/WDSP/IB/2003/06/30/000094946_0306190405396/Rendered/PDF/multi0page.pdf.

Collier, Paul; Hoeffler, Anke; and Söderbom, Måns. "On the Duration of Civil War." *Center for the Study of African Economics.* University of Oxford. October 2003. Available at http://users.ox.ac.uk/~ball0144/warduration_oct03.pdf.

Collier, Paul and Hoeffler, Anke. "The Challenge of Reducing the Global Incidence of Civil War." *The Copenhagen Consensus Project Challenge Paper.* May 2004. Available at www.copenhagenconsensus.com/Files/Filer/CC/Papers/Conflicts_230404.pdf.

Davis, S.; Murphy, K.; and Topel, R. "War in Iraq Versus Containment." (2003). Available at gsbwww.uchicago.edu/fac/steven.davis/research.

Drakos, K. and Kutan, A. "Regional Effects of Terrorism on Tourism: Evidence from Three Mediterranean Countries." *Working Paper* 26. Bonn: Centre for European Integration Studies. 2001. Available at: www.zei.de/download/zei_wp/B01-26.pdf.

Eisenhower, Dwight D. "Farewell Address to the Nation" speech delivered by U.S. President Dwight D. Eisenhower on January 17, 1961. Abilene, Kansas: Dwight D. Eisenhower Presidential Library. Available at http://www.eisenhower.utexas.edu/farewell.htm.

Enders, W. and Sandler, T. "What Do We Know about the Substitutions Effect in Transnational Terrorism?" April 2002. Available at http://www-rcf.usc.edu/~tsandler/substitution2ms.pdf.

Ergas, H. "Some Economic Aspects of the Weapons Systems Acquisition Process" NECG 2003. Available at www.necg.com.au/pappub/some_economic_aspects_of_weapons_systems_acquisition_HE_Aug_03.pdf.

Estevadeordal, Antoni; Frantz, Brian; and Taylor, Alan. "Rise and Fall of World Trade, 1870–1939." *National Bureau of Economic Research.* Working Paper No. w 9318. Available at www.nber.org/~confer/2002/itis02/taylor.pdf.

Fernandez, Richard. "What Does the Military Pay Gap Mean?" *Congressional Budget Office.* June 1999. Available at http://www.cbo.gov/showdoc.cfm?index=1354&sequence=0&from=1.

Fiftieth Anniversary of the Treasury-Federal Reserve Accord. Federal Reserve Bank of Richmond. 2001. At http://www.rich.frb.org/research/specialtopics/treasury/index.html.

Frieden, B. and Baxter, C. *From Barracks to Business: The M.I.T Report on Base Development.* Economic Development Administration. U.S. Department of Commerce. March 2000. Available at www.eda.gov/Research/ResearchReports.xml.

Goldich, Richard. "Military Pay and Benefits: Key Questions and Answers." Congressional Research Service Report for Congress. March 19, 2003. Available at http://hutchison.senate.gov/Foreign4.pdf.

Grimmett, Richard F. "Conventional Arms Transfers to Developing Nations, 1995–2002." Congressional Research Service Report for Congress. September 22, 2003. Available at http://fas.org/man/crs/RL32084.pdf.

Gropman, Alan. *Mobilizing U.S. Industry in World War II.* McNair Paper Number 50. National Defense University. 1996. Available at www.ndu.edu/inss/McNair/mcnair50/m50cont.html.

Gupta, Sanjeev; Clements, Benedict; Bhattacharya, Rina; and Chakravarti, Shamit. "Fiscal Dimensions of Armed Conflict." Berlin, Germany: Deutsches Institut für Wirtschafts-forschung. *The Economic Consequences of Global Terrorism Workshop,* June 14–15, 2002. Available at www.diw.de/deutsch/produkte/veranstaltungen/ws_consequences/docs/diw_ws_consequences200206_gupta.pdf.

Holcombe, Randall. "The Growth of the Federal Government in the 1920s." *The Cato Journal.* Vol. 16, No. 2. Available at www.cato.org/pubs/journal/cj16n2-2.html.

Hosek, James and Sharp, Jennifer. "Keeping Military Pay Competitive." *RAND Corporation Issue Paper 205.* Santa Monica, CA: RAND Corporation. 2001. Available at http://www.rand.org/publications/IP/IP205/.

Huang, Reyko. "The Financial War Against Terrorism." Center for Defense Information Terrorism Project. March 5, 2002. Available at www.cdi.org/terrorism/financial.cfm

Hufbauer, G.C.; Schott, J.; and Oegg, B."Using Sanctions to Fight Terrorism." November 2001. *Institution for International Economics.* Available at www.iie.com/research/topics/sanctions-hot.htm.

Hufbauer, G.C. "Sanctions Happy USA." July 1998. *Institute for International Economics.* Available at www.iie.com/publications/pb/pb98-4.htm.

Humphreys, Macartan. "Economics and Violent Conflict." Boston, MA.: Harvard University. February 2003. Available at www.preventconflict.org/portal/economics.

Labonte, Marc. "Financing Issues and Economic Effects of Past American Wars." Congressional Research Service Report for Congress. November 1, 2001. Available at fpc.state.gov/documents/organization/6271.pdf.

Morris, I. "The Athenian Empire (478–404 B.C.)." (2003) Available at www.stanford.edu/group/sshi/empires/morris.pdf.

Murray, Carla Tighe. "Military Compensation: Balancing Cash and Non-Cash Benefits." *Congressional Budget Office.* Issue Brief. January 16, 2004. Available at http://www.cbo.gov/showdoc.cfm?index=4978&sequence=0.

National Security Council Report to the President. "NSC-68: United States Objectives and Programs for National Security." April 14, 1950. Available at http://www.fas.org/irp/offdocs/nsc-hst/nsc-68.htm.

National Defense Budge Estimates for FY 2001 Green Book. United States Department of Defense. Office of the Under Secretary of Defense (Comptroller) March 2000. Available at http://www.defenselink.mil/comptroller/defbudget/fy2001/fy2001_greenbook.pdf.

The NATO Handbook on the Medical Aspects of NBC Defense Operations.1996. Available at www.fas.org/nuke/guide/usa/doctrine/dod/fm8-9/2toc.html.

Nelson, Edward. "The Great Inflation of the Seventies: What Really Happened?" *Federal Reserve Bank of St. Louis Working-Paper Series.* January 2004. Available at research.stlouisfed.org/wp/2004/2004-001.pdf.

Nitsch, V. and Schumacher, D. "Terrorism and Trade." Paper for Workshop. *The Economic Consequences of Global Terrorism.* Berlin, Germany: DIW/German Institute for Economic Research. June 2002. Available at http://www.diw.de/deutsch/produkte/veranstaltungen/ws_consequences/docs/diw_ws_consequences200206_nitsch.pdf.

Nofi, Al. *Statistical Summary: America's Major Wars.* The United States Civil War Center. Available at www.cwc.lsu.edu/cwc/other/stats/warcost.htm.

Nordhaus, William D. "The Economic Consequences of a War with Iraq," in Kaysen, Carl; Miller, Steven E.; Malin, Martin B.;Nordhaus, William D.; Steinbruner, John D. *War with Iraq: Costs, Consequences, and Alternatives.* American Academy of Arts and

Sciences. 2002. Available at www.econ.yale.edu/~nordhaus/homepage/AAAS_War_Iraq_2.pdf.

Oxfam. *Up in Arms: Controlling the International Trade in Small Arms.* Paper for the UN Conference on the Illicit Trade in Small Arms and Light Weapons in All Its Aspects. January 2001. Available at: www.oxfam.org.uk/what_we_do/issues/conflict_disasters/up_in_arms.htm.

Perl, Raphael. "Taliban and the Drug Trade." Congressional Research Service Report for Congress. October 5, 2001. Available at http://fpc.state.gov/documents/organization/6210.pdf.

Raby, Geoff. "The Costs of Terrorism and the Benefits of Cooperating to Combat Terrorism." Paper presented to Asian Pacific Economic Cooperation Senior Officials Meeting, Chiang Rai, February 21, 2003. Available at http://www.dfat.gov.au/media/speeches/department/030224_costsofterrorism_graby.html.

Riedl, Brian. "Most New Spending Since 2001 Unrelated to the War on Terrorism." Heritage Foundation (2003). Available at www.heritage.org/research/budget/bg1703.cfm.

Sandler, T. and Enders, W. "An Economic Perspective on Transnational Terrorism." Berlin, Germany: German Institute for Economic Research (DIW). *The Economic Consequences of Global Terrorism Workshop,* June 14–15, 2002. Available at www.diw.de/deutsch/produkte/veranstaltungen/ws_consequences/docs/diw_ws_consequences200206_sandler.pdf.

Schneider, F. "Money Supply for Terrorism–The Hidden Financial Flows of Islamic Terrorism Organisations." Berlin, Germany: German Institute for Economic Research (DIW). *The Economic Consequences of Global Terrorism Workshop,* June 14–15, 2002. Available at www.diw.de/deutsch/produkte/veranstaltungen/ws_consequences/docs/diw_ws_consequences200206_schneider.pdf.

Schram, M. and Taube, M. "The Institutional Foundations of Al Qaida's Global Financial System." Berlin, Germany: German Institute for Economic Research (DIW). *The Economic Consequences of Global Terrorism Workshop,* June 14–15, 2002. Available at www.diw.de/deutsch/produkte/veranstaltungen/ws_consequences/docs/diw_ws_consequences200206_taube.pdf.

Schwartz, S. *Atomic Audit: Cost and Consequences of Nuclear Weapons Since the 1940s.* Washington, D.C.: Brookings Institution. 1998. Available at http://www.brook.edu/fp/projects/nucwcost/weapons.htm.

Squassoni, Sharon. "Weapons of Mass Destruction: Trade Between North Korea and Pakistan." Congressional Research Service. March 11, 2004 unless otherwise cited. Available at www.fas.org/spp/starwars/crs/RL31900.pdf.

Stockholm International Peace and Research Institute (SIPRI). *Year Book 2003: Armaments, Disarmament and International Security.* New York: Humanities Press.
Chapter 10, "Military Expenditures": http://projects.sipri.se/milex/mex_trends.html.
Chapter 11, "Arms Production": http://projects.sipri.se/milex/aprod/trends.html.
Chapter 13, "International Arms Transfers": http://projects.sipri.se/armstrade/Chap13YB2003.pdf.

Truman Presidential Library. "Special Message to the Congress Recommending the Establishment of a Department of National Defense." December 19, 1945. Available at http://www.trumanlibrary.org/publicpapers/index.php?pid=508&st=&st1=.

U.S. Congress, Office of Technology Assessment. *Proliferation of Weapons of Mass Destruction: Assessing the Risks.* OTA-ISC-559. Washington, D.C.: U.S. Government Printing Office. August 1993. Available at www.wws.princeton.edu/~ota/disk1/1993/9341_n.html.

U.S. General Accounting Office. *Military Base Closures: Overview of Economic Recovery, Property, Transfer, and Environmental Cleanup.* August 2001. Available at www.gao.gov/new.items/d011054t.pdf.

Viscusi, W. Kip. "The Value of Life: Estimates with Risks by Occupation and Industry." *Economic Inquiry.* January 2004, pp. 29–48. Available at papers.ssrn.com/sol3/papers.cfm?abstract_id=416600.

Viscusi, W. Kip and Aldy, Joseph E. "The Value of a Statistical Life: A Critical Review of Market Estimates Throughout the World." *Journal of Risk and Uncertainty.* December 2003, pp. 5–74. Available at http://papers.ssrn.com/sol3/papers.cfm?abstract_id=362840.

Wesbury, Brian. "The Economic Cost of Terrorism." U.S. Department of State. 2002. Available at http://usinfo.state.gov/topical/pol/terror/02091107.htm.

Weschsler, William F., and Wolosky, Lee S. *Terrorist Financing.* Council on Foreign Relations, November 25, 2002. Available at www.cfr.org/pdf/Terrorist_Financing_TF.pdf.

Wintrobe, Ronald. "Can Suicide Bombers be Rational?" Berlin, Germany: German Institute for Economic Research (DIW). *The Economic Consequences of Global Terrorism Workshop,* June 14–15, 2002. Available at www.ssc.uwo.ca/economics/faculty/Wintrobe/Solidarity_and_Suicide.pdf.

Index